A Science of Mind
The Quest for Psychological Reality

A Science of Mind
The Quest for Psychological Reality

Peter du Preez

Department of Psychology
University of Cape Town
7700 Rondebosch
South Africa

ACADEMIC PRESS
Harcourt Brace Jovanovich, Publishers
London Boston San Diego New York
Sydney Tokyo Toronto

ACADEMIC PRESS LIMITED
24–28 Oval Road,
London NW1 7DX

United States Edition published by
ACADEMIC PRESS INC.
San Diego, CA 92101

Copyright © 1991 by
ACADEMIC PRESS LIMITED

All Rights Reserved

No part of this book may be reproduced in any form by photostat, microfilm, or any other means, without written permission from the publishers

This book is printed on acid-free paper

British Library Cataloguing in Publication Data
Du Preez, Peter
  A science of mind.
  1. Science. Psychological aspects
  I. Title
  501.9

ISBN 0-12-224960-7

Typeset by J&L Composition Ltd, Filey, North Yorkshire
and printed in Great Britain by St Edmundsbury Press, Bury St Edmunds, Suffolk

Contents

Acknowledgements	vi
Prologue	vii

Part I Research traditions in psychology

1	The knowledge matrix	3
2	Paradigms and disciplinary matrixes	19
3	Research traditions and theories	29

Part II Rhetoric and change in research traditions

4	The uses of metaphor: or a hatful of larks	51
5	Displacements: metaphor/metonymy/myth	79
6	The fulcrum of reason: truism/axiom/tautology	95
7	Problem-solving and the evolution of theory	114
8	Problem-solving and strategies of competition	140
9	Values	163
10	The quest for the real	181

Part III Towards a reflexive psychology

11	Polyphonic beings	193

Epilogue	209
References	212
Author index	223
Subject index	227

Acknowledgements

How can one ever acknowledge all the help one has received? We are rooted like trees in our families, our friendships and our societies. I have had the good fortune to be rooted in a wonderful family, wonderful friendships and a wonderful society. How can that be? Isn't the man callous or crazy, people may think, seeing that he comes from South Africa? Yet certain times and places in history are wonderful because they are full of movement, like skies before a storm. When I think of the clouds rushing across our skies, where would I rather be?

Now to get down to earth. The people who typed this manuscript have been – yes! – wonderful: Sue Thorne, Pearl Symons, Priscilla Wolters and Heather Steyn. (And, Jane Hutchings, long ago.) Characteristically, Colin Tredoux helped out with word processing expertise when others were baffled.

Finally, I acknowledge the friendship and example of Don Bannister, no longer here to dispute, feast and joke with those who loved him. But who, having known him, can ever forget?

I should end with a line of Greek to dignify the occasion, but I shan't. Academia isn't what it used to be.

Prologue

In this book I attempt to describe the evolution of psychological knowledge; and this attempt requires a description of both its structure and environment. What is it that evolves and how does it evolve?

What evolves is a research tradition – or, rather, a number of research traditions which compete with each other. A research tradition is a line of workers who believe that they are solving the same kind of problem in the same kind of way. Their feeling of continuity appears to result from the fact that they share a metaphorical picture of their field of study, use the same symbols and symbolic generalizations, refer to the same model solutions or empirical studies, and share the same values. This is what Kuhn referred to as a 'disciplinary matrix'.

The structure of the book flows from this concept of what a tradition is. After discussing what a disciplinary matrix is and how it can be used to identify some research traditions in psychology, I go on to elaborate the elements of that matrix. In Chapter 4 I look at the first element of the disciplinary matrix: metaphor. In Chapter 5, metonymy is introduced as an additional resource in constructing theory. Then, in Chapter 6, I look at symbolic generalizations and the work they do. However, it is when we arrive at problem-solving in Chapters 7 and 8 that the account of how traditions change gathers momentum. Research traditions compete with each other to solve problems and to carve out niches of their own. An important weapon in this competition is the values (Chapter 9) which workers in a tradition try to impose on their own membership and on others, both to enforce a style of work and to maintain quality. Formal expression, empirical testing and prediction are among the values used. Realism is another, though we may have some doubts about it. I devote the penultimate chapter (10) to trying to clear up what kind of realism psychologists profess.

This is where I should end. However, I cannot resist the temptation to add a final chapter, sketching an approach to psychology which seems compatible with the activity of working in a research tradition. This is an impertinence. Strictly speaking, a reflexive psychology is an impossibility, since it suggests that out method of inquiry (the reflexive theory) is what we find after using it to make our inquiries. This is like expecting to find one's own corpse after excavating the tombs of the Pharoahs. Yet, one goes at it in the spirit that the approach one adopts should be an approach which explains one's approach.

Naturally, the reader will decide what to do about all this.

Part I
Research traditions in psychology

1 The knowledge matrix

Given that there are many approaches to mind and behaviour – psychoanalysis and personal construct theory and genetic epistemology and cognitive psychology derived from automaton theory, to list some of the principal ones – the impatient student of the subject is inclined to rank them. Which tradition solves the most problems, comes closest to the truth, and has the manners of science – that is, goes in for conjecture and refutation, is logically coherent, permits tight deductions, predicts events in detail, and turns up a crowd of data based on experiment and observation? Our difficulty in ranking these approaches is that they tend to take one to different parts of the territory of mind and show one different views, though sometimes there are blurred similarities. Aha, one thinks, that's something I saw in gestalt territory (as one wanders through cognition). Another difficulty is that these approaches tend to solve different kinds of problems, do not have all the manners of science, and claim equal familiarity with truth. Can it be the case that they are simply incommensurable, in the sense that the things we see along one route are not visible when we take another? These problems are familiar to us by now, coming as we do after 'the sociology of knowledge', 'language games' and 'scientific revolutions'. Knowledge, it seems, is not simply a matter of uncovering the truth, like lifting a napkin off the hot scones, or like inventing a periscope to look round and over obstacles. The old images of holding up a mirror to nature or finding a theory which is like a perfect lens for the understanding, a lens of absolute transparency and wonderful focus through which to see things as they are, turn out to be no more than images, perhaps illusions. They belong to a 'spectator theory of knowledge' (Dewey, 1950). Instead of simply looking, we have to 'twist the lion's tail' (Bacon, 1974) to make nature dislose its presence in various ways – by roaring or leaping or biting – so that we can guess what sort of beast it is. In other words, we prod, pummel, pinch, twist, tickle and bombard 'nature' in order to discover what it will do under various circumstances. We call this 'observing', and it is a long way from taking a good clear look at 'things as they are'. To observe, we must have theories, methods and technologies for carrying out the prodding and pummeling, but there is no simple opening of a box on the experimenter's lucky day to find nature reposing like a Barbie doll. What we have to do is to make the lion roar in more or less the same way when we prod in more or less the same way. We then come to a conclusion: it's a ten-decibel roar per prod kind of beast.

How, then, should we look at psychological approaches, traditions and theories? The first way is to ask how they enable us to intervene – to make observations and produce phenomena. The second way is to ask why we should do all this, in the sense of the human and social interests that are being served. Taken together, these questions about the interventions our theories make possible and about the interests they serve, define what we may call a knowledge matrix, which is simply an orderly arrangement of questions we attempt to answer in arriving at an understanding of a theory. This understanding, one should immediately say, is quite distinct from the understanding of the working psychologist who hopes to bring the theory to bear on events in order to produce experiments, data and interventions. Instead, it is an attempt to understand theories among other theories. To understand a theory in terms of a knowledge matrix is not to ask such questions as

- how should I explain this set of data here? or
- what sort of experiment would test this hypothesis? or
- what can I do to get rid of Mrs Casey's lower back pain?

No, to understand theories in terms of a knowledge matrix is to ask about theories as theories, it is to look at theories in the context of theory. To be specific, we attempt to understand a theory by asking and answering the following sorts of questions.

Questions about the social context of theories:
- What social functions do theories perform and what social structures determine that they shall perform these functions? since psychological theories reflect on the nature of persons, they must carry a heavy ideological freight (Ash and Woodward, 1987).
- When we study the 'manufacture' of knowledge (to use an expression which some prefer because of its no-nonsense materialist resonance), what sort of scientific practices, habits, rhetorical manoeuvres and discourse do we come across? Studies of this sort lead us to a close examination of the behaviour and talk of scientists in laboratories and in their other natural habitats.

Question about the intellectual contexts of theories:
- Is it possible to describe an intellectual *zeitgeist* – a sea of received ideas in which particular kinds of theory will multiply and swim?

Question about the content of theories:
- How can we compare, in a non-evaluative way, what various theories do? One possibility (which I shall adopt in this book) is to use Kuhn's concept of a disciplinary matrix, which refers to the metaphors, the symbolic generalizations, the internal values and the exemplary solutions which we find in a particular scientific enterprise.

A matrix is composed of ordered elements, each requiring further specification. It is in this sense that Kuhn (1977: 463) lists metaphors, symbolic generalizations and exemplars as elements of the disciplinary matrix of scientific traditions. To this we can add 'values', since these are central to the judgements which theorists working in particular traditions make of the success or failure of solutions to problems. I have also added the concept of a 'social matrix', which comprises the elements 'social structure', 'discourse' and 'intellectual climate' as factors in the cognitive operations of scientists. Each of these is discussed in the pages which follow.

Various people, at various times, have seemed to suggest that a 'real' understanding of science can only be achieved by asking the question in one of the ways listed above, with some refinement or twist to make it more precise. My own view is that we should conceive of these questions as leading to an understanding of the matrixes of knowledge. In other words, we have to decide in each case we are studying what the most interesting question is. Let me give an example. Suppose that we are studying what Danziger (1979a) calls 'the positivist repudiation of Wundt' in America, a repudiation which led to the rejection of his distinction between social and physiological or experimental psychology. Should we focus on intellectual climate; on the demands of a class of industrialists for a science which would make the prediction and control of behaviour possible; on an intra-disciplinary process which rewards those who advance new 'theories', however thin they might be, rather than those who deepen and extend older theories; on personal rivalries, such as the rivalry between Wundt and an ambitious assistant, Kulpe; or on the greater truth values of new theories? Surely, each of these would yield its own insights.

These are dazzling prospects. In this chapter I shall give examples of the discoveries we might make were we able to investigate psychological theories by bringing to bear all the questions suggested by the knowledge matrix. Then, I shall turn to an examination of the disciplinary matrix of psychological sciences. Finally, I shall turn back to examine some of the epistemological questions which psychology must provoke. The point is, quite simply, that psychology is reflexive in the sense that any theory of psychology must tell us about processes which occur in the scientist who is producing the theory. This is particularly relevant when we are examining theories which intend to tell us about persons, theories which are ambitious in the range of phenomena they explain. All the theories discussed in this book are of that kind. Hence, in the end we shall have to ask what the consequences of adopting a particular psychological theory are for a theory of knowledge. The knowing subject, or person, is at the centre of knowledge, asking questions and suggesting answers. This does not imply individualism. Our knowledge matrix makes it quite clear that we will often be interested in the social provenance of knowledge and in the interpersonal activities which shape it.

Let me now illustrate what I have been saying by describing studies which have focused on different features of the knowledge matrix. They are:

Social matrix
- Social structure
- Discourse
- Intellectual climate

Disclipinary matrix
- Exemplary studies and problem solutions
- Symbolic generalizations
- Metaphors and images
- Values and goals in a scientific discipline

Knowledge matrix: 1. Social structure

The main feature of attempts to link social structure to knowledge is that they indicate specific cases in which the two affect each other in a specific manner and to a specific degree, and the main problem which has arisen out of this is that of relativism. If theories are socially conditioned, how can we, as members of society, know whether our theories are true? Suppose we divide the problem in the following way: (1) we admit that different theories arise in different cultures and social structures, yet (2) we claim that we can compare and evaluate these theories.

The first form of relativism is called epistemic relativism and the second is called judgemental relativism (Bhaskar, 1979; Knorr-Cetina and Mulkay, 1983). It doesn't require much to convince us of the truth of the first proposition, since we immediately find, in the work of anthropologists and historians, a variety of theories. It seems to make perfect sense to ask how these theories come about, what social institutions produce them, and what functions they serve. When we turn to the second proposition, that it is possible to evaluate and hence to prefer some theories to others, we soon find convincing reasons to assent. The proposition does not state that it is always possible, or that any theory can be compared with any other, but merely that in certain significant instances we can judge one theory to be better than another. Where we are not able to do this, it is usually because theories are indistinguishably bad or because they work in totally different domains, as a theory of magnetism and a theory of angels must. In the social sciences, it may often be difficult to prefer one theory to another because it is not clear what problems these theories solve. On the other hand, modern theories in chemistry and physics are indisputably better than older theories because

(a) they enable us to do things we could never do with the older theories (utility);
(b) they enable us to explore the universe in more and more surprising ways (information); and
(c) they solve concrete scientific problems (problem-solving).

In this section, though, we are concerned with epistemic relativism, with the ways in which social factors shape the enterprise of producing knowledge. As Danziger says:

> The development of new scientific specialities and subspecialities involves a shift in the division of labor. The production of certain kinds of knowledge becomes the prerogative of a group with a particular professional identity (1979b: 34).

Let us revert to the 'repudiation' of Wundt's distinction between social and physiological psychology in America, and ask: What were the differences between Germany and America a little before the turn of the century and how did these influence the rate of Wundt's psychology?

Germany
- University psychology was dominated by philosophy
- Psychology had to be made legitimate to philosophers
- Psychological experiments were often questioned

USA
- University philosophers were few in number
- Philosophy was subordinate to psychology, which was more 'practical'
- University appointments were controlled by those interested in 'techniques of social control and in tangible performance' (Danziger, 1979b: 35)

In Germany, the relation between professional psychologists and the sources of social power was mediated by the established position of philosophy; in the USA, this relationship was relatively direct. American psychologists promised a practical, useful science, to which all other social sciences would be subordinate. It was no accident that American psychologists were initially interested in behaviour rather than in mind, or in the measurement of intelligence rather than in the processes of cognition. They were pragmatists, who wished to make their influence felt in education, industry, counselling, military affairs and wherever important and busy things were being done. Retrospectively, we have distorted Wundt's contribution to fit our image of modern psychology. We see him as the founder of experimental psychology but ignore the fact that he distinguished between two kinds of psychology – 'physiological and social, the former employing experimental methods, the latter, nonexperimental methods' (Danziger, 1979b: 31). Wundt was deeply aware of the fact that psychological laws are historically situated – they are 'developmental' and must be understood in their social context, and he warned against abstract laws of behaviour, calling them 'metaphysical'. American psychology, however, took the road of metaphysical abstraction, with the consequence that human action was stripped of its social context and reduced to 'behaviour' and social reality was reduced to 'stimuli' (Danziger, 1979b: 40).

The power of the natural sciences and the scientific model ensured the imitation of experimental methods, even where these were grossly inappropriate. Every effort was made to treat subjects as though they were objects by pretending that they are 'naive' and the subject's theories were usually either ignored or regarded as a contaminating factor. Possible goals for psychology, such as emancipation and radical social change, were initially subordinated to control and prediction, for the reasons which have already been given.

One might object that explanation in terms of social structure neglects the internal logic of a discipline, the metaphysical context, and the use of powerful models (such as the natural science model); and one would be correct. Our concept of a knowledge matrix prevents us from developing only one kind of explanation of the growth of particular forms of knowledge. The sociology of knowledge directs our attention to the interests of social groups and to the ways in which institutions are organized, but it can never give us the whole story.

We can also point to a flaw in the kinds of relations uncovered by traditional 'sociology of knowledge' studies. Most strikingly, they show a relation (or suggest an influence) which runs from established power to some form of inquiry, such as science. However, when sciences become highly developed, the very societies in which they exist are transformed by scientific innovations. Knowledge creates new centres and kinds of power. As Bruno Latour observes, in his study of Pasteur's laboratory:

> This interest of outsiders for lab experiments is not a given: it is the result of Pasteur's work in enrolling and enlisting them. This is worth emphasizing since there is a quarrel among sociologists of science about the possibility of imputing interests to people (Latour, 1983: 143).

We should not aim to discover a permanent, static or relentlessly pressurizing set of interests in dominant groups: rather, we should look at the ways in which people try to interest others in particular kinds of activities. Interests are created as well as 'found' and utilized. Social activity is more like rhetoric, persuasion, games and theatre than like astronomy, in which one might aspire to watch the eternal and unchanging heavens. The search for fixed interests misses the point, as Latour observes. 'He who is able to translate others' interests into his own language carries the day' (Latour, 1983: 144). We should look for the processes of invitation and persuasion as well as pressure. American psychologists were not the victims of practical men of affairs, we might argue; on the contrary, they conned these practical men into supporting an ambitious enterprise – that of creating experimental psychology – by making promises that could only be fulfilled (if at all) in the distant future. They translated the concerns of men of affairs into their own language and created the enormous enterprise of American psychology, with its tens of thousands of psychologists, enormous budgets and vast student enrolments. What should be examined is the ways in which this discipline has created new social forms, new ideas, new activities and new forms of power.

These few remarks are merely illustrations of the kind of work that needs to be done in construing the history of psychology. Much more detail is required to understand the interplay of influences which led American and German psychology to diverge in their early days, at the turn of the century.

Let us now turn to the next element of the knowledge matrix, which is a study of the actual discourse and practice of scientists in their laboratories and in the networks which create (or 'manufacture') science.

Knowledge matrix: 2. Discourse

Discourse is to the social sciences what matter is to physics. In other words, it is impossible to define, though it is necessary as an object of study. Russell said that matter is whatever satisfied the equations of physics; similarly, discourse is whatever we choose to include in the theories of social scientists attempting to understand significant interaction among people. There is no theory of discourse, just as there is no theory of matter. We study discourse in all the various forms it takes: rhetoric, war, theatre, illness, practical affairs, science, love, fiction, banking or teaching. Wherever we find disciplines, audiences, speakers, texts, gestures or acts which constitute social realities, such as marriage, crime and madness, we are studying discourse. What, then, is the value of studying 'scientific' discourse? How could it possibly contribute to our understanding of the creation of psychology? Indeed, the question is still an open one, but a preliminary answer is that the study of discourse enables us to understand how science is dressed up for public consumption in journals. When science is formally presented, we see nothing of the process of discovery (Medawar, 1963); writing is impersonal, the logic of the world apparently dictates the course of events and when the author does appear in the text, he is presented as being subject to the unequivocal demands of natural phenomena and the rules of experimental procedure (Bazerman, 1981). Scientists regularly present correct theory as arising unproblematically from the experimental evidence, while incorrect theory is explained as a consequence of various distorting effects, whether personal, social or other extraneous factors (Latour and Woolgar, 1979). On the other hand, when we study the 'manufacture' of knowledge before it has been dressed up, we find no such rationality. Scientists attempt to 'sell' their ideas, to persuade, to shape the data in various ways, to find new angles, and make irrational leaps and connections. Discourse, as we see, takes different shapes among different participants at different stages of presentation. Is this important? Jonathan Swift was fascinated by various stages of dress and undress, and satirized beauty by showing its various layers. Here, a beautiful nymph goes to bed (*Corinna, Pride of Drury Lane*):

> There, seated on a three-legg'd chair
> Takes off her artificial hair;
> Now picking out a crystal eye,
> She wipes it clean and lays it by . . .
> Now dext'rously her plumpers draws
> That serve to fill her hollow jaws,
> Untwists a wire, and from her gums
> A set of teeth completely comes;
> Pulls out the rags contrived to prop
> Her flabby dugs, and down they drop.

And so forth. The registers of discourse may be no more significant than the registers of dress. We do, in fact, dress differently and discourse differently on different occasions, but what does this tell us about the manufacture of knowledge? Knorr-Cetina invites us to take the process of production seriously.

> If we take the metaphor of the manufacture of knowledge seriously, science emerges from the constructivist interpretation as a 'way of world-making' (Goodman, 1978). A factory is a production facility, and not an establishment designed to mimic nature' (Knorr-Cetina, 1983: 135).

The various shifts of register, the negotiations about what was actually seen and what really happened, the discussions about what evidence is relevant, the sudden changes in angle, the compromises about method and decision rules, the taking into account of grant agencies, administrators, publishers and others, are all part of the process of manufacture, the constructivist process in which science is conceived of as a 'process of embodiment and incorporation of objects in our language and practice' (Knorr-Cetina, 1983: 136).

There is also a more sceptical view of analyses of this kind (e.g. Agassi, 1984). Studying science from the outside, without reference to the search for truth, is rather like training pigeons to play ping-pong. There's something missing. Shouldn't we direct the sort of argument at this kind of microscopic analysis that used to be directed at operationism – that it makes physics into the science of meter-reading? Here, we seem to imagine that science is a kind of rhetoric without reference to reality, one in which unicorns and hartebeest are indistinguishably real. Some analyses would be more vulnerable to this kind of criticism than others, but Knorr-Cetina would undoubtedly defend herself by referring to her position as an empirical constructivist epistemology, which is directed at the 'unknown world' (Knorr-Cetina, 1983: 135). What we have to study is science as a process of engagement with that unknown, a process which leads to an increasing stock of problems. We may contrast this with a problem-solving approach, which would assume that as we solve the problems of the universe, we decrease the stock of remaining problems. We can now return to Jonathan Swift. The plumpers, the wires, the rags and all the other gear are important in the production of beauty; and perhaps the metaphors, the twists, the negotiations, the rule-fiddling and the transformation of data are equally important in the production of knowledge. And maybe not. It is just as likely that we are still at the surface, collecting data and imagining that they are explanatory principles. My own view is that, for the moment, discursive practices are the object of social science theory, but that they do not explain very much. To revert to the analogy with which I began this section, discursive practices are like material phenomena – like bodies falling in space, like magnetic deflections, like light and heat – which must be studied until we arrive at an understanding of them. Till then, our close observation of these things will be like a close observation of ants hurrying in various directions to collect grain or seed. We shall be interested, but without the ability to understand what makes them behave as they do.

Knowledge matrix: 3. Intellectual climate

New knowledge is generated in the context of existing knowledge; but how shall we describe that knowledge? One way is to make an inventory of existing theories. Soon we see, provided that we step back a little, that the theories of an age resemble each other, and our problem is to describe that resemblance. It is clear, for example, that psychological theories have arisen in three contexts. The first we may describe as that of theology, which led to dualism; the second we may describe as that of mechanistic natural science, which led to behaviourism; the third we may describe as that of information and ideology, which leads to cognitive psychology and discourse analysis.

How can we describe these knowledge systems? The approach which I shall present here is the 'semiotic' approach to culture, which proposes that cultures are composed of sign systems or 'languages'. This is the approach of the Moscow – Tartu group, and is well reviewed by Winner and Umiker-Sebeok (1979). 'Culture is information', as Lotman (1977: 213) says, and this is true even of those 'monuments of material culture' which serve practical purposes. Such 'monuments', whether they be buildings, machines, clothing or agricultural fields, serve both a practical, immediately obvious purpose, and pass on information from person to person. In other words, practical arrangements and implements also have 'textual' functions, which can be read off in various ways, as though they were utterances in a language. We see this in the work of Michel Foucault, who reads the various discursive practices of surveillance and punishment in the architecture of prisons and lunatic asylums as well as in the texts of criminologists and psychiatrists, of pedagogues and ministers of religion (Foucault, 1972).

Suppose, then, that we look at the arrangements of a culture as though they had both practical and textual or semiotic functions in order to construct its 'language' or 'code'. How, in other words, do the various details of the text hang together in what Foucault (1972) calls an 'episteme' and others might call a world view or an ideology? The important thing is that knowledge is produced within such a world, at once material and significant, at once practical and textual. Everything has both its immediate, obvious utility or function and its place in a system of signs which must be 'read' if we are to understand any culture.

Let us now look back at the cultural context in which psychology has arisen, as a system of knowledge and practice. Lotman (1977) contrasts two cultural types, the medieval and the enlightenment, and to these I would add a third and a fourth, the ideological and the discursive. It is very likely that the last two types will be collapsed into one, when seen from a greater distance, but they do have some interesting features which separate them, and the additional detail will serve our present purpose of understanding the relation of forms of psychology to forms of culture.

Before I say anything more about types or 'codes', we must bear in mind that we will always find a mixture of codes in any period of history. All that we are interested in, for the moment, is the dominant code.

Let us now attempt to describe the four codes briefly and see what kind of psychology is implied by each.

In the medieval code, we see that the primary objects of knowledge are God and Spirit, the eternal rather than the temporal. God is to be known by interpretation of holy texts, by prayer, by meditation and, ultimately by revelation. Power is maintained by controlling permissible interpretation. The world is 'saturated' with the presence of God, and hence with meaning; all things may be signs and derive value from this. Things often mean by resemblance: man is created in the image of God, icons are sacred, and true knowledge is a knowledge of images and names – the name of God (which may be too sacred to be uttered) and the blasphemous names of demons who might be conjured up by correct modes of address. The essential mode of understanding is mythical or participative (through rituals and observances). Myths reveal the true story and the real names of the world. Texts which bear this truth are sacred.

The psychology which arises in this context is a psychology of the Spirit and its relation to God. The rational is eternal and divine. On the other hand, when we are mad, we are possessed by demons. We can see, also, how features of this psychology (dualism, for example) have persisted and how the difficulties come to a head in the work of Descartes.

When we turn to the enlightenment, we see that the focus of interest is the material world. Men strive to discover the machinery of nature. A new mode of inquiry, experiment and observation rises to prominence to supplement mathematical or demonstrative reasoning. None of these things happen suddenly, but it is not my intention to attempt detailed history here. Mythical understanding is excluded in favour of functional understanding of the relations between events. Words are arbitrary, things are real. We should abandon our theories if they do not fit the world.

What kind of psychology arises here? The first is a drive towards understanding the brain as an organ which secretes thought, as the liver secretes bile. The climax of this is the study of the process of conditioning. The second is a drive towards the creation of mental machines, or engines of thought, which will carry out mind-like processes and eventually enable us to understand the mind as a machine. The climax of this is the study of artificial intelligence and its embodiment is the computer. The computer then becomes a major metaphor in our understanding of the mind as a material machine.

We now turn to the ideological code and discover that the primary object of knowledge is the social origin of our ideas and the primary mode of inquiry is 'unmasking'. When individuals or classes present ideas, these are to be treated as the masks of yet deeper ideas, interests or motives. Given any picture of the world, our task as social scientists is to show that it is a rationalization of some hidden interest or motive. The primary relation of signs to objects is that signs serve hidden interests or motives. The major epistemological problem of the ideological period is relativism. In the medieval period, God was the measure of truth; in the enlightenment, truth was to be found in experiment; in the ideological period, truth is to be found by asserting that there are definite keys to knowledge. In Marxism, the key is to be found in the system of production of material goods; in Freudianism, the key is to be found in the biological and particularly the sexual nature of the human species.

These are fragile assumptions, and when they are questioned, we find ourselves in the discursive code (which might also be regarded as a subtype of the ideological). Before I go on to describe the main features of the discursive code, though, let me refer briefly to the forms of psychological theory which are associated with the ideological code. These are psychoanalysis and Marxian social psychology. In both, the process of inquiry leads to a progressive uncovering or unmasking of the true state of affairs, as we show how various symptoms, rationalizations and ideological errors disguise the underlying truth. In the former, this truth is the fixed system of instincts or drives; in the latter, it is a system of class interests. These instincts and interests are the 'master code' of social understanding.

What happens when motives and interests are relativized? This is when we enter the discursive type of knowledge formation, in which our main object of interest is a study of the codes themselves, and a compar son of these codes. There is no 'master code' into which all others are translated. Every decoding is a further encoding; every translation is merely a translation into another code which is just as detached from any fixed basis. It is said that objects are constituted by discourse and the modes of understanding are rhetorical. In fact, rhetoric is the main form of social knowledge and the production of rhetoric seems to be the main form of social activity. However, rhetoric is embodied in discursive practices and not merely in words. Ploughs, guns and cathedrals are part of rhetoric, as we see when we examine them aesthetically.

What is radically new about both the ideological and the discursive codes is that they embody change. The medieval and the enlightenment approaches to the world saw it as essentially fixed in its order and nature. There was only one set of problems to solve, even if it was an immense set. Even Marx saw the world as progressively changing towards a socialist system, but the new 'master code' of knowledge has removed the concepts of 'progress' and 'end'. Evolution and change are not progressive. Every problem we solve creates new problems, just as every new species creates new problems for other species.

What kind of psychology is consonant with a discursive code? In general, psychology which treats mind as historically formed and localized becomes the obvious choice. This is the general approach in modern cross-cultural psychology. The fundamental assumption here is that mind is social and that the social is rhetorical and discursive, though the word 'practice' may be thrown into the soup as well. As an example of this kind of approach, let me refer to Gergen's (1982) book, which favours what he calls 'sociorationalism'. What was wrong with the 'positivist–empiricist' programme, according to Gergen, was that it assumed that:

- scientific knowledge is cumulative (contrast this with Kuhn's concept of 'scientific revolutions'),
- scientific truths are eternal and ahistorical,
- facts determine theories, and
- there is a clear distinction between facts and values.

What Gergen is rejecting is the materialism of the enlightenment code; instead, he takes the view that knowledge is generated not by the internal mental processes of individuals, but by 'a social process of communication' (Gergen, 1982: 207) and 'Truth is the product of a collectivity of truth makers' (1982: 207). This echoes Habermas's concept of truth as a predicate of communicative acts under ideal speech conditions of free and equal opportunities to participate in discussion. (Mary Hesse (1980) asks the question: What if truth has to be brought down from the Mount by Moses, inscribed as a tablet as Divine Law? Isn't our notion that free and equal participation is an essential characteristic of truthful communicative acts simply one perspective from one position and moment in history?) To summarize, sociorationalism:

- focuses on collective activities and communication;
- argues for a socially constructed reality; and
- does not distinguish sharply between values and facts, but invites the investigator to place intellectual expression at the service of a vision of the good (Gergen, 1982: 208).

The difficulties in this approach are not hard to find. The obvious one is that your vision of the good may not be mine, and mine may not be yours. Even if this is transferred to the plane of social life (since the collective and its rhetoric are primary), there are sure to be various parties, gangs, classes and factions, each with a vision of the good and a lively rhetoric to support it. A second difficulty is that a careless interpretation of the notion that 'reality' is socially constructed leads us to suppose that coelocanths and mermaids are real in the same way. Both are social constructions. The difference is that they refer to different kinds of entities, one to be found only in picture books and stories, and the other to be found in the natural world (however problematic some may find that notion). It might be useful to distinguish between 'dubbing' various objects (such as moons, planets, coelocanths, atoms and quasars) and entering them into a variety of theoretical systems. Natural scientists attempt to do both. They attempt to dub, or to refer to real natural entities – and sometimes they are wrong – as well as to enter these real entities into theoretical systems. Sometimes, as Kuhn (1979) points out, an object changes its theoretical status: what was thought to be an element is found to be a compound. Nevertheless, we track its various theoretical allocations without losing faith in its identity. It is the 'same' entity, but we understand it differently.

And what of the social sciences? Are we interested in 'realities' or only in the creations of rhetoric? This is a question which we shall keep referring to in this book. It seems to me that the only interesting line for us to take is that we are interested in discovering the real. There are obvious realities, the ones we refer to all the time, such as persons, languages and social institutions. What changes continually is our understanding of these. The concept of rhetoric and the primacy of interpersonal processes is a new way of understanding (or attempting to understand) persons, but we can still identify persons without difficulty. Occasionally, sciences introduce new entities in order to explain events and claim for these entities the same status in reality as would be claimed for those we are already familiar with. Electrons are referred to. Are they 'real'? Superego and id, unconscious and conscious are referred to. Are they 'real'?

These are immense questions. I shall take the line that we are in pursuit of the 'real', even if we do find ourselves deep in rhetoric; but how can we study the rhetoric in which we find ourselves immersed? There are various ways, and we should avoid despair. The first is by historical study, as we have implied in comparing the various culture codes which have dominated European thought over the last millenium. The second is cross-cultural, which proceeds by the same methods as historical study, with the difference that there are sometimes representatives of various cultures about, more or less ready to be studied. The third is by dialectical exchange within what we think of as our own culture. This exchange may be therapeutic, analytical or participative. We may, in a therapeutic exchange, discover different parts of ourselves which were previously hidden from us. By analysing political and literary discourse we may discover forms of social life which are hidden from various participants. By participating in social activities and then reflecting with others on our participation we may discover meanings and structures of which we were not previously aware. Finally, by studying our reactions to others in critical situations (transference and counter-transference) we discover significant social and personal facts.

The problem with most social psychology is that it has been ineffective because it has attempted to adopt an objective or 'spectator' approach to knowledge. We have administered questionnaires and performed trivial experiments. We can only 'twist the lion's tail' by entering into skilfully directed relationships with other persons. Controlled rhetoric is the psychologists' neutron gun, cyclotron or X-ray. This is what Freud and Marx showed, and we are slowly absorbing that lesson into the knowledge theories (epistemology) of the social sciences.

I have indicated some difficulties in working within the intellectual climate of the discursive code, using Gergen's sociorationalism as a peg to hang the discussion on, and then I have indicated a distinct preference for the 'real'. This is rather like a bankrupt declaring a preference for a million dollars. How do we get a million dollars? – or the 'real'? Those who live by the discursive code had better have a good philosophy handy when they come to be judged by it. We shall have to find a way of drawing back from relativism; we shall have to find a master code; reality is too good an idea to let go of. We shall see how it goes but pilgrims do not always make it to the holy land. I hope, though, to find a master code in the concept of the evolution of knowledge, a concept which will be developed from Chapter 7 on.

Conclusion

We have opened up more questions than we can properly answer in our discussion of the first three components of the knowledge matrix. Knowledge, it has been suggested, is influenced by social structure, by discourse, and by intellectual climate. In all of these, we seem to converge on something which we might call the structure of discursive practices, or a treatment of culture as rhetorical practicality. That is to say, artifacts have primary purposes, for which they are ostensibly designed, as well as rhetorical purposes, which shape the style of manners and thought in society.

Now we come to the inner circle of the knowledge matrix, to what Kuhn (1970) called the disciplinary matrix. This is the immediate intellectual anatomy of a body of knowledge.

2 Paradigms and disciplinary matrixes

To capture attention it is often necessary to state a point of view boldly and without qualification. This is sure to stir up a noise. One may then begin to qualify, but one has defined the subject of debate. Evolution by natural selection; determination of the superstructure by the relations and forces of production; and the non-cumulative advance of science by revolutionary changes of paradigm are bold sketches of the views of Darwin, Marx and Kuhn. It may turn out, subsequently, that 'natural selection', the 'relations and forces of production', and 'paradigms' are puzzling notions and that the ways in which they are supposed to determine speciation, superstructures and the practice of science are obscure, but these formulations are like navigational instructions. They tell us the direction in which we must sail, though they do not give a complete set of instructions for the voyage. They are like the order: 'sail west and find the Spice islands'. Of course, the task may be impossible, but we know which way to go and what to look for.

Kuhn points us towards the study of revolutionary change in science and the non-rational factors which lead scientists to choose a revolution rather than adhere to old modes of thinking. Others have drawn the conclusion, to which Kuhn reacts with dismay, that he sees scientific change as a largely irrational process, in which people are 'converted' from one view to another; as solipsistic since people adhering to one paradigm cannot understand people adhering to another; and as relativistic, since the paradigms are incommensurable in the sense that they do not refer to the same problems and entities. We have, then, a picture of scientists in different closed worlds unable to communicate with each other except by conversion, which defeats the object of communication.

Kuhn quite justly points out that this is an absurd distortion of his views. He can refer to many passages in his book, *The Structure of Scientific Revolutions*, which show that he is not committed to irrationalism. When one draws attention to non-rational factors in a choice, does one imply that there are no rational factors? When one shows that some revolutionary changes lead scientists to abandon old concepts and problems, so that these have no place in the new paradigm, is one saying that comparison is totally impossible? When one learns a new 'language' (in the sense of a new theoretical approach) one may lose facility in the old 'language', and those who have never learnt the old 'language' may not even understand what it was about; but is any of this mysteriously solipsistic, implying that communication is in principle impossible and that we advance from one closed world to another, without any possibility of knowing that we have progressed rather than simply changed?

It is the fate of those who point us in new directions to be associated with slogans and simplifications. That is the only way in which the non-specialist can remember these directions. 'Westward!' he mutters. 'Find the paradigm.'

Let me now give a brief account of Kuhn's approach to science and then spell out the particular version of it that I wish to use: his expansion of *paradigm* as *disciplinary matrix*.

Paradigms

The key words in Kuhn's schema are paradigm, normal science, crisis and revolution, followed by normal science once more. Let us take them in order.

Scientists are said to share a paradigm. An energetic critic (Masterman, 1970) has discovered 21 ways in which he uses the term. Here are some of them:

- universally recognized scientific achievement
- myth
- philosophy or constellation of questions
- textbook as classic work
- analogy
- standard illustration
- gestalt figure which can be seen two ways
- general epistemological viewpoint.

Some of these differences are significant, others are not, but this analysis has forced Kuhn to clarify his concept and reduce his images to two. A paradigm, in his 1970 revised edition (Kuhn, 1970: 175), is either:

- a model solution of a scientific problem; or
- an entire constellation of beliefs, values and techniques shared by the members of a given community.

How do scientists learn to do science? They learn by example, by practice in solving standard problems which exercise them in the language and habits of thought of an established science. Physicists, during their training, solve many problems in their textbooks and learn to perform standard experiments; radical behaviourists learn to see behaviour in terms of contingencies of reinforcement; psychoanalysts learn to detect the impulses which are disguised in symptoms. In each field, practitioners use their own theoretical language and refer to classic examples when asked what their science is about. Furthermore, it is well-nigh impossible to translate from one language into another, even where they seem to be talking about similar events.

This is clear enough when we cross disciplinary boundaries, as when we try to picture a physicist, a physiologist, a behaviourist and a psychoanalyst explaining a gesture of the hand. Each of these must refer to different theoretical entities and to different processes. Even in 'psychological' accounts, the radical behaviourist will omit any reference to intention or to fantasy and concentrate on the stimuli which elicit the behaviour: the psychoanalyst would explain the gesture in terms of displacement, or as an expression of an unconscious impulse, or in terms of hysterical conversion, or some such thing, depending on the precise meaning which he could read into it.

When we contrast psychoanalysis and behaviourism we can see, quite easily, what is meant in saying that people who share different paradigms have different techniques, different values, different concepts and refer to different examples. We could illustrate this equally well by referring to the new paradigm of cognitive psychology, with its vocabulary drawn from information science and the computer. At a later stage of this book we shall turn to these examples once more, showing how important the imagery of science is in establishing pictures of 'reality'. Now we turn to the next key word in Kuhn's scheme – normal science.

Once a paradigm has been accepted, scientists have the job of working on the many puzzles it creates. Psychoanalysts, cognitive theorists and behaviourists attempt to fill in the gaps in their approach to empirical questions. Normal science is, as Kuhn says, puzzle-solving science. We repair anomalies, we show the power of the new paradigm, we invent new methods, we discover technical applications. It is inevitable that difficulties accumulate during the course of this puzzle-solving activity. We become increasingly aware of the anomalies and the limitations of our approach. There are so many important questions which we find ourselves simply unable to answer in any satisfactory way and even to ask intelligibly, that we look round for approaches which will lead to new solutions. The young, in particular, want new solutions to new problems.

Finally, the discipline reaches a state of *crisis* and scientists (particularly younger ones) no longer have faith in established theories. At this stage they are ready to attach themselves to a new vision of reality, and to new solutions (even if these solutions are full of difficulties). In fact, they are ready for revolution. Kuhn adds that revolution entails conversion; sometimes a choice between theories is made on insufficient grounds, because the new theory promises solutions which we no longer expect of the old theory. In psychology there are many examples of choices being made on the basis of promise rather than achievement. Many people chose psychoanalysis because it seemed to them to solve fundamental problems in psychopathology, aesthetics, the interpretation of dreams, mythology and religion. And many others bought the hardnosed promises of behaviourism for its apparent practicality. The choice was not made on clearly rational grounds, but on the basis of interests, assumptions, values, expectations, chance contacts, training and intellectual climate.

As we have already seen, the learning of a new approach in science is like the learning of a new language *and* the acquisition of a new set of practical skills. The behaviourist cannot (as a rule) psychoanalyse; the psychoanalyst cannot (as a rule) perform conditioning experiments. Nor can they apply their reasoning to the same concepts, since these concepts exist in one but not in the other theory. Concepts such as 'complex', 'cathexis', 'superego' and 'defence mechanism' exist in psychoanalysis and not in behaviourism, though a laborious translation may be attempted. What seems to follow from this is that these approaches are incommensurable and that all truly revolutionary changes introduce approaches which are incommensurable. Taken to its extreme, this would suggest that we live in different worlds when we adopt different paradigms and that comparison of these worlds is impossible. Suppose a psychoanalyst were to convert to behaviourism, would he still be concerned with cathexis and superego and conscious/unconscious mind? Would he see any *point* in trying to identify these ideas in behaviourist language? I think this is the significant thing. Even if it were possible, it might no longer be worth doing. Truly revolutionary science, like revolutionary politics or religious conversion, introduces a new set of ideas and there is simply no point in attempting to find the old ideas in the new theory. However, we may still demand that the new theory give a satisfactory account of important empirical findings. This appears to be obvious, but it is not necessarily so. Are schedules of reinforcement significant problems for a theory of cognitive psychology? Possibly, but it is not clear that they should be. A cognitive theory might ignore schedules of reinforcement and focus on an entirely different set of problems – say problems of memory or perception. Schedules of reinforcement might be ignored until they become theoretically important for cognitive psychology.

Let us now summarize the main criticisms of Kuhn's contribution.

- It was said that he used the term *paradigm* in 21 different ways (Masterman, 1970). Kuhn acknowledged the difficulty and attempted to make his usage more consistent.
- Emphasis on 'gestalt change' and 'conversion' from one paradigm to another suggest that science is largely non-rational or even irrational. This introduces relativism.
- 'Incommensurability' of paradigms appears to suggest that we live in closed worlds and that comparison and criticism is not possible. This substitutes collective solipsism for individual solipsism.

The first criticism is effectively dealt with in Kuhn (1970). We have already said something about both the second and third criticism, but it would be valuable to draw our comments together.

Kuhn retorts that to point out the significance of non-rational factors in scientific revolutions is hardly the same as a denial of rational factors. Even though scientists draw on other values in choosing theories, 'the demonstrated ability to set up and solve puzzles presented by nature is, in case of value conflict, the dominant criterion for most members of a scientific group' (1970: 205).

It is not always clear at first which of two theories is better at solving problems, and then it is inevitable that some will back the right one and others the wrong one. It may also be the case that both theories are bad bets. This is inevitable in human affairs, and to admit such a thing is not to deny rational activity, but to assert that reason must often operate under conditions of uncertainty.

What of relativism? Is it true that if we must sometimes choose on non-rational grounds, we are committed to a malignant relativism? Kuhn denies this, making the point that 'later scientific theories are better than earlier ones at solving problems' (1970: 206) and hence it is usually possible to distinguish later from earlier theories. Can we say, though, that theories get closer to 'the truth', in the sense that they represent what is 'really' there in nature? To this, Kuhn replies that he can see no coherent direction of ontological development. Do sciences yield functional/pragmatic knowledge only, or do they 'cut nature at its joints' (to use Boyd's 1979 phrase)? Are we in pursuit of real entities and do we get truer and truer pictures of them?

It is not in the interests of orderly progress to start such hares at this stage of the book, much less to go off chasing them. We shall therefore resolutely continue the procession, which is towards disciplinary matrixes, and try to catch a hare or two later in the book. Then we shall see how real they are.

Disciplinary matrix

In his 1970 revision of his book on scientific revolutions, Kuhn expands the concept of paradigm to disciplinary matrix; and it is this expansion that I shall use to complete my concept of knowledge matrix. Disciplinary matrix is the inner circle of knowledge matrix. What, then, is a disciplinary matrix?

Kuhn discusses four elements of the disciplinary matrix, namely *symbolic generalizations, beliefs in particular models, values,* and *exemplars.* What are these?

Symbolic generalizations are most easily demonstrated in physics and other natural sciences, where we find equations such as

$F = ma$ (Force is mass m × acceleration a)
$I = V/R$ (Current I is potential difference V divided by resistance R)
$PV = k$ (The volume V of a given mass of gas at a constant temperature is inversely proportional to its pressure P)

In the social sciences, such laws are less common, but they do exist in economics, sociology and psychology. To concentrate on psychology, we find such equations as:

$$\frac{DI}{I} = K$$ (Weber's law: The least added difference in stimulus DI that can be noticed is a constant proportion of the original stimulus I)

These generalizations are often taken to be 'laws of nature', but they may also be definitions of the terms they employ, as Kuhn observes. Thus, laws of gravity and of pressure/volume/temperature (Boyle's law) seem for a while to be unbendable and unbreakable laws of nature. On the other hand, some generalizations function as definitions; hence they are axioms. Axioms are important in defining our vision of nature. Here are some that I would add. They are 'research programmes' (Lakatos, 1978; Popper, 1972), or basic assumptions about what can and what cannot happen if nature is what we assume it to be. These axioms are expressed as 'laws':

The law of conservation of matter
The law of conservation of energy
The laws of thermodynamics
The law of evolution by natural selection.

The law of the conservation of matter is an axiom about what happens to matter during a chemical reaction. When a reaction occurs in a sealed container, no matter can be gained or lost. If there is either gain or loss, the container has not been properly sealed. Furthermore, the chemical equation for that reaction must be so written that the mass on the left must balance the mass on the right-hand side of the equation. The law of the conservation of energy states, in similar vein, that energy may change its form but cannot be created or destroyed. The first law of thermodynamics states that the energy in a system equals the energy input less the energy output. These laws of mass and energy were the axioms of classical physics and chemistry.

The law of evolution by natural selection states that speciation is brought about by the differential survival of the offspring of certain kinds of individuals in each generation. A psychological axiom within the tradition of radical behaviourism is that positive reinforcements increase the probability of operants on which they are contingent, thus shaping behaviours.

These axioms define our terms and also our conception of reality. If they are wrong, reality will have to be conceptualized quite differently. If matter were not conserved in chemical equations, then some non-material agency would be at work in them. If energy were not conserved, or the first law of thermodynamics did not hold, then the energy equations of physics would be nonsense. If organisms did not evolve by natural selection then some other force would be at work. These axioms define the terms of our observation and hence our conception of the fundamental realities of nature. When they are violated in any particular observation, we conclude that the observation is faulty. We look for the missing matter, the energy, the environmental factor that is affecting breeding rate, or the reinforcements which have gone unnoticed. These axioms direct us to look upon nature as having a certain structure and are essential for coherent science.

To summarize: Generalizations may (a) be laws of nature; (b) define terms; and (c) define research programmes.

When we assess the coherence of any theoretical position, we must examine its axioms, particularly its commitment to a research programme which defines the 'reality' it confronts. Since psychologists rarely attempt to state axioms, our task is relatively difficult. We can only hope that, in the event of our stating an axiom incorrectly, other theorists will correct the mistake.

The next feature of the disciplinary matrix to which we should turn is the way in which we are committed to particular metaphors. Some of these may be purely heuristic (we may think of an electric circuit as though it were 'a steady-state hydrodynamic system' and the molecules of a gas as 'tiny elastic billiard balls in random motion' (Kuhn, 1970: 184). However, our commitment to an image may, especially in psychology and the social sciences, become a moral vision. This leads to considerable (and often well-justified) heat. Do we commit ourselves to a model of persons as:

- actors,
- scientists testing hypotheses,
- clever automata, processing information,
- products of schedules of reinforcement,
- autonomous and reflective individuals, or
- victims of childhood experiences?

The point of view which will be advanced in this book is that these images are important in opening up space for research programmes, and hence considerable attention will be paid to the metaphors of modern psychology. If we conceive of persons as rhetoricians, we direct our attention to different problems that if we conceive of persons as products of reinforcement. We might even conceive of persons in terms of many metaphors, acknowledging the insufficiency of any single metaphor for capturing the diversity of human processes. This is Freud's virtue, according to Jahoda (1980). Freud employs, in different places, a variety of metaphors – economic, energetic, physiological, rhetorical and topological – in his attempt to construe human psychology. This makes for rich construing, but it also leads to confusion, when different models are employed in the same text.

What we ought to do is to attempt to explore the range and power of each metaphor as a heuristic device. Each opens up a set of problems, questions and possible answers. Each can be no more than a 'slice' of the total. By keeping each one distinct and clearly before our attention in the solution of a problem, we shall avoid confusions about the nature of the reality we are construing.

Each discipline has its values, and this is particularly so of the social sciences. To the values which we find in the natural sciences – quantification, mathematization, simplicity, consistency, explanatory power – we add moral values. Are certain kinds of solutions morally acceptable? Is a certain kind of research morally permissible? Are certain images of human beings morally tolerable? Thus, psychology and the social sciences are said to have communicative and emancipatory functions (Habermas, 1972) which act as values in guiding psychological activity. We are, after all, not merely 'reflecting' nature, like mirrors. We engage reality in whatever ways we can to co-constitute possible worlds of experience and knowledge. When we change the direction and form of scientific discourse, we change the kinds of reality we bring into being. A thousand worlds cling to our attitudes. Psychology, we may insist, is not simply picking up facts like stones, it is a directed effort to achieve certain kinds of result. The point of view that I put here is not that we can create anything we choose, or that there are no constraints on what we construct, but that we can engage different potential worlds, depending on our activities.

Finally, each discipline has its exemplars, or model solutions, from which we learn how to do our science. We learn to see our problems, to apply our generalizations, to employ our techniques by reference to such a set of exemplary instances. A science without exemplary studies is pretending to be a science. Psychoanalysts refer to Freud's studies of Anna O, of Dora, of Little Hans, and of the Wolf Man. They undergo a training analysis and learn to interpret and see relationships and phenomena that were previously hidden from them. Behaviourists learn to do operant conditioning experiments and to find reinforcements in the natural environment. They learn how to manipulate them to alter behaviour, as we shall indicate in the next chapter. Piagetians refer to classic studies on the conservation of mass, of number, of volume; and to experiments on morality and classification as evidence for stages of intellectual growth. These are the exemplary studies that must be done in order to understand psychology in a particular way. In the course of doing these experiments, we develop a mode of analysis and problem solution.

Conclusion

What we shall find, as we scrutinize the work of psychologists working in various traditions, is that theories are not so much finished pictures of the world as resources – rather like maps or tools for getting to various places and intervening in specialized ways. Our success in reaching our destination and in getting particular results will depend upon our maps and tools, but these are instruments rather than complete pictures of the world. It is when we begin to think of theories as complete pictures that we become troubled by solipsism and wicked relativism. Yet no-one is troubled by the fact that a variety of maps can be drawn of the world, showing very different features and relations. Tools and maps enable us to do various jobs, practical and intellectual. We need them; their imperfections and specialized nature limit what we can do, but nobody imagines that there is a final tool or instrument, like a genie in the

Arabian Nights. Yet that is what the search for the final or complete theory is like.

What I shall do now is to use Kuhn's concept of disciplinary matrix to analyse various classic traditions in psychology.

3 Research traditions and theories

We see immediately that psychology is more like gang warfare than harmonious family life. Why should this be so? Sidney Smith summed it up (in more or less these words) when he saw two women abusing each other from across a street, from separate tenements: 'They cannot agree since they are arguing from different premises.'

In Chapter 2, we introduced Kuhn's (1970) concept of 'disciplinary matrix', and it is this concept which will now be applied to an analysis of scientific traditions and theories in psychology. To recapitulate, each scientific tradition or theory (I shall distinguish between the two terms at the end of this chapter) attaches itself to particular models and metaphors of 'the real', and in addition, a scientific theory refers to exemplary studies which show us how things can and should be done. Then, there are values. What form should data take? What should the theory accomplish? Finally theories contain symbolic generalizations.

In this chapter, I shall sketch the following traditions, applying the concept of the disciplinary matrix outlined by Kuhn. These examples are merely used to illustrate the main features of research traditions. Though each is an important tradition, other traditions such as ethology or cognitive psychology could have been selected. Furthermore other traditions will be referred to in later chapters.

Traditions
  Existential phenomenology
  Psychoanalysis
  Genetic epistemology
  Marxist social psychology
  Skinnerian behaviourism

Tradition 1 – Existential phenomenology

Primitive objects: Conscious being; intentions
                     Co-constitution of reality

Metaphors:	Encounter
	Dialogue
Exemplars:	Biography (Sartre, 1963), case history (Boss, 1978)
	Studies of perception (Merleau-Ponty, 1962), emotions (Sartre, 1962)
Values:	Intelligibility rather than prediction
Axioms:	Conscious being is intentional
	Existence precedes essence.

Why is the primitive object of existential phenomenology conscious *being* rather than mind? The reason is that we are all embodied; we are not abstracted minds. Phenomenologists hope to escape the Cartesian trap of mind/body dualism. The world is *lived* by us, not simply thought about or reflected on.

What is intentionality? It is an ancient concept, derived from Aristotle by way of the medieval schools, particularly William of Occam, and postulates that to be conscious is always to be conscious of something. Consciousness is never empty. Conscious being is filled with its objects, as we see from statements such as *I see John; I hope to win the race; I believe in God.* Each of these statements links a subject and an object. The object and the subject are bound in one reality, that of the intention. Pre-reflective consciousness is a consciousness of objects, directed entirely upon them. Nevertheless, this consciousness is not simply a mirror of the object. When I am angry, happy, or when I think the object is of a particular kind, my state will, together with the object, make for a particular lived consciousness of it. Annabel is not the same girl when I am in love with her as she was before. Perception transforms the objects which are present to it. It is intentional, a presence to a certain mode (angry, happy, believing this or that) of being.

Reflective consciousness takes the intentional act itself as the object of consciousness. I think about what I see, feel, hope.

If conscious being is intentional, and intentions always link subject and object, then subject and object must co-constitute each other. Consciousness takes the form of the object, the object takes on the particular intentional state of the subject. The phenomenon cannot be described by referring to either the object or the subject. It is intelligible only in terms of the intentional act. The metaphor here is dialogue. When we attempt to understand a person's state, we hope to make it *intelligible*, in terms of reason, choice and intention.

What kinds of events fall entirely outside the domain of phenomenology? The world of mechanistic physics is constituted of events which act externally upon each other, in the sense of one billiard ball knocking another one. When we talk of causes in this sense, we have abandoned phenomenological description. Thus, if we say that a childhood trauma 'causes a neurosis', as though it were one external event acting upon another, we are incorrect, according to phenomenologists. We violate its fundamental axiom, which is that conscious being is intentional and that we co-constitute reality, including our own reality. For the same reason, the existential phenomenologist would not speak of the person's life as being determined by his innate nature. (Nor would most other modern theories.)

We have what the existential phenomenologist calls 'situational freedom'. For this reason, a biographical explanation of a person's life must examine what he makes of himself, or what Sartre called the 'constituted – constituting itself' (Sartre, 1960). We search for the person's original projects and in this way may make his life intelligible. Choice is not in a vacuum; we are not entirely free. The metaphor is dialogue and co-constitution.

How would we violate the fundamental axiom of existential phenomenology? By discussing a person's life in terms of 'causes' and omitting his projects. This seems inconceivable, yet it has been proposed as a programme by Skinner in *Beyond Freedom and Dignity*, as we shall see.

The phenomenologist would direct the inquirer to find the intentional state, to search for the project by which the person has become what he is. No matter how convincing an explanation you offered in causal terms (I am not analysing the concept of causation at this stage), you would still be requested to proceed to the intentional stage of explanation before you would have completed your task.

Existential phenomenology attempts to cross the Cartesian divide between mind and body by starting with the reality of *conscious being*, on the ground that all experience is the experience of embodied beings, not of minds in the abstract. Starting with the world of phenomena, of consciousness, we may begin to abstract various features, such as subject and object, but consciousness is primary. 'Without consciousness there is no world' (Luijpen, 1966: 33) and consciousness is 'the quality of every conceivable world' (Husserl, 1928: 701). The world is full of significance for us, not because of our purely 'mental' properties or qualities, but because of our biology (Thinés, 1977). Each species has its own objects, related to its own life space, as J. von Uexküll pointed out in 1921, and these objects are 'bearers of meaning' to it, significant for its mode of life. In von Uexküll's example, the mated female tick climbs a bush and waits for a mammal to pass by. When it detects butyric acid, it releases its grip and drops. If it hits something warm, it searches for an area free of hair and bores through the skin to suck. Ethology has continued to explore the life spaces of various species, showing how signs and 'bearers of meaning' are related to modes of existence.

Perhaps this seems obvious, yet we continue to think of our own knowledge of the world as independent of our embodiment and life space. The things we value, our modes of grasping reality, have often been treated as absolutes. The approach of evolutionary phenomenology leads us to relativize our own world.

If there is a psychological equivalent to the concept of gravitation, which plays such a central role in physics, it is the fact that people *recognize* each other in various ways, using recognition as a general term for the ways in which people constitute each other. By this, we understand the whole range of confirmation, disconfirmation, evasion, collusion and condemnation, conveyed in the *regard* or the *look* (Sartre, 1957). These are the outward manifestations, the instruments of recognition. We recognize each other as heroes or villains, as good or bad, as admirable or contemptible, as honest or dishonest. This is what makes people move towards or away from each other, which splits or unites them internally so that they become fragmented or all of a piece. It is what makes people love and hate, murder or spend fruitless years of toil to achieve pre-eminence in the hope of some future and postponed recognition.

If recognition is the gravitational force of society, then various groups are the social equivalent of solar systems. It is in these constellations that recognitions give rise to the trajectories of plot and conspiracy, collusion and conflict as people attempt to arrive at stable multi-personal social configurations, in which self-image and recognitions are tolerably matched. The resultant of a mismatch may be described, from the individual perspective, as a project. One becomes something to reduce the mismatch. One may become what others recognize one as being; one may vacillate where there are several images in several primary groups; one may emigrate or cause others to emigrate by physical displacement or death. These are the manoeuvres described in existential case studies (Valle and King, 1978; Van den Berg, 1961, 1971, 1974) and existential biography (Sartre, 1963).

Let us now turn to the psychoanalytic tradition.

Tradition 2 – Psychoanalysis and the politics of mind

Primitive objects: Sexuality
The unconscious
Metaphor: Figurative language (there are many others, but figurative language is primary)

Examplars:	The analysis of hysteria (Anna O; Dora)
	Oedipal conflict (Little Hans; Paul Lorenz)
	Analysis of dreams
Values:	To discover causes (intelligibility follows analysis of causes)
	Therapeutic effectiveness
Axioms:	The conservation of intentionality under repression. That is, all psychological events have intentional meaning, though we may have to find a meaning in the repressed.
	Symptoms are psychological events to the extent that they can be interpreted.

The fundamental move in psychoanalysis was to discover the intentional meanings of neurotic symptoms and to define psychology as a science of meaning. Meaning was conserved by introducing the concept of the unconscious. The mode of utterance of the unconscious can only be understood as a series of elaborate troops, or figures of speech, the key to which is a series of inadmissible impulses. It is interesting to discover that Freud did, for a while, attend Brentano's lectures – and Brentano (1973) was the person who re-established the axiom that psychology is the study of intentions. Freud's contribution was to explain the bizarre, the incomprehensible, in terms of the intentional systems of different parts of the personality, each with its own logic and syntax. What we observe is a politics of mind; a power struggle between the id, the ego and the superego, each with its own goals. This power struggle is a consequence of the internalization of an external power struggle in the real world of the family. It is the internalization of a narrative, of a story about how to deal with desire. This is not an arbitrary story. It is a story which is appropriate to the real relations of power in a given society, as mediated by the family and the kinship system. Power is internalized as a set of *prohibitions*, which is the system of censorship, and as a set of *positive suggestions* and displacements, which are the things that ought to be done and desired. Each family has stories with both elements, each family is a power field in which the child must become structured by both elements. But since the child is never completely penetrated by any one narrative, what emerges is a series of compromised utterances as different stories are acted by different parts of the child and the adult.

Freud's account is intentional and causal. His interpretation of events relies on grasping the intentions of different systems in the person – or the way in which the person acts out different systems of intentions. In this way, he takes an *intentional* stance to the subject. In addition, he takes a *design* stance. He asks – how is it that the person comes to have intentions of a particular kind? He also takes a *physical* stance at times, proposing physiological structures which could explain dreams, for example. (See Dennett, 1987 on these three stances towards intentional systems.)

There is nothing contradictory, as many phenomenologists seem to believe, in adopting these various stances and in attempting to relate them to behaviour. Sometimes it is prudent to adopt an intentional stance, to credit a system with beliefs and goals and psychological states. Why prudent? Because we are too ignorant to go beyond this. At other times, we may be able to go to the design stage. Freud entered the design stage when he postulated three systems of personality – the id, the ego and the superego – and three states of mind – conscious, preconscious and unconscious – to account for his observations.

He also offered a causal account of how we come to have the intentions we do have and perform the compromised acts we do perform. His causal account depends on his analysis of the war between adults and children which is waged in the heart of every family. The child cannot escape; nor can the parents. There is no simple dichotomy between causes and reasons. Causes are not all of the external, billiard-ball-acts-on-billiard-ball type. There is the transformation of systems by information or by programming; there is the replication of genes and the interaction of chemical structures fitting into each other and forming each other. What Freud begins to see is the formation of mind by narrative, the linking of events to each other towards an end, under general assumptions about what follows what.

Given the struggle, given the fact that both parents and children are locked into narratives which carry a heavy investment of meaning (to depart from this is to lose their positive directions as well as their prohibitions) and a heavy investment in secondary gain (there are rewards and sanctions for meshing with the narratives of others), it remains true that we have 'situational freedom'. But now we can see, with some clarity, the costs and the limitations of this freedom.

What kinds of events are prohibited by psychoanalysis? The meaningless symptom and the meaningless dream would cease to be psychological events, since it is an axiom of psychoanalysis that meaning is conserved, even in the compromised utterances of neurosis and censored expression. To understand the compromise, we have to grasp the facts of power; to recover the meaning, we have to discover the impulse that is repressed. The unconscious is postulated to save the axiom that mind is the realm of meaning and intentionality.

Psychoanalysis can, therefore, be regarded as a phenomenology which recognizes the transformation of meaning by power. Just as, in physics, it was necessary to modify the concept of the conservation of matter when it was discovered that matter and energy are interchangeable, so it has been necessary, in psychology, to modify the concept of intentionality when it was discovered that internalized power transforms meaning. Meaning is conserved only if we recognize the effects of power.

We see clearly how the fundamental axiom or tautology works. When we fail to understand a dream, we assume that we have missed the key to its narrative, not that the axiom is wrong. It would be like coming across a tablet inscribed in a forgotten language. By definition, the inscription must have a meaning if it is a language. If there is no meaning, then the inscription is not a language. The odd case in which someone deliberately jots down random words is not an example of language, for obvious reasons; he merely makes use of language elements and we would understand this peculiar act by understanding his purpose.

What other moves are possible? We might, on a question of detail, ask whether the symbols uncovered by psychoanalysis are properly understood. This is what Jungians have done. Is the emphasis on sexual content universal? It is possible that the significant aspect of the unconscious will be whatever is socially prohibited. And then, to take up the second power theme; may not many difficulties arise from weak positive suggestions rather than from prohibitions? In other words, people have no story to act out, nothing to invest in. In Freud's day, prohibition and censorship might have been the problem; in a permissive society, a lack of structure or of positive desire may become the problem. People amble along in a desultory fashion towards no discernible end. They have not been able to invest in anything and there is no reciprocal interlocking system of powerful rewards and sanctions to make them work their story into anything.

It is my own view that both command, with its investments, and prohibition, with its structures of denial and censorship, must be stressed in the composition of human lives. We have stressed censorship too much and command too little.

Tradition 3 – Genetic epistemology

Primitive objects: Structures of intelligence. Schemes; operations
Metaphors: Homeostasis and biological equilibrium
Embryology: morphogenesis and a homeorhesis
Examplars: Experiments on the conservation of mass, number, transitivity

	Classification
	Egocentricity etc.
Values:	Prediction (from one observation to another within a stage)
	Explanation
Symbolic generalizations:	Lattices and groups
Axiom:	To know an object is to act on it; mental operations are interiorized and generalized actions.

Piaget regards himself as a genetic epistemologist. Why 'genetic'? Because he is concerned with the very general problem of how one kind of knowing develops into another. Whenever we are concerned with systems which develop new forms (morphogenesis) and yet preserve their internal coherence while doing so, we are concerned with a special version of adaptation. Homeostatis refers to the capacity of fundamentally unchanging systems to maintain equilibrium. Homeorhesis refers to the more difficult capacity of a system to maintain equilibrium while being transformed. This is a common property of biological systems. Piaget believes that there is a continuity between biological adaptation and psychological adaptation (1967: 44).

In order to illustrate the concepts of homeostasis and homeorhesis, let us use a commonplace example in which a child learns to attract attention in socially acceptable ways. Suppose that at the start of our account it attracts attention by bad behaviour. Whenever it is getting too little attention, the child screams. The system, consisting of child plus family, is a kind of homeostat – a system for maintaining a certain level of attention to the child. The developmental problem is to allow the child to gain attention without bad behaviour. This can only be done by changing the actions of the system as a whole, so that attention is now paid when the child behaves well and not when it behaves badly. This changes the behaviour of the child and, indeed, of everyone in the family. The system 'develops' – that is, it preserves its capacity to give the child the attention it needs in new and more differentiated ways. This is homeorhesis, whereas a homeostat is stable and not necessarily developmental.

Why epistemology? Because he is concerned with the foundations of knowledge. He distinguishes genetic epistemology from two other positions: empiricism and realism. Genetic epistemology stresses the formation of new structures which did not exist before (1970: 77). The empiricist believes that knowledge is the discovery of what exists in external reality. The nativist believes that the forms of knowledge are pre-determined in the subject.

From this outline it can be seen that Piaget is a genetic phenomenologist. He accepts the premise that mind is intentional and that relations between mental processes are intentional. Relations are implications, not causes. We say that a premise and a covering law imply a conclusion, not that they cause it. We say that, given the rules of arithmetic, $2 + 2 = 4$ *implies* that $4 - 2 = 2$, not that the one causes the other. Cause is a concept which is inappropriate to relations between mental events. Piaget's great contribution has been his remarkable observation of the ways in which children learn to classify, to conserve number and mass to test hypotheses, to follow rules, to make moral judgements. He is an imaginative experimenter, guided by certain heuristic assumptions.

The first is that intelligence grows in stages. These are the sensorimotor, the concrete operational and the formal operational stages. Each level is organized as a unity, with its own coherence. He has attempted formal mathematical descriptions of these stages. The main point to be made about these descriptions is that they were made with such intellectual tools as were available at the time and that they are static. They do not describe processes. To do that, Piaget would have needed programs, which can describe action, or sequences of different operations over time. He did not have these tools. Furthermore, the kinds of internal organization of these processes (hierarchical, flexible control, partly and fully joined, heterarchy) could not be described by him.

What are the processes of internal transformation of the system? Why should a child move from the sensorimotor to the concrete operational stage? The basic concepts here are disequilibrium and abstraction. The child exists in a field which is made up of itself and an environment (which includes other persons). Disequilibrium arises when the child tries to act on that environment and fails: there is an imbalance between accommodation (which is the modification of internal schemes to fit reality) and assimilation (which is the filtering or modification of the input). In feedback terms (and we should remember that Piaget began formulating this theory well before Wiener's discussion of feedback), there is an unacceptable difference between the value of the feedback and a demanded value, or test. It is in the presence of this gap that the process of equilibration occurs. Equilibration is a structural change due to reflective abstraction which transforms the system so that it becomes adapted to a wider range of circumstances. It is this continual process of abstraction from action that builds up more and more general schemes, or systems of operations. The internal structure is not a reduced or minimal version of the external world, rather it is an abstraction from the acts of the individual, the end result of which is a system of logically co-ordinated operations or mental processes.

Is there any way in which Piaget could be proved wrong? Several studies have shown that the details of some of his experiments may be incorrect (e.g. Bryant, 1974; Donaldson, 1982).

The matter is not clearcut, since what is needed is a much more exact statement of hypotheses. There is little doubt that Piaget's descriptions of the mental structures which underlie task completion need revision. It is also clear that the concept of equilibration is not precise enough to serve as a solution to the problems of morphogenesis which Piaget identified (e.g. Boden, 1982).

Why does Piaget remain important? First, he was one of the most original experimenters psychology has ever had. Second, he provided a broad framework for research still being pursued by theorists such as Sternberg, Case and Pascual-Leone. Third, he stressed mental structure and an epigenetic approach to mind at a time when most Anglo-American theorists were naive empiricists or nativists. Fourth, while most psychologists were still concerned with homeostatis – an important problem – Piaget (1967) was concerned with homeorhesis, or the genesis of structures capable of equilibrium.

Tradition 4 – Marxist social psychology

Primitive objects: Relations of production
Classes and class interests
Metaphors: Hegel's dialectic (substituting classes for nations)
Messianic Judaism
Examplars: Analyses of fetishism, alienation, class interests, ideology, relations of production
Values: Revolutionary change, not contemplation, is the goal
Axioms: Ideology is a function of class interests
Mind is a function of social organization

Many great men work out the implication of a single theoretical idea. Freud worked through the idea of sexual repression; Marx worked through the idea that class is determined by the relations of production. For both, the relations of power are important. First, the power which forbids, censors and drives underground. Second, the power which displaces, substitutes and fills. The meanings of symptoms can be understood by the psychoanalyst only if he bears both of these in mind. His primary scene is the family. The primary scene of the Marxist analyst is the industrial world in which goods are produced and consumed. For the psychoanalyst, the key to the gestures of illness, to dreams and to perversions, is the fate of sexual drives in the force field of the family. For the Marxist, the key to the gestures of ideology is the disposition of classes in the relations of production. The relations of production and the reproduction of these relations are primary. Society is kept alive by what it produces. As Raymond Aron (1967) said, Marx saw society as though it were a gigantic factory; instead, it has become more like an enormous bureaucracy.

The important thing is that the ruling ideas are the ideas of the ruling classes, to cite a well-known expression. Yet these ideas cannot express the interests of the ruling classes too directly. If they did, they would be ineffective. Marked propaganda is not likely to fool people. Thus, the ideas which make people act as they are acted (Althusser, 1971), which they adopt as their own, are great, general visions of society. Liberalism, for example, is said to benefit the bourgeoisie and impoverish the proleteriat. Individual freedom is good for those who have money, property to protect, education and a start in life. It is not in the interests of those who are poor and who are likely to be crushed by free competition. Individualism, the protection of private property, free trade and free economy are all, it is said, designed to serve the interests of the middle classes. They were revolutionary ideas when the bourgeoisie were in revolt against the aristocracy; they are conservative when they are used to keep the working class in place. What place is this? It is their place to be commodities, to be bought and sold in the relations of production of capitalist economy. The ideas are noble, we accept them as timeless truths, and we are prepared to defend them against our own true class interests. This is false consciousness. It is an example of the way in which we are ruled by false ideas.

The general principle should be stated as follows, rather more broadly than it was stated by Marx. Every ideology serves, not merely its immediate and patent function, but the general function of keeping a society going. The question is, then, how do our ideas about education, economics, politics, marriage and morality keep the present system functioning? How do they relate and complement each other, like organs in the body politic? These ideas may keep the ruling class ruling, but they are not necessarily the result of a conspiracy (though they may be). The more generally they are accepted as 'right' and as 'universal' by everyone, the more effectively they function. When such ideas are detached from the interests they serve, we are dealing with symptoms, with displacements, with metonymy, as in hysteria. The meaning can be recovered only by studying the secondary gains of the ideology, attaching it once more to the economy of class interests and the relations of production which are, to the Marxist, what sexuality is to the psychoanalyst. Ideology serves the social unconscious. The social unconscious, we might add, could be generalized (as the individual unconscious was) to whatever is inadmissible and neglected and repressed in a given epoch.

Hegel, from whom Marx borrowed, attempted to show that ideas determine the course of history. Marx attempts to show that ideas are produced in the very relations of production which they serve. Yet how is this production of ideas mediated? Who produces these ideas? Individual people, acting in concrete situations. A system of mediating structures is required, as Sartre (1960) pointed out. Isiah Berlin adds: Marxism 'set out to refute the proposition that ideas decisively determine the course of history, but the very extent of its own influence on human affairs has weakened the force of its thesis' (Berlin, 1963: 284).

Is there a conspiracy of the ruling class to maintain a set of ideas or are all, the ruled and the rulers, simply blindly acting out the ideas which reflect the relations of production?

Whatever the case, the social analyst will look at ideological expressions with one question: How do they serve class interests and which class interests do they serve? This is what defines ideology. It is as tautologous as the concept of evolution by natural selection, and as powerful. It defines the data. If class interest cannot be found, then either ideas are not ideological or the analysis is wrong.

Are there political ideas which are not ideological, in the sense that they are not determined by class interests? This must be so if Marxism itself is not to be one more ideology among others. It is a weakness of the theory that it does not show how this may be possible. The dialectical account is that the view which is carried by the most inclusive and largest class is also the truest and least ideological. This would be like a theory of evolution which stated that natural selection acts on all organisms except those which are most numerous. We should be amused, but not convinced.

In the outline at the beginning of our discussion of this position I said that one of the metaphors for Marx's theory is Messianic Judaism. This is how Bertrand Russell (1961: 361) draws up a table of equivalence:

Yahweh	=	Dialectial materialism
The Messiah	=	Marx
The Elect	=	The Proletariat
The Church	=	The Communist Party
The Second Coming	=	The Revolution
Hell	=	Punishment of the Capitalists
The Millenium	=	The Communist Commonwealth

This aesthetic or mythical figure is one of the reasons for the powerful appeal of Marxism and one of the sources of its authority and conviction.

What sorts of problems does a Marxist social psychology investigate? First, it takes as its starting point the relations of production, not the individual, and it asks how individuals are adapted to these relations. Then, it investigates the ways in which society ensures the reproduction of these relations by socialization, child rearing and education practices which fit people for their roles. How do people become ideological instruments? How do they become the sort of ideological subjects they are, speaking and maintaining views which support the system?

The fundamental axiom of a Marxist psychology is the sixth thesis on Feuerbach, which develops the ideas stated above.

> The human essence is no abstraction inherent in each individual. In its reality it is the ensemble of social relations (Marx, 1975: 423)

This is what Sève calls the 'excentration of the human essence' (1974: 529), or the Copernican revolution of Marxist theory. He contrasts it with 'human relations' theories which are ahistorical and presuppose *human being* prior to social relations. This is 'a fetishism of the individual' which corresponds to commodity fetishism. Fetishism is the attribution of powers to objects which should be attributed to the social relations which produce those objects. We think of them as facts of nature rather than as derivations of social existence. By modifying the forms of social existence we can modify 'human nature'.

It is fundamental to Marxist thought that 'consciousness is from the very beginning a social product' (Marx, cited in Sève, 1975: 32) but is Sève correct in drawing the conclusion that:

> The consciousness of the individuals cannot therefore pass beyond the limits nor escape the problems – and solutions – characteristic of their class. The institutions and objective conditions of a given epoch determine the life process and the consciousness of individuals. (1975: 32).

Before we agree, we must confront the perennial problem of deciding what a 'class' is. Class is merely one of many possible groupings in society. Whenever Marx confronted a real problem of analysis, he had to abandon the fiction that society consists of a small number of classes and resort to the notion of 'fractions'. There are interest groups, ethnic groups, religious groups, and a myriad of ways in which people are related to the same process of production. The interests of the bureaucracy, the petty shopkeepers, the peasants, the large farmers, the entrepreneurs, the politicians, the medical doctors and other professionals, do not necessarily conflict or coincide in any simple way. Marx observes that in England 'the stratification of classes does not appear in its pure form. Middle and intermediate strata even here obliterate lines of demarcation everywhere' (Marx, in McClellan, 1971: 152). For Cohen (1978), a person's class is 'established by nothing but his objective place in the network of ownership relations' (1978: 73) and it is a false argument (by people such as E.P. Thompson) that: *Since* production relations do not mechanically determine class consciousness; *therefore* class may not be determined purely in terms of production relations.

This kind of argument (so it is said) confuses objective and subjective class. It confuses the cause and the effect, the independent and the dependent variable. True, but why do people lapse into this kind of error? They lapse because it is claimed (and we see the claim in Sève) that class determines consciousness, that no-one can transcend his class, and so forth. Therefore, when they find differences in class consciousness where there should be none, they begin to question the assertion that class is entirely a matter of objective conditions. This is more the case since 'objective class' turns out to be very poorly defined. It is not at all clear, in theory, what all the members of a given class have in common and why their differences should not be important in many issues.

McClellan (1971) points out that class is never defined clearly in Marx. And, when we look at class in terms of 'identity of revenues and sources of revenues', we find that society divides into many 'classes'.

We may divide objections to Sève's statement into two kinds: logical and factual. The logical objections are:

(a) Class is not a clear concept and 'objective class' is sleight of hand.
(b) It is not clear what forms of consciousness are determined by class (all forms? music? science?).
(c) It is not clear what would be accepted as falsification of the generalization that one cannot 'transcend' class problems and solutions.
(d) It subsides into a form of group solipsism. The only interaction between classes is liquidation.

The factual objections are:

(a) Detailed historical studies, such as those by E.P. Thompson in *The Making of the English Working Class,* fail to reveal any simple relationship between class and consciousness.
(b) Platt (1980) cites complications such as the following:
   (i) Members of the Nazi and Social Democratic Parties in pre-War

Germany were equally heterogeneous in social origin. Forty per cent of SDP support was *not* working class.
(ii) Brunton and Pennington found, after statistical studies of the long Parliament in the English Civil War, that there are no specifiable social English and economic characteristics that differentiated the leadership of the Royalists from the Parliamentarians.
(iii) Similar studies of the Paris mobile guard of 1848 have shown that its class composition was not significantly different from that of the insurrectionists.

These studies lead us to be sceptical of the proposition that consciousness is a product of class. What, then, of the more general proposition that the structures of mental activity changes in the course of historical development (Luria, 1976) which is the proposition that guided the research of Vygotsky and Luria, among others, in the Soviet Union? All that one can observe is that this hypothesis is not notably 'Marxist'. In Luria's studies, the most significant 'social organization' to affect cognition was schooling. There is little that distinguishes this kind of Marxism from traditional educational theory.

Yet the guiding assumption has inspired work in the Marxist tradition: relate consciousness to history and search for ways of understanding the position of the actor. One of the transformations of Marxism is into discourse theory (which does not, of course, derive from Marxism in the sense that there is a straight line of descent, since many modern movements in linguistics, philosophy and social analysis have contributed). What is left is a tendency to explain social action by referring to social position and available ideological forms.

Tradition 5 – Behaviourism (Skinnerian)

Primitive objects: Operants; Stimuli (both discriminative and reinforcing)
Metaphors: Selection of behaviour by its consequences: evolution
Examplars: Numerous experiments demonstrating the control of behaviour under various contingencies of reinforcement.
Values: Prediction and control
Quantitative data
Axiom: Behaviour in a given situation is a function of reinforcement

One way out of the Cartesian dilemma in which mind is separated from body, is to study neither mind nor body, but behaviour. The dichotomy is denied. I shall examine only the radical behaviourism of Skinner.

Behaviour must always be observed in a triple or set of three terms consisting of a *discriminative stimulus* (which is the situation or the features of the situation that the organism is sensitive to), an *operant* (what does the organism do), and a *reinforcing stimulus* (what is the consequence of what the organism has done?). All of these are classes of events. The operant, to give an example, may vary from time to time, provided that it produces within the environment in which it is being studied, a particular reinforcement. The three terms are written S_D, O and S_{rein}.

I shall not define these terms more carefully in this short summary, since the main concepts are clear enough. Behaviour cannot be studied without the most careful analysis of the environment and the contingences which maintain it. The consequence of a thorough-going application of this method is that we do not find the causes of deviant or good behaviour 'in' the individual, but in the contingencies of reinforcement. This leads to an examination of natural communities of reinforcement.

The fundamental axiom that behaviour is a function of its reinforcing consequences is as powerful as the fundamental axiom of evolution by natural selection, which is a model for it. Just as natural selection is supposed to produce, without the intervention of any design, the staggering variety of forms of life, so reinforcement is supposed to produce, without appealing to inner powers or the mental capacities of the organism, the variety of behaviour which can be observed.

The operation of the fundamental axiom can be seen in the assumption that when an organism emits one behaviour rather than another the reinforcements contingent upon the former are greater than the reinforcements contingent upon the latter. This is an axiom of the same kind as the conservation of matter or the conservation of momentum. That is, any problems of measurement may be assumed to be just measurement problems and not violations of the fundamental axiom.

What kind of treatment of mind do we find in this theory? Why, simply that mind is not given any status as a substance or entity separate from behaviour. There may be private operants which can be conditioned in the way that public operants are, but there is no *res cogitans* which is of a kind different to *res extensa*.

And what status, if any, is accorded to intentional statements such as 'I see John', 'I believe ten and ten make twenty', or 'I want a sweet'? The argument is that they are not explanations; they are items in need of explanation. Under what conditions (contingencies of reinforcement) will you come to see, believe or want various things? It is a problem of reinforcing responses, as Skinner sees it.

Finally, what would lead to a suspension of the axiom of the shaping of behaviour by reinforcement? If we could show that, in learning, no reinforcing consequences are necessary, the theory would either collapse or possibly become a theory with a limited domain of application.

In later chapters, I shall return to the behaviourist position and supplement this sketch with more details.

Conclusion

Here we have a rather mixed bag of discourses, committed to different metaphors, values, generalizations and exemplary problem solutions. What are these discourses and how should we choose among them? Are they 'theories'? or 'approaches' or 'disciplines'?

The best general term for them seems to be Laudan's 'research tradition'. Behaviourism, psychoanalysis, genetic epistemology, cognitive psychology based on the computer metaphor, existential phenomenology, Marxist social psychology and evolutionary theory are research traditions, some old and some new, rather than theories. Let us distinguish between the two.

A theory is 'a very specific set of related doctrines (commonly called 'hypotheses' or 'axioms' or 'principles') which can be utilized for making specific experimental predictions and for giving detailed explanations of natural phenomena' (Laudan, 1977: 71). On the other hand, a research tradition refers to 'much more general, much less easily testable, sets of doctrines and assumptions' (1977: 71). Research traditions may comprise several specific theories: the Marxist research tradition comprises more specific doctrines on economics as well as approaches to the analysis of social conflict; the psychoanalytic research tradition comprises specific theories such as the formation of the Oedipus complex, the origins of hysteria, and the origins of the 'self' in infancy; the behaviourist tradition of research must contain specific theories about stimulus sampling and 'prepared' learning, or species-specific learning programmes. Research traditions are broad movements within which research problems are generated, supported and understood. Psychoanalysts and Marxists, behaviourists and genetic epistemologists, recognize those within their own research tradition, find that they share a common language, and can evaluate what their fellows are doing. To summarize, *research traditions*:

— include specific theories, either simultaneously or successively
— have distinct metaphysical and methodological commitments
— persist for a long time, even though their specific theoretical content may change.

(Laudan, 1977: 78–9)

What Kuhn calls a 'discipline' and what Laudan calls a 'research tradition' share the characteristics of the disciplinary matrix, and the terms can be used interchangeably. Within a research tradition (as within Kuhn's 'discipline') there are methods of analysis, observation and experiment; and only certain kinds of reality are recognized. The example of behaviourist attempts to create 'intervening variable' may be given. As we have already seen, behaviourists are committed to account for events in terms of publicly observable stimuli and responses. In the work of certain behaviourists, intervening fractional responses and internal, unobserved stimuli were postulated, of the form

$$S\text{------}r\text{------}s\text{------}R$$

but the commitment to S, R and ultimate observability remained.

Another example of how a research tradition can guide and shape research is the tradition of Cartesian physics. Laudan points out two characteristics: (1) only matter and mind exist, and other forms of substance are not allowable; and (2) particles can interact only by contact, not at a distance. These two commitments gave rise to great problems for both psychology and physics, since the question of how mind and matter could make 'contact' was not satisfactorily resolved (mind being 'thinking substance' and matter being 'spatial substance'); nor was the question of gravitational attraction at a distance resolved.

Within the Marxist tradition, as we have seen, there is a commitment to analyses of the following kinds:

- interaction between entities is economic;
- the real entities are classes, the forces and relations of production, base and superstructure;
- the direction of causation is from base to superstructure; and
- change is dialectical.

A research tradition can, when we analyse its ingredients, be conveniently described by means of the commitments of a disciplinary matrix. However, it has the advantage of making the position of theory and tradition clearer. Hence I shall use the term 'research tradition' when describing the clusters of theories and commitments which we have described above.

Each research tradition evolves through its constituent theories; it is these which solve problems and lead us to work within a research tradition. A rational choice between research traditions can rest on two kinds of estimate, according to Laudan. The first is *present performance*: 'choose the theory (or research tradition) with the highest problem-solving adequacy' (1977: 109). The second is *pursuit* or *promise*: 'it is always rational to pursue any research tradition which has a higher rate of progress than its rivals' (1977: 111).

All other considerations, such as falsifiability, coherence, simplicity, elegance, 'rationality', and extensibility are secondary to the problem-solving capacities of theories, according to Laudan. Let us attempt to apply the criteria of present performance and promise to the traditions sketched above. Suppose you were a behaviourist, would it be rational for you to become interested in, let us say, gene-culture co-evolution? Yes, it would, if you saw that rapid progress was being made in problem-solving within that tradition. Then, you might continue to commit yourself to the behaviourist tradition while paying close attention to any emergent tradition which appeared to be doing well. This is one of the reasons why we often have mushroom growths: new approaches which suddenly emerge and then fizzle out. An example is the adoption of transformational generative grammars in psychological research. It was rational to get in on a promising new movement, because it seemed to solve a large number of problems in the psychology of language. In particular it offered hypotheses on the kinds of rules that children might use in producing and comprehending language, and in this way seemed to be a great advance on models based on imitation and conditioning.

But is there any way of persuading a behaviourist that he ought to be a psychoanalyst; or a genetic epistemologist that he ought to be a Jungian? Probably not. In addition to success in problem-solving, we have to allow for *significant focus* in each research tradition and its constituent theories. Where theories belonging to different research traditions focus on different kinds of problems, they cannot be serious competitors since there is no way in which we can compare their relative success in solving problems. It is only when they focus on the same problems that we can prefer one to another. Suppose, for example, that behaviourists and genetic epistemologists were to attempt to account for the main features of language acquisition, and suppose that a convincing solution of a major problem were achieved in one or the other tradition, then we should have reason to prefer one to the other. To date, there is no such *convincing* demonstration, though there may be minor or partial success in (say) relating stage of cognitive development to use of grammatical form (e.g. Sinclair de Swart, 1967). But this success is not striking enough to pose real difficulties, and behaviourists might easily point to successes of their own, in other areas, to counter this example.

We can, therefore, introduce a principle of undecidability. It is not possible to make a rational choice between research traditions when: (a) they focus on different problems, and (b) no theory in any tradition has solved an outstandingly important problem. When an outstandingly important problem has been convincingly solved by any theory, it may seem to us that theories which do not address that problem are not worth attending to. What is more common, though, is the sort of eclecticism that we find in therapy. In the treatment of anorexia we may find the principles of behaviour modification being employed to change eating behaviour while psychodynamic principles are applied in an attempt to give the patient insight into his or her condition.

Thus, when we are confronted by any specific problem, we may simultaneously employ methods and insights from a variety of research traditions without becoming aware of metaphysical or methodological incoherence. Is this rational? Yes, it is, if by rationality we mean doing (or believing) something for good reason. Our 'good reason' in solving an applied problem is purely pragmatic. We find a mixture of techniques that work. This is not a 'scientific solution', yet we find that such practices strengthen the research traditions which nourish the methods we use. What would 'good reason' in science be? That we believe we have solved a problem – that is, we have offered an explanation which enables us to solve a whole class of similar problems.

Rationality is different in the two cases, but both sets of 'good reasons' have their place in the social activity of producing knowledge.

To summarize: We have described different research traditions, we have applied the concept of disciplinary matrix to them, and we have proposed a way of choosing between research traditions which, though rational, is difficult to use. We shall return to the question of progress in science in the second half of the book.

Now, we shall proceed to look at the making of scientific knowledge, and in particular at the way in which rhetorical manoeuvres suggest fresh ways of opening up problems. These rhetorical manoeuvres are, in fact, the components of the disciplinary matrix which give internal structure to traditions. Another way of looking at metaphors, generalizations, values and model solutions is to regard them as the resources of a tradition. They are the intellectual tools used by practitioners for crafting new theories.

Part II

Rhetoric and change in research traditions

4 The uses of metaphor; or a hatful of larks

Suppose that you are trying to understand how one piece of matter resembles another, or how talking–moving–thinking beings really work. Are they machines of a kind? Are they robots controlled by computer-like brains? Are they actors on the world's stage, performing pre-determined parts? Are they the sleepwalkers of ideology or fabricators of marvellous novelties? You search for images which capture some of the things you already see and suggest even more things. You perform experiments and try to look at your problem in various ways. Your first difficulty, though, is to find a way of seeing, a way of placing your object in a new intellectual space which will reveal unexpected properties. Eventually, you may have a theory, yet initially you really have no choice but to start inquiring metaphorically.

Furthermore, and this is very important, if you did not see events in terms of each other you would be living in a world of isolated and unconnected happenings. The metaphorical basis of thought is not, therefore, a lamentable intrusion of poetry into the world of hard facts. The world begins in poetry.

The physicist might start off by saying: What would happen if I thought of all matter as being composed of various mixtures of the elements of earth, air, fire, water (Empedocles)? Some substances would be volatile (lots of fire and air), others would be sluggish and difficult to burn (lots of earth and water). The physiologist might take this valuable insight over and think of the body as being regulated by humours formed of these elements: blood, black bile, yellow bile and phlegm (Hippocrates). The metaphor of harmony or balance is added and sickness is then interpreted as a consequence of a lack of balance in the humours.

Still later, the physicist might think of all matter as being composed of tiny particles or even waves. This would constitute the underlying similarity of all material events. But hasn't the theory fallen into a trap? How can we then account for differences? Well, the elementary particles might be arranged in different patterns, or they might travel at different velocities. Waves can have different frequencies and amplitudes.

Combinations of these might be shown to make up all perceptible qualities of matter. Here, to refresh memory, are *some* of the important metaphors of physics:

waves (light, sound)
particles (atoms)
currents (electricity)
empty space (Newtonian physics)
curved space (Einsteinian physics)
vibration, oscillation
elasticity (gases)

Now, what about psychology? Suppose we are interested in giving an account of *mind* or of *social life* (which may, in some theories, be very closely linked). How should we start? What is similar about different minds? What makes them different? And what about the ideas, feelings and impulses that seem to go on in minds or be otherwise associated with them?

Then, should one concentrate on one metaphor and shoulder all others out of the way? Should one admit different metaphors to different domains of psychological reality? Before we think of all these complications, let us look at some psychological metaphors.

Metaphors of individual minds

'The ghost in the machine'	(Ryle on Descartes)
Thinking substance	(Descartes)
Container, or empty cabinet	(to be filled with ideas, thoughts – Locke)
Blank slate	(to be written on by experience – Locke)
A computer program	(modern functionalists)
A system of constructs	(Kelly)
A two-chambered space, conscious and unconscious	(Freud – we might add 'pre-conscious')
An active, organizing space with a priori ideas or theories	(Locke, Kant, Mills, Bain, Chomsky)
Secreted by the brain as bile by the liver	(Tyndall, Cabanis)

Metaphors of contents of mind

Atoms in motion in the brain	(Hobbes)

Elementary ideas	(Locke, associationists)
Waves and particles: 'vibratiuncles'	(Hartley)
Intentions	(Brentano – and many before him)
Constructs	(Kelly)
Operations – acts	(Piaget)
Complexes	(Jung)

Metaphors of processes or of combinations of ideas

Chemistry: Automatic processes of frequency, recency, contiguity, vividness	(Associationists)
Programmed logic	(Modern functionalism)
Language	(Freud)

Metaphors of social life

Rules	(Wittgenstein)
Games	(Wittgenstein)
Rhetoric	(Harré)
Drama	(Goffman)
Language	(Wittgenstein)

Here we have a fair collection of metaphors – by no means all the metaphors that could be assembled! Is this, then, what the science of psychology is all about? Should we collect metaphors and see what they tell us? The more the better?

Often, one gets the impression that this is what psychologists do in their active hours, but it is not the whole story. The next stage is to work through the implications of a metaphor or closely related system of metaphors.

Working a metaphor

If a metaphor is to work, it must have an internal structure which is adequate to the task. Consider the metaphors of mind as a blank sheet which has to be written on by experience, or as a cabinet which has to be furnished. These are good illustrations, but it is difficult to take them very far. On the other hand, the metaphor that social behaviour is rule-governed can be taken some way. We may ask: Are people aware of the rules? How do we know when to apply them? What happens when we make mistakes? Here, we are obviously into something that looks promising.

How close should a metaphor be to the thing we are studying? The immediate answer seems to be: As close as possible. But is this true? Imagine that we hope to understand language and the target is English. Should we use German as a metaphor? Or should we use a more abstract and remote metaphor, such as a rule system? Obviously something which is too close presents all the problems of the original. We may fail to see it as a metaphor at all, though it is.

'Look at English as though it were German' might expose some of its idiosyncracies, but it would not (it seems) take us very far into the abstract nature of language.

Metaphors must show up similarities in a range of different objects. English, German ... Xhosa. We cannot stand too close to any of them if we hope to get something general.

Thus: The metaphor must have a rich structure, we must be able to see the relevance of its structure, and it should not be too similar to the object of study. It should lead the mind to interesting *new* thoughts about the object of inquiry and not merely summarize or reflect things we already know.

Think of the periodic table of the elements. The model (metaphor) is an atomic structure like a solar system. Could it be that periodic similarities in the number of electrons in the outer orbits will explain similar chemical properties of groups of elements? This is a new thought; a new possibility.

This reminds us that intellectual traffic between the metaphor and the object of study is in two directions. The atomic metaphor has been enriched to support inquiry, gradually changing it from its particle beginnings to a solar model of protons, neutrons and electrons and then to a system of sub-atomic particles of questionable behaviour.

Let us collect our thoughts again. A metaphor is, if well-chosen, a good starting place for an inquiry. It creates 'intellectual space' – the room for intellectual manoeuvre which brings new knowledge into being. What is intellectual space? It is a system of implications, a park containing many paths, which can be followed to unexpected places. Metaphors are interesting if they have many implications which help us to make a coherent picture of what we wish to know. They lead to discoveries. In the course of inquiry, the metaphor may be enriched – should be enriched – by new discoveries, till its origins are barely remembered. We see its faintest shadow, almost erased, in the plans of the park as it exists today. Yet we may wonder why things are as they are. Often the answer lies in the original design.

It might help if I were to become more concrete and show how a metaphor changes, little by little, into something which begins to look like science. Because it is so accessible, because it remains close to what we all know, I shall use Goffman's dramaturgical metaphor of the presentation of self as my illustration.

Scenes from social life

A theatre has a stage (and an off-stage area); it has actors and audiences, it has roles, parts, a script, acting conventions, and a setting within which the action is interpreted. We know that what happens on stage is not real. Events do not *happen*. It is *as if*. We are accustomed to that. In many respects we are *as if* beings. There are different traditions of acting, ranging from Stanislavksy (real tears!) to Brecht (distances) and these demand different relations between the actor and his role. Stretch the imagination yet further, and acting traditions become even more distinct, relating to the entire material of the play: Noh plays demand extreme stylization (from our point of view); farces demand a subtle degree of over-acting; opera achieves a heightened, and unnatural, emotion by demanding that the actors burst into song at astonishing moments, such as while dying.

What use can be made of all this in suggesting an approach to social psychology? Goffman (1968, 1971, 1975) shows us some of the ways. There is, firstly, the general notion of a *frame* within which action is apprehended and perceived as normal. Singing and murder are natural within the frame of opera, but not in Oxford Street. Nor is singing acceptable in a very wide range of other forms of theatre, as a means of *rendering* the performance. Where it occurs, it is a *representation* or statement: 'X is singing, at this moment, while pottering about in the garden'. In opera, he might *render* his experience of the garden by singing, and he would not simply be representing X-singing-in-the-garden. We understand all this without difficulty. It is part of role-taking within a reality frame which is as important in everyday life as on the stage. There are, as Goffman points out, off-stage areas in everyday life where we may be out of character. The husband, loosening his belt after dinner, is no longer Sir Charles, the distinguished diplomat; his wife, abandoned to curlers and cream, has temporarily given up any attempt at being the most ravishing beauty in Europe. Stanislavsky and Brecht give us various degrees of *role distance*. What should the actor do? He may be cool about his performance and display full command by his nonchalance while carrying out difficult tasks with skill; or he may be fully immersed in his role, unable to see himself and his performance.

In order to perform successfully, performances of self and others must be monitored. Whatever happens, the show must go on, performances must be skilful enough to maintain face. When actors fail in their roles they lose face and discover each other's social nakedness. The embarrassment of being out of role, of failing to carry it off, must be avoided. It is the first sin of society, the descent into barbarism (where intentional) or shame (where unintentional). Certain conditions have to be concealed or managed most carefully to prevent social incoherence. These are *stigmas*. Inability to read, a coleostomy, or a skeleton in the cupboard may dominate people's lives as they play for all they are worth to prevent disclosure and loss of face. We can study their methods of impression management as they go about their performance.

Since skilled performance is the way we escape the embarrassment of naked encounter, we admire skilled performance for its own sake. The trapeze artist, the brilliant actor, the blind person whose blindness we cannot detect, are admirable. When the performance falters, we avert our eyes lest we be overwhelmed by embarrassment.

Why has Goffman been so highly praised for his extensive use of this metaphor? How does it combine reason and imagination in a way which advances our thinking about psychology?

The first thing I would draw attention to is the notion of *ensemble*, of co-performances. Many theories start with the individual and then laboriously try to put individuals together into some sort of scene. It is often difficult to imagine why they should care to do anything in common. We may ask: Given individuals, how is social life possible? Or, we may reverse the question and ask: Given social life, how are individuals possible? This is not quite the question that Goffman has asked, though it is an important one. What he has asked is: Given social life, what must people do to live it? And, what happens if social life fails? One must distinguish between suspension of social life, as far as that can occur, and failure. Suspension is off-stage; it is only embarrassing if we are caught off-stage and the assumption is that we should be on-stage. A trivial example: I am eating a sandwich in my office at 11.30 a.m. and my boss walks in. We are both embarrassed. The assumption is that I am on-stage for consulting with clients and others about work and that eating a sandwich in the middle of the morning puts me off-stage. More embarrassing situations can easily be imagined. Failure occurs when I attempt to present myself in a certain way and do not quite pull it off. I slip on the high wire, I lose the thread of a lecture, I forget a name during an introduction, etc. This leads to a flurry of repairs.

The performance is social, an ensemble effort; the repairs are also an ensemble effort, because embarrassment is something we face collectively, and the pleasure of skilled performance is something we achieve together.

Yet there are different conventions. Discomfiture of particular people is often a feature of cruel comedy or farce. Then, we admire the skill with which the discomfiture of a particular person is achieved and we laugh at the safely focused danger.

Apart from the important concept of ensemble which is directly entailed by the metaphor of theatrical performance, what has Goffman contributed? The *management* and *monitoring* of performance are two essential features of behaviour that are also entailed by the theatre model. We have to respond appropriately to the actions of others. Together, we make society according to an elaborate though often unknown set of conventions.

Finally, the concept of *embarrassment* is central to failed social performance. Skilled performance of difficult roles exhilarates by keeping embarrassment under control. At any moment, we could be overwhelmed. The artist conceals his art in such a way that only afterwards do we realize how close we were to disaster.

Goffman's contribution is important when we consider the way in which it shifts the focus from sexuality (in Freud), reward (in learning theory), or work (in Marx). It is a social metaphor for social beings. Goffman has uncovered the social structure of embarrassment.

Can we use the dramaturgical model to go beyond the commonplace; can we make it yield the unexpected? Point-by-point analogy with social life is not enough if we want to know what we did not know before.

What we could do is to link embarrassment and self-representation and construct a story about the development of social life. This is a possible extension, a way beyond Goffman to make Goffman more interesting.

Suppose that we develop self-representations to guide our actions from scene to scene. We act in terms of the ways we represent ourselves and others in scenes. It follows that a child cannot experience embarrassment until it has a self image (or 'face'). Parents have to cultivate the child's face as rapidly as possible (as Mead, 1934, tells us, in a slightly different context) in an attempt to make a social being of it. From the moment the child looks responsive (within weeks), it is being told that it 'is a good girl', 'is clever', 'wants to be Papa's lollipop', 'loves Mama', 'is Charlotte' and is 'scrumptious'. When it knocks over the porridge it is 'horrible'.

In the course of building up a set of self-representations (always relations to others), the child discovers how difficult it is to maintain them. Good one moment and bad the next. Mama's own baby now and beastly monster the next. A glaring eye and an angry voice convert her instantly from a good girl to a bad girl. Her mother is transformed into anger. Charlotte is stripped of her identity as 'good'. It makes nonsense of the self-representation which was ticking over nicely a moment ago. Charlotte begins the lifelong business of repairing the difference between what she apparently is in Mama's glare and what she thought she was a moment ago. She is frightened. Then she is ashamed. Then, even in the absence of Mama, she is guilty.

To be ashamed is to discover one's nakedness. It is in relation to another that we are naked. To ourselves, we are simply without clothes. Nakedness is what we discover in the gaze of another (as Sartre has said). Doubt enters us.

Shame is our failure to be what others expect us to be and the way out of shame is to manage the impression we make on them. We become the sort of self they want us to be, if we cannot make them want the sort of self we are, or escape the relationship altogether. We may give up with particular others (parents, teachers, perhaps even the whole law-abiding circle) and find those who help us to become the sort of people we think we are. An incongruity of expectations leads us to wriggle until the incongruity is over, if ever.

Shame, as I have said, is our failure to meet the scrutiny of others. Guilt is a failure to meet our own scrutiny. Shame must come first.

This failure before others has the general name of embarrassment. It covers our feeling for the failure of others in their attempt to perform well, as well as our feeling for our own failure. We may repair our own embarrassment by learning manners and going to a good tailor. The manners of a dancing master and the morals of a whore might do us very well.

Repairing the peculiar embarrassment of guilt, of wishing to hide from our own scrutiny, may require a deep and extensive change. The flashing and skilful presentation of self may no longer seem enough. We may put it about that we no longer wish to be actors and pretenders, that sincerity is all we aspire to. Carried through, it makes social liabilities of us. We introduce a regime of sincerity and denounce hypocrisy. This is very disruptive, but it does happen.

In his emphasis on being-for-others, on face-work, Goffman has ignored what Sartre calls being-for-one's self. Is there a self to be discredited? Is there anything behind the mask in Goffman? One is often left with the impression that he is concerned with charades, with the various masks which conceal nothing very much.

Scenes from social life are real, gripping and engaging because there is someone to become, someone to defend, someone who is ashamed, guilty and anxious, someone who is trying to make a connected story of life or simply to keep afloat. What is missing in Goffman is the story line, the continuity from scene to scene, the attempts to make sense as well as to make impressions. People are making their lives as well as making scenes. In the course of it, a person becomes someone. There is the someone we are for others, the someone we continually find as others approach or avoid us, bring praise or ridicule, love or contempt. There is the someone we attempt to become, starting from the situation in which we find ourselves.

In other words, one needs more commitment, more engagement with the real world, a stronger attempt to link scenes and discover what people are trying to make of what others are making of them, in a good theory.

When we think about the aptness of theatre metaphors, we can see another implication. Why is it that we spend so much time looking at theatre (in the broadest sense of the word – television, films, advertisement, whatever the media can deliver)? Isn't it because it exercises our moral and sentimental life, shows us how to be human according to the conventions. It is also simple play. It relieves us of the serious business of maintaining serious selves.

What do we learn from this exercise? We see how a metaphor is used as a vehicle for thought. We see, also, that it can be used too concretely, in a point-by-point comparison. Metaphors are important for *differences* as well as *similarities*. We see that at the edges of the metaphor we must begin to feed back the results of observation. How should the metaphor be changed? Might it be fruitful to think of the presentation of self, as Sartre does, in terms of becoming a self? Engagement or commitment, projects or a long-term quest for design; dread, *angst* and fear lest one fail to carry out these projects (in addition to embarrassment); and the different aspects of self (see the section on existential phenomenology for more detail) might be added to fill in the picture.

In other words, scenes are soon tiresome if they are not connected by stories.

Symbol machines, connection machines, and possible minds

Let us consider another metaphor, which is that the mind is a machine, something like a computer.

What is a machine? A machine is the physical embodiment of a theory. If the theory is simple, the machine is simple. If the theory is about the transfer of force from a point of application to another point, then the machine will (if successfully constructed) transfer force. If the theory is about the transfer of signals, then the machine, when completed, will transfer signals.

The great change in theories is this: Older machines were, generally, constructed to convert and/or transfer energy. Wind, fire, electricity, the traction of mules, provided energy which was captured in various ways at one place and applied at another. These were the *energy machines*. They released humanity from the burden of physical toil. There are also *perceptual machines*, which enable us to see more, or further, or to detect forms of energy that we cannot detect with our own sense organs.

Symbol machines

The new machine models of mind are symbol machines, which run programs of ordered transformations on symbols. A realist theory incorporating these assumptions would adopt the view that cognitive processes are algorithmic and that thought is 'purely a matter of symbol manipulation'. In addition, the mind is 'disembodied' (see Lakoff, 1987: 339–40).

When one considers the activity of the perceptual system in adapting to the wearing of inverting spectacles, or in locating the source of sound in an anechoic chamber, the plausibility of the above two assumptions, which are dominant in current cognitive psychology, must be regarded as very low indeed. Adaptation of the perceptual system is very unlikely to depend on symbol manipulation by rules and most certainly occurs in the embodied mind. Ashby's *Design for a Brain* (1952) made it quite clear that the multistable system of connections he was envisaging included variables in the entire system of the 'body' of the machine and the environment. Taylor (1962), using Ashby's theory, also made it clear that the mind is not in the disembodied brain, or even in the nervous system, but is an emergent feature of a system of behaviour reaching into the world.

Approaching embodiment from a different angle, Lakoff (1987) suggests that metaphors are both informative and possible because we are embodied in certain ways (in Popper's words, the eye or any sensory organ embodies a 'theory' of the world). When we study systems of metaphors, such as the metaphors of anger or lust, we see that they are closely related to bodily experience. Anger is physiology. In it, you lose your cool, you burst a blood vessel, you foam at the mouth, you wrestle with your emotions, you turn red, you do a slow burn, you get hot under the collar, you have heated arguments, you see red, your blood boils, you stew, you seethe (Lakoff, 1987: 380–415). You are a body in a certain condition, as Sartre (1962) would say.

Colour perception, our knowledge of emotions, our preferences for certain experiences, can only be studied as embodied knowledge. We need to look at their evolution, at the operation of epigenetic rules which bias our learning in certain ways, at the complementarity of ontogeny and philogeny.

Why did the symbol machine become popular?
The first reason for the popularity of symbol machines is that they are 'good to think with'. The more clearly we understand the workings of symbol machines, the more clearly we seem to understand the workings of mind – if the mind is a symbol machine. If the mind is not, then we may be misleading ourselves very thoroughly and seductively.

The second reason for using symbol machines as metaphors of mind is historical. The model of language introduced by Chomsky (and others) in the late 1950s was perfectly assimilable to the symbol machine. This model of language not only separated syntax from semantics, but appeared to give syntax a precise, mathematical form. Since this model grew out of work on computer languages, this is hardly surprising, but the effect was overwhelming at the time. The aim of syntactic theory was to define the set of grammatical elements and their rules of transformation, and it was almost certain that a semantic theory of the same kind would follow, once 'knowledge of the world' had been separated from 'knowledge of the language'. The theory of language sustained by these analyses, with its sharp distinction between competence and performance and its clearly formulated set of symbolic operations was used to demolish Skinner's *Verbal Behavior* in Chomsky's (1967; original 1959) review. This syntactic approach plays an important role in recent philosophy, as in Stich's (1983) theory of mind.

The third reason for embracing the symbol machine metaphor was that a level of representations could now be formulated. Mentalism was defined as an approach which operated at this level and which did not reduce every account of behaviour to s and r elements, whether fractional, mediating, external or anticipatory. Having a theoretical tool to work with is the most important methodological imperative. If we don't have geometry, we use figures in the sand; if we don't have figures in the sand, we use our fingers.

As we climb the methodological ladder, we take notice of the imperfections of the theoretical tools we leave behind. Psychology is a rusting heap of discarded metaphors. The symbol machine metaphor may be about to join the heap, for the reasons given above. Though it is useful to test theories, it is not useful to conceptualize them. It neglects the embodiment of knowledge, the ways in which knowledge is affected by psychodynamics, by sociodynamics and by culture. It is poorly structured to model sub-symbolic adaptive processes, such as the adaptations of perception, kinaesthetics or aesthetics for that matter. Human knowledge is based on a system of pre-symbolic or sub-symbolic responses to the world. I have already mentioned the way that metaphors of anger reveal our embodiment; let me give examples of the way that lust is embodied. We find that lust is hunger (he is sex-starved; she looks luscious); lust is animal (he's a wolf; she's cold); lust is madness (he's crazy about her; she's delirious); lust is a game (he'll score; she'll lose); lust is war (he's well-armed; she'll surrender); lust is a physical force or reaction (we were drawn to each other; she's devastating) (Lakoff, 1987). And many more examples of the system of desire can be given. Concepts interact emotionally and experientially because we relate to the world in ways determined by our biology and our culture.

Symbol machines are useful to think about representations, about the possibility of different discourses running in the machine like different programs, and about partly joined operations. These are the things that were persuasive in the past, but they are no longer the problems in the foreground.

It may turn out that modern cognitive psychology is, by and large, a barren subject based on an approach at least as faulty as that of Clark Hull in the 1930s and 1940s. Because it is based on a faulty image of mind, it can reach no correct view of its subject, though it may turn up the odd fact.

The horizons of the computer metaphor
The difficulties at the horizon of the metaphor of the brain as a symbol machine and its theoretically developed consequences are three-fold: (1) In what sense can we think of mental processes as *computations*? (2) What is it to *understand* a problem? and (3) What is it to *be* a particular mind?

The first consequence, which is the treatment of mental processes as though they were computations, may be harmless as long as we do not make any claims about the design or physical reality of those computations. Suppose we find that 'yellow-eyed juncos' (a kind of bird) avoid risky options if they are not very hungry, but take risks if their lives depend on it' (Beardsley, 1983) and suppose that we find mathematical models based on optimality theory to be useful in predicting the feeding decisions which these birds make, can we produce an account of their behaviour by introducing the mathematics of optimality theory into their heads? Obviously not, it would seem. Optimality theory is strictly a theory about the evolutionary benefits an animal obtains by behaving in a certain way and is not committed to any account of the mechanisms in that animal's head which make it behave the way it does. Have we any reason to suppose that computer models are any better? In fact, there is no obvious justification for believing in the realism of any particular program. A program is merely a conceptual answer to the question: How does the organism maximize its rate of food intake under various risky conditions? One way of responding is to write a gambling program and put it in the animal's conceptual head, but this goes wrong the moment we suppose that a conceptual head is the same as a physical head. We have, in terms of Putnam's (1960) criteria, produced a *how to* model, but we have skipped all the problems of trying to specify the biological mechanisms which enable the animal to behave in a way which is modelled by the mathematical theory of optimality. We have confused *causal* and *conceptual* accounts of how an organism might behave in a particular way. Conceptual accounts might terminate in a computer program which models the behaviour successfully; causal accounts attempt to uncover the physical machinery of the organism whose behaviour we are modelling, and that machinery need not use anything like a computer program and might not carry out anything like a series of computations. Daniel Dennett (1981) makes the point: 'Presumably a diving bell does not compute its equilibrium depth in water, though it arrives at it by a process of diminishing "corrections". Does a fish compute its proper depth of operation?' (1981: 70).

Consider Fodor's distinction between cognitive psychology and psychophysics in the light of what has just been said.

> Psychophysical truths express the lawful contingency of events under *psychological description* upon events *under physical description;* whereas the truths of cognitive psychology express the computational contingencies among events which are homogeneously (psychologically) described (Fodor, 1976: 201).

According to this account, the work done in cognitive psychology is an attempt to specify the psychological machinery for carrying out an operation, such as remembering, recognizing, or solving a problem, and is not concerned with the psychophysical problem of the kind of machine in which the program is executed. Exercises in computational theory have led to a vivid distinction between psychophysical realism (which we may call *type* functionalism) and cognitivism (which we may call *token* functionalism). According to the former approach, a theory of mind and mental operations must be a theory of the ways in which nervous systems carry out psychological functions. According to the latter approach, though 'all the mental processes in existence happen to be neurological' (Fodor, 1981: 7), there is no reason why this should always be the case (if it is the case). If we adopt token functionalism or cognitivism, then mental operations in nervous systems are simply a special case in a general theory of mental operations. This leads to the conclusion that 'there are possible – and, for all we know, real – information processing systems which share our psychology (instantiate its generalization' (Fodor, 1981: 9).

The significance of the distinction between psychophysical truths and cognitive truths as formulated by Fodor (1976) is that it appears to 'free' psychological explanation; but that freedom may be bought at the price of confusing conceptual and physical explanations of behaviour, where 'conceptual' refers to the fact that we substitute a 'logical' for a 'real' answer, a series of calculations in the bird's head for whatever biological machinery may be present.

The second problem at the horizon of a machine metaphor of mind is the question: Can we say that the machine understands what it is doing? Is it a 'semantic engine' (Fodor's 1981 words); that is, a machine which could operate on symbols in such a way as to produce beliefs or experiences? Unfortunately, we have no theory of mental representations, though machines can certainly 'make decisions' on input, 'interpret' input, 'transform' input, and embody 'maps' and 'assumptions' about the world. What is the difference between these operations on symbols and mental representations? Perhaps it is a matter of degree; perhaps it is only a matter of appropriate sensorimotor links with the environment. Given the right equipment, machines might develop points of view, commitments to reality, and interests. When this happens, we may have to give them the vote. At the moment they are like skilled bridge players who don't know why they are playing. In phenomenological terms, a machine is a thing 'in itself', not 'for itself'. It does not give an account to itself and to others of its purposes.

We can now turn to a third problem at the horizon of the machine metaphor, a problem which is closely related to mental representations. Quite simply, there is no theory of consciousness or qualitative states of mind. How do we *experience,* apart from the question of how do we *operate on* or *transform* or *manipulate* symbols. Information-processing models have added to the range of possible models for doing things with symbols but have not been able to tell us how these operations might lead to conscious experience of anything. Without consciousness, we cannot imagine any use of language, representation, or reasoning in the sense of exploring points of view, inquiring into the nature of the universe, or reflecting on ourselves.

A recent trend, embryonic as yet, is the development of sub-symbolic or connectionist models. Is this a return to the efforts of people like Ashby in the 1950s – attempts described by Minsky and Papert (1968) as 'fearfully simple'? No. In fact, we should take warning from the start that many of these models are as disembodied as symbolic models. Yet they may be more plausible.

Connection machines

An alternative to the symbol machine approach to mind is the connection machine approach. According to this approach, our problem is to see how, starting with a relatively unorganized brain or nervous system, connections of an adaptive kind are formed. It may be asked why we should attempt to assimilate mind to yet another machine? The reply to this is that machines are the best things we have to think with. Since the eighteenth century, there have been persistent attempts to assimilate the human mind to the best machinery available. As the machinery improved, so our understanding of the human mind seemed to improve. At first, human beings were rather remarkable automata, then complicated telephone exchanges, and finally symbol machines or connection machines.

The methodological point is that this attempt may be entirely misleading. It is part of the 'spirit of the age', part of the desire to discover the algorithms or programs of mind. To the extent that this is misleading, our methodology will lead to us to systematically wrong conclusions about mind.

Let us continue, though, with an account of connection machines. They are sub-conceptual and do not depend upon the manipulation of symbols for their operations.

> Connectionist models are large networks of simple parallel computing elements.... Much of the allure of the connectionist approach is that many connectionist networks *program themselves*, that is, they have autonomous procedures for tuning their weights to eventually perform some specific computation (Smolensky, 1988: 1).

Why is there an interest in connectionist models? The first reason has nothing to do with psychology. It depends on the promise of self-programming, highly adaptable machines for performing inventive work. The second reason, which has more to do with psychology, is that connectionists offer better models of the nervous system than symbol machine theorists. The third is that a better model of the nervous system may lead to a better model of the mind. At this stage, connectionism is no more than an approach and many are sceptical of its claims.

What are the possible relations between connectionist (sub-symbolic) and symbolic machines? Do we have to choose between them? Woodfield and Morton (1988) suggest three possible relations, and to these we shall add a fourth.

The first possibility is a division of labour in the brain. It may carry out computations of different kinds with different systems, using a sub-symbolic or a symbolic system where appropriate. The second possibility is 'killing two birds with one stone' (Woodfield and Morton, 1988: 58). Thus, one may practice archery and add to the larder and impress one's lover simultaneously. Similarly, the two cognitive processes of symbolic and sub-symbolic computation may be carried out simultaneously by one connectionist set of neural events.

The third possibility is the 'by' relation. One may launch a ship by breaking a bottle of champagne; one may 'carry out a symbolic process by performing sub-symbolic operations' (1988: 58). It is the 'by' relation that Woodfield and Morton favour, proposing that symbolic thinking is indeed an emergent property of connectionist systems and that it really exists: the human brain functions as a symbol manipulator by being a sub-symbolic or connectionist system. Perhaps the difference between symbol machines and connection machines should be first stressed in considering this point of view. In symbol machines, there really is a program written in a programming language and entered into the machine; in connection machines, there are only connections of different patterns and weights. The information is *in* the network and the connections. They are 'self-programming' in the sense that these networks and weighted connections are altered during learning.

Yet emergence is a common enough phenomenon in biology. 'Ethologists have proposed that some social behaviour in animals (display, courtship rituals) evolved out of displacement activities produced by conflict between basic instincts' (Woodfield and Morton, 1988: 58).

One might imagine how, with the advent of language, operating with symbols becomes an essential part of the programming of the system. Self-directions of all kinds are evident, but are they simply output of a system of connections, rather than a real, separate element in the operation of the mind?

This leads to the fourth possibility, which is that the symbolic and

THE USES OF METAPHOR 67

sub-symbolic are *not* levels, but different paradigms of cognitive modelling. Nor are they separate systems which can connect or disconnect, but different modes of explanation. The different approaches may be analogous to the approaches of Newtonian mechanics and quantum mechanics. Quantum mechanics is supposed to tell how things 'really are', but Newtonian mechanics is essential for accounts of the world at the macro level. In a strict sense, if the microtheory is right, the macrotheory is wrong. Yet, for a large range of circumstances, the macrotheory is the best we have. In the same way, connectionism may be right. The nervous system may operate sub-symbolically, by altering the weights of connections and their patterns of firing. Yet at the macrolevel, symbols are a necessary ingredient. We refer to symbols which represent intentions, beliefs, desires. Or, if we search for greater generality, we include only semantically uninterpreted, syntax-like symbols rather like those in a Chomskyan theory of syntax. The argument is hardly settled and both versions are, strictly speaking, wrong according to the connectionist account. There is no 'real' level of symbol operations in the connectionist machinery of mind.

Is there any reason why one should prefer connection machines to symbol machines as metaphors of mind or vice versa? The reasons are fairly weak but they are worth going over.

1. The symbolic approach is more plausible when we approach problems from a macro level. The sub-symbolic approach is more plausible when we consider the structure of the nervous system. Ideas and symbols are then explained by referring to patterns of firing of the nervous system, but are not essential parts of the explanation. This resembles the explanation of heat by reference to vibrations of molecules, although they are qualitatively so different.
2. Many adaptations, such as the adaptation of the perceptual system to inverting spectacles, do not seem to involve any symbolic operations at all.
3. It is clear that connectionist models leave even less room for 'folk psychology' than syntactic theories of the mind (Stich, 1983). (This is something I shall return to later in this book.) They have the potential of really 'deep' theory. Their possibilities of self-programming appear to offer verisimilitude of a degree not found in symbolic approaches.
4. The dynamic variability of networks seems to give us a better grip on intuition, on metaphoric thinking, than working with a well-defined list of symbols.

At the end of all this, perhaps a dash of cold water is healthy. Smolensky (1988) observes, after a long debate, that the coupling of connectionist and neural modes is a long way off. The distance between connectionist and psychological models is correspondingly greater.

What, then, is the value of the computer metaphor of mind (apart from its utility as a method of modelling specific processes such as those which *might* be involved in retrieving information or in other cognitive processes)? Perhaps its greatest value is that it enables us to think about problems at the outer limits of convenience of the metaphor.

Conclusion

We might wish to say that the mind is a machine of some kind or that it is a machine like a computer. At the moment, we are tempted to say the latter. This may do as a temporary metaphor, but it is likely to mislead as often as it assists, resulting as it does in the assimilation of mental processes to computations.

Furthermore, a machine-functional foundation metaphor runs into almost as many problems as dualism in attempting to account for qualitative experience (Searle, 1987). It seems likely, though, that investigations in artificial intelligence could lead to the construction in principle of machines which could if it were desired approximate human cognitive functions more and more closely, and that the machine metaphor may be replaced by a genuine theory of intelligent operations, including those of human intelligence.

Now let us turn back to a more general consideration of metaphor and its uses.

Fitting the world

Suppose that we attempt to understand one thing in terms of another, as in the following:

- The mind is a computer
- Love is war
- Love is a game
- People are machines

then, is it only the thing which we are trying to understand or represent that is seen in a new light? In other words, is the traffic one-way? When the conjunction is ephemeral, this may appear to be the case, but when there is a protracted development of metaphor, then both terms in the metaphor are changed or understood in a new way. The more love is thought of as war, the more war is thought of as love ('that sweet enemy, France'). Where the conjunction is temporary, reciprocal influence is less obvious, and the metaphor may achieve its effects as much by pointed differences as similarities.

An example may illustrate this. Consider the metaphor 'office wife' for secretary. It suggests drudgery, sexual exploitation, low pay, male dominance, and enables us to see secretaries in a new light. On the other hand, we begin to see wives in a new light as well. Why should wives not be paid, have limited 'office' hours, be able to leave the 'office-house' at certain hours, be free to change jobs? Even more important is the fact that the equation enables us to grasp both categories as exploited people. Thus, both are conceived of in a new way.

Piaget summed up the tensions of transfer under the headings: 'accommodation' and 'assimilation', both of which seemed to him (however poorly understood) to be essential to the growth of understanding. Metaphor is merely the most striking and obtrusive form of a universal process of transfer, in which new events are assimilated to old constructs and old constructs are accommodated to new events.

Every action in the world must accommodate to its properties. A sucking mouth must accommodate to the formation of a particular teat; a grasping hand must accommodate to the form of a particular object and to its movement and surface, its density and mass. When we count, we have to accommodate our numbers to apples and elephants. In his graphic *The Origin of Intelligence in the Child*, first published in 1936, Piaget describes the growing co-ordinations of schemes which children apply to the world. Here is an oft-quoted example. Lucienne is trying to remove a watch chain from a match box with an opening of only 3 mm. She cannot insert her finger. She knows only how to turn the box over to empty it (Scheme 1) and how to slide her finger into the opening of the box to ease out an end of the chain and then pull (Scheme 2).

She has failed. There is a pause. 'She looks at the slit with great attention; then, several times in succession, she opens and shuts her mouth, at first slightly, then wider and wider!' (Piaget, 1977: 375). Possibly the opening of the mouth represents an action, a transformation of the box. She then puts her finger into the slit and, instead of trying to reach the chain, she pulls the box open.

Here we may speak of the conjecturing mouth, the application of the construct of opening to a new object. A metaphor is a conjecture about the nature of reality; a significant metaphor is an insight into unexpected properties of the object of an inquiry: both accommodation and assimilation must occur. To assimilate what we see to an existing construct is to know something about it, but not a great deal. It is like a child using a block of wood as a car and ignoring, for the moment, all those properties which are not car-like. The fit is loose. To generate new knowledge, constructs must be changed by the objects on which they act as well as changing these objects. Metaphors not only help us to understand new things in terms of old constructs – they change old constructs as well.

We see that metaphor is the most visible tip of the iceberg of transfer of old constructs to new contexts. However, there is an additional feature which we should take note of, and that is the purpose of metaphorical transfer.

Think of the following series:

>the rules of bridge
>the rules of the game
>the rules of language games
>the rules of dying

Think also of the following series:

>Lucienne opens her mouth to take a nipple
>Lucienne opens her mouth to explore a block
>Lucienne opens her mouth to 'represent' opening and closing a box

What we have in each case is an increasing abstraction; an increasing distance between the 'proper' use of the construct and an 'improper' use of it. Looking at the first series, we can discern the following: (1) the use of 'rules' becomes increasingly hypothetical, (2) the use of 'rules' becomes increasingly metaphorical, and (3) the use of 'rules' becomes metalinguistic.

We may postulate a use of 'rule' in a language at level n, at which 'rule' appears to be the natural term for the event or object. This is the level at which there is no apparent transfer of terms (though we have seen that all constructs and their terms must transfer). However, by the time we have reached the phrases 'rules of dying' and 'rules of language games', we are clearly speaking metaphorically. We are conjecturing that there are regularities which could be understood as though they were rules. Our terms are now parts of a metalanguage, $n+1$, the object of which is rules in language at level n. (Here, I shall note in passing that there is a kind of language at level $n-1$, where we attempt to discover the 'real' or 'sacred' or 'proper' names for things. This is mythical language – and I shall be discussing it in a subsequent chapter.)

How do we go on from here? If our purpose is scientific, we might investigate the rules of dying in various societies and situations. We should attempt to conjecture about 'rules' in such a way as to be able to incorporate them in propositions which would be tested. We might discover different 'rules' governing the behaviour of the person who is about to die at the gallows, before the firing squad, in a hospital bed, at home, etc., and we might conjecture that violation of these rules produces the sort of embarrassment that we experience when lapsing on other grave occasions, such as when we fail to produce a ring at a wedding.

Referring to our other example, which is Lucienne's use of her mouth, we observe changes of level and the achievement of new combinations which are similar to those we find in verbal metaphor. When Lucienne opens her mouth to take the nipple or to explore an object, she is performing actions at a first-order level. When she opens her mouth to represent the opening of the box, she has transferred the action to a higher level, at which new transformations of reality are possible.

Not all hierarchies are constructed for metaphorical use. Piaget describes the development of classifications, which are hierarchies: both canaries and ducks are birds. Metaphor requires the construction of new and unexpected systems of equivalence. Where 'rule' is used metaphorically, we construct a new classification which can include both 'rules of bridge' and 'rules of dying' and lead to a fresh understanding of one or both.

Metaphorical language produces examples of the set of provisional constructions of reality. The insights produced may be ephemeral and appropriate to particular circumstances only, or they may be the foundation of new intellectual adventures.

Intellectual space

In creating new configurations of ideas, metaphors provide us with intellectual spaces in which to work. Viewing social life as a game, a drama, or a discourse, we start out with different charts and explore different worlds. The reason for this is that each metaphorical transfer carries with it a new system of implications and possibilities. If social life is to be thought of as a game, then we should look for rules, for ways in which rules are learnt, for guidelines on how to score points, for lessons on tactics, strategies and manoeuvres, and for fields of play. Which game does social life resemble most closely, or is it a set of games, some still being invented?

We could also look at the metaphors people use in their daily life and wonder what might happen if we persuaded them to change these (Pollio et al., 1977). Would a couple who construe their marriage as a kind of reciprocal exploitation be better of with another metaphor?

Or, when we attempt to understand the universe of matter, we could either build our inquiry upon the assumption that space is a void or on the contrary assumption that space is an active structure. Here is Einstein's description of the dominant metaphor:

> Since it would have seemed utterly absurd to the physicists of the nineteenth century to attribute physical functions or states to space itself, they invented a medium pervading the whole of space, on the model of ponderable matter – the ether, which was supposed to act as a vehicle for elecro-magnetic phenomena, and hence for those of light also (1954: 477)

An alternative construction of space is:

> Since the gravitational field is determined by the configuration of masses and changes with it, the geometric structure of this space is also dependent on physical factors. Thus according to this theory space is – exactly as Riemann guessed – no longer absolute; its structure depends on physical influences. Physical geometry is no longer an isolated self-contained science like the geometry of Euclid (1954: 482).

Here we have two foundation metaphors of modern physics. We see, also, that such foundation metaphors are conjectures about the nature of reality, which have to be transformed as they are more and more rigorously applied to physical problems. The metaphor is itself a complex set of terms, the relations of which have to be rigorously defined as it is developed. New elements are introduced into the metaphor and existing elements are suppressed as they are found to be inappropriate to the problem, until one arrives at theory which is far removed from its original metaphorical beginning. Nevertheless, buried in theory is the foundation metaphor which formed the basis of inquiry. As we can see, a foundation metaphor of space as the inert and rigid container of physical action has to be abandoned to permit solutions of relativistic physics.

It is worth noticing that our conception of metaphor itself is also being changed as we apply it to the question of how an inquiry begins and is sustained. At first, we saw metaphor merely as a transfer of terms from one event to another to which it is 'inappropriate', and we might have supposed that its function is mainly decorative and fanciful. Then, as we examined different kinds of transfer, we saw that it might occur *within* a language level n, as when we use *rule* consistently in contents which are so similar that we mistakenly suppose them to be identical, and that transfer might also require us to change the level of our language, so that at level $n + 1$ our use of 'rule' has as its object properties of *rule* at level n. Finally, we saw that when we transfer a term from a language n

to a language $n + 1$, we take along much of the internal structure of the term, but not all. This process of selection can be summarized as the accommodation of the term to a new environment of discourse. We may call this process 'working' a metaphor and we may understand the process by referring to Goffman's working the metaphor of theatre to describe social life and even occasionally explain some of its features. To 'work' a metaphor is to discover its implications and to test them in the context of inquiry. How far can a dramatic metaphor be taken? Which elements of the metaphor have to be ignored and which developed? Should relations between elements be changed in any way? The dramaturgic metaphor leaves us with significant problems about scripts (who writes them?), learning roles, realism and commitment, and the question of whether there is any 'real' self to be discussed apart from roles. After all, actors pop in and out of roles in different plays. What happens to their 'real' selves?

The import of this is simply that, no matter how hard we work any given metaphor, it is likely to solve only a small set of problems and leave many others untouched. Furthermore, most metaphors never become more than quasi-science, in the sense that they carry far too much surplus meaning and that there is no exact statement of the elements and their relations which are being abstracted for the problem. There is a failure of both prediction and falsifiability. At a more ordinary level, there is even a confusion about what, exactly, in the metaphor is explanatory for the new science and what is to be sent back. Obviously, we can't swallow the theatre whole; yet, what should we discard? What is needed is a degree of formality in selecting props and parts for the new task of scientific explanation.

As soon as we recognize that metaphors require a change in level of language and that their application requires a selection of elements and relations, we see that metaphors are not inert, or a sort of wallpaper plastered on to the surface of events; rather, they are intellectual spaces, active fields of inquiry. The change is rather like the change in the conception of physical space referred to at the beginning of this chapter. At first, physicists thought of space as an empty framework within which physical events occurred; then, they began to think of space as having a physical geometry which depended on the configuration of masses within it. Psychological space has undergone a similar change. On the one hand, we may suppose that psychological spaces consist of unrelated events which have to be associated by such processes as conditioning. Older theories of 'ideas' or 'responses' in the empty space of mind or the physical world (depending on whether the psychologist was a mentalist or a behaviourist) closely resembled the empty spaces of physics. The real difficulty with such empty worlds is how things ever connect, except by collision and proximity. In psychology, a 'physicalist' solution depended upon the laborious conditioning of responses.

Psychological space is not like that at all, if the view adopted in this book is correct. It is much more like the world of *gestalten*, of *good figure* and *insight*, in which the individual composes the world. Metaphorical composition is, it is maintained here, an important process in achieving this active psychological space. That is, the composition of this space is changed by the introduction of metaphors, rather as its composition is changed when we see a reversible figure first one way and then another. Metaphorical composition is by no means the only process by which new configurations of psychological space can be achieved (as we see from the reference to reversible figures), but it is an important process for setting up new compositions. There are other processes, such as deductive reasoning, which can lead to important new conclusions and hence to new configurations of psychological space. What I am concerned with, for the moment, is the opening up of active new psychological configurations within which problem solutions can occur.

How metaphors work

Metaphors appear to represent relations between things, like charts and maps, graphs and models – all of which represent significant relations between things rather than simply how things are (Black, 1979). A vivid example of this, from Max Black, is the metaphor: 'Nixon is an image surrounding a vacuum'. Whatever we may think of the accuracy of this metaphor, we must conclude that its value lies in its portrayal of certain relations between things rather than its accurate portrayal of Nixon's many other properties. Similarly, when we examine metaphors in which love is systematically treated as a physical force, a journey, a sickness, a madness, a form of art, war, wealth, or nourishment (Lakoff and Johnson, 1980), we are portraying relationships between things. These relations may be essential or superficial, enduring or ephemeral, practically useful or aesthetically striking. They may form the basis of a new theory or of a new joke. In this way, a metaphor is like a map which may represent real or imaginary or funny islands. When a map is useful, it is because it represents real relations in the world. Some maps are more useful than others when we intend to explore the world, others are more decorative or amusing. Similarly, some metaphors are worth exploring as a basis of psychological theory, but others are not. Metaphors, like maps, are a product of, and a tool in, our exploration of the world. As we explore, we improve our maps: as we improve our maps, so exploration becomes easier.

We have already had some examples of how metaphors can be worked – in particular, the theatre metaphor – but let us look at the interaction between the terms of a metaphor. When we think a metaphor (e.g. 'winter of our discontent'), how do we interact with its terms and make them interact with each other? Black proposes the following:

> (a) The presence of the primary object incites the hearer to select some of the secondary subject's properties; and (b) invites him to construct a parallel implication – complex that can fit the primary subject; and (c) reciprocally induces change in the secondary subject (Black, 1979: 29).

This is an account of a psychological process, a personal response to the terms of a metaphor. What does this process work on? We have already seen, in the many metaphors of love, that it is hardly plausible to suppose that a selection of pre-existing attributes (like cards in a pack) is extracted and then matched with another pre-existing set. Indeed, Black writes of 'constructing' an implication-complex, so we conclude that he has something more elaborate than the use of pre-existing feature-sets in mind. What is more likely is that some attributes are so rapidly generated as to seem ready-made, whereas others are reached only by turning over images, uses, contents, implications and structures. In other words, our use of words draws not only on a 'dictionary' of definitions but on a wider range of experiences and perceptions (Paivio and Begg, 1981). In considering love as divine frenzy and as a work of art (not to mention its appearance as hard labour, a journey, or a form of sickness), we do not derive much help from the dictionary.

When we think of matching the attributes of terms in a metaphor, therefore, we should bear in mind the possibility that we are constructing and matching 'implication-complexes', and that the reach of this process will depend on the purpose of the metaphor. Where a metaphor has a scientific purpose, we will tend to compare implications quite thoroughly and the processes of reciprocal change of implication-complexes will be sustained and complex.

We have ignored (or taken for granted) the difference between literal and metaphorical similarity. What is the difference between 'his intellect is a razor' and 'this knife is a razor'? In both cases, there is an intersection of attributes on which the comparison is based. When we compare intellect to razor, though, we are aware of the sudden illumination of a feature of intellect; an indication of the direction we wish our use of the term to move in. A salient feature of razor, its sharpness, is used to draw attention to a quality of mind. The greater the intersection, the greater the similarity, and the less we rely on drawing our implications to discover the point of the similarity.

Ortony (1979a) uses the concept of interaction of a set of attributes to explain similarity, and imbalance in salience of matching attributes to explain both metaphorical direction and the differences between literal similarity and metaphor. The greater the intersection, the greater the similarity between two terms. The greater the imbalance of salience of matching attributes between two terms, the more likely we are to see the similarity as metaphorical. Thus, knife and razor are both used for cutting, are both commonly constructed of the same sort of materials, and are both commonly sharp. The combination of the two is not usually perceived as metaphorical, since all these features are equally salient for the two terms, though 'sharpness' may be slightly more salient for razor than for knife. However, when we compare 'intellect' or 'mind' with razor, there are not many common attributes and these are likely to differ greatly in their salience. 'Sharpness' is much more salient for razor than for 'intellect' or for 'mind'.

This difference in salience is referred to as the diagonality of the attributes which the two terms have in common (Ortony, 1979a). For this reason, 'razor', can be used to draw attention to the 'sharpness' of intellect, but intellect can hardly be used to draw attention to the 'sharpness' of razor. This implies that metaphors have directions. Thus, we say: 'the winter of our discontent' but not 'the discontent of our winter', when speaking metaphorically. The latter expression is literal. It does not invite us to find any unusual or sharply focused attributes of either 'winter' or 'discontent'. Whereas the salience of 'cold' in the winter of the first expression leads us to focus on cold, a low salience attribute of discontent. Provided that we bear in mind the argument that attributes or relations are not simply present in the terms but have to be constructed, and that some of these constructions are more obscure or complex than others, we can use Ortony's concept of diagonality to explain the directions of metaphor.

Not all metaphors have interesting implications, but the fundamental metaphors of science do. Significant metaphors, such as the computer metaphor of mind, are 'theory-constitutive' and become 'an irreplaceable part of the linguistic machinery of science' (Boyd, 1979: 358).

To this we may add that metaphor is an irreplaceable part of the linguistic machinery of metatheory, or judgements *about* science. Boyd, to take an example from the paper already cited, argues that metaphor is a device available to the scientific community to accommodate language to the causal texture of the world, and he uses the graphic expression, 'cut the world at its joints', to convey the image of a science which is continually getting deeper into the real anatomy of the world.

THE USES OF METAPHOR 77

There are other significant metaphors of the way in which science works. One of these is that nature contains mechanisms or generative structures which produce events, and that it is the business of the scientist to discover and understand these mechanisms. Thus, where we explore the implication of the computer metaphor in psychology, we are attempting to understand mental activity as if the brain were a mechanism of some kind.

The search for theory-constitutive or foundation metaphors is, of course, no more than a first step in the construction of theory, but it is a vital step. Let us now summarize what has been said about metaphor in this chapter.

Summary

- Metaphors are conjectures about events.
- Metaphors can open up new intellectual space. They can be, in Boyd's words, 'theory-constitutive'.
- Metaphors have structure – 'implication complexes' as Black calls them – and this structure constitutes working space for inquiry.
- Metaphors are the most notable form of the general process of transfer of terms from from event to another. However, they differ from generalization in that literal similarity is not insisted on, and we remain aware, as a rule, of our figurative treatment of a subject.
- Metaphors change the level of language.
- Metaphors do not only assimilate events; they also accommodate to them. The result of this process of assimilation and accommodation is new knowledge.
- Metaphors are used to initiate inquiry but they do not complete it. Part of the work of metaphor is the gradual selection and formalization of elements and relations of new theory.
- Each metaphor has a focus and a horizon; at the focus, problems seem to be clearly soluble, whereas at the horizon we have doubts about the nature of reality and often run into problems of a kind we call 'metaphysical', such as the real nature of mind and its relation to the body.
- Every science has its foundation metaphors, which represent the first successful attempts to solve significant problems and get hold of the subject. In social psychology, the foundation metaphor is theatre (roles, actors, role-distance, role-relations, scripts), in cognitive psychology the foundation metaphor is the computer (information processing, programs, storage, retrieval).

There are many other metaphors in psychological theory – theatre, games, narrative and dialectic – but the two metaphors which have been selected for discussion will be sufficient to demonstrate the theory-constitutive function of foundation metaphors.

I shall now discuss other forms of rhetoric and their contribution to psychology.

5 | Displacements: metaphor/metonymy/myth

The time has come to show the relations between metaphor, metonymy and myth in the development of social theory. This is a set of rhetorical manoeuvres for probing the similarities, associations and 'essences' of the world. And when we speak of 'rhetoric' here, we are not speaking of quaint figures of speech introduced like garden gnomes to disfigure the severe decorum of science, but of fundamental processes of intelligence. To think metaphorically is to attempt to see similarities between things; to think metonymically is to seek new combinations, contiguities and associations, and to think mythically is to attempt to reduce the distance between discourse and reality by creating a sacred language or, for that matter, a language consisting of proper names for the 'facts' of the world.

We can represent these elements by displacements along two axes. The first axis indicates the degree to which a search for similarity or a

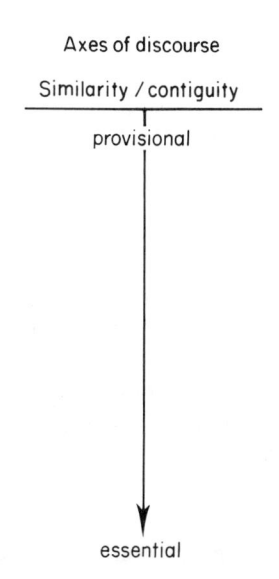

Axes of discourse

Similarity / contiguity

provisional

↓

essential

search for combinations and associations predominates in discourse; the second axis indicates the degree to which the relation between discourse and events is thought of as essential or provisional and arbitrary.

From what has been said above we can easily construct a triangle within which we might place samples of discourse. The extreme forms are identified as 'pure' metonymy, metaphor and myths, but any given example of discourse would show mixtures of these.

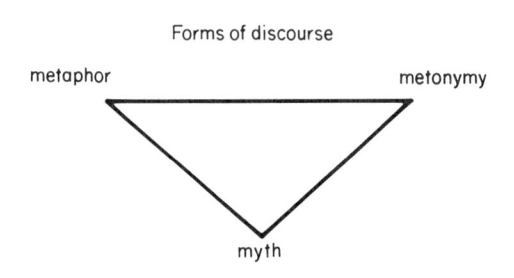

Forms of discourse

```
metaphor                    metonymy
         \                /
          \              /
           \            /
            \          /
             \        /
              \      /
               \    /
                \  /
                 \/
                myth
```

Before we elaborate on the relations between these forms of discourse, let us give a brief definition of each.

Metaphor

In metaphorical discourse we look at one thing as though it were another, while remaining aware that it is not. When we cease to be aware of a distinction, similarity becomes identity. Thus, we might start off saying that the brain is a computer (metaphorically) and end believing that it is a computer (literally).

Metonymy

In metonymical discourse, we describe a thing by 'some accompaniment or significant adjunct, instead of naming the thing itself' (Nesfield, 1899: 249). We do not view one thing as though it were another, in order to discover surprising implications, but rather systematically select features or accompaniments of the event we are referring to. Here are some examples:

- he is a good *hand* at bridge
- she has gone over to *Rome* (Catholic Church)

- soul of this age, the *applause, delight* and *wonder* of our stage!

In these examples, we see that the adjuncts (hand, Rome, applause) do not lead us to view the original in a new way, as though the bridge-player were a hand, or the writer an applause, or the Catholic faith were Rome. There is no illumination to be had in this way. What has happened is that the focus of attention is displaced to an accompaniment of an event. The process becomes particularly interesting when the connection between the accompaniment and the event is lost or suppressed, as in the processes of displacement, condensation and hysterical conversion (Freud) or fetishism (Marx). The process of metonymy, or 'change of name' has occupied a central place in analyses of the relations between consciousness and society. Let us complete our definitions, though, before discussing this question in greater detail. We have not yet attempted a definition of myth.

Myth

In mythical discourse we attempt to discover a 'world of proper names' (Lotman, 1977: 238). Myths may be stories, but this aspect does not interest us in this chapter. What is significant is that mythological thinking is, in the prototypical case, an attempt to search sacred texts for the real names of events in the world. Mythical understanding is based on naming and showing events as they really are rather than on an attempt to form propositions about them in conceptual languages.

A few examples of mythological thought may aid understanding here:

- a peasant says: 'Measuring the distances to stars may be difficult, but how do you discover their names?'
- the true and only name of God is Jehovah
- the real name of the substance of the universe is matter.

Discussion: Myths and zero displacement from reality

Both metaphor and metonymy are forms of rhetorical displacement, whereas myths attempt zero displacement, or a language in which the true names of the real world are revealed. In other words, mythical discourse aims at the creation of sacred texts. We can see how important this is in ideological texts of all kinds and, therefore, what a central place myth occupies in the social sciences. The words 'free enterprise', 'class', 'capitalism', 'production', 'relations of production', 'proletariat', 'democracy', and 'socialism' have all been mythologized in some or other sacred text. We also see this in the continual search for the proper names of various ethnic groups, in terms such as 'negro', 'black', 'African', 'bushman', 'San' and others. We may acknowledge that these terms are signs of changing social practices or we may regard them as the proper names of these groups. Naturally, our discussion of myth does not imply contempt for mythical thought, but an attempt to recognize a particular form of rhetoric. The person who uses mythical forms attempts to reduce his distance from reality to zero, or to attach himself directly to it. Thus, the ideologue who has discovered the truth about society can recognize its forms all about him, rather like the believer who can see evidence of God even in disease and earthquakes. He can see the hidden machinery of history propelling us towards a classless society (Marx), or the spirit of the world working, by way of the Prussian state, towards the ultimate rationality in which 'thought thinks itself' (Hegel).

The ways in which people name events are indeed important; when people insist that the true name of God is Jehovah rather than some other name, it is likely that they are insisting that *the* God is *their* God, rather than anyone else's. Similarly, when scientists insist that the substance of the universe is matter (and no other substance is allowed), it is likely that they are insisting that rationality is *their* rationality, and that no other form will do.

Tags are important in keeping track of events; it may be important to identify and tag a heavenly body and know that it passed us 35 years previously. Tags, though, are not mythical names which reveal essences of inherent nature. 'Matter', on the other hand, is either an 'essence' or a term which we can extend indefinitely. Tags keep track of events which must be referred to conceptual language for understanding; whereas sacred or mythical names are part of the essential nature of what we study. When we tag a particular body, we might, without changing its tag, change its conceptual status (as Kuhn, 1979, says). What was a star might become a satellite or a planet. This would not disturb us. We might even change its tag to fit into a new conceptual series without feeling that we had mislaid it.

Can we now state briefly what the function of mythical thought is? As we attempt to reduce our distance from the world to zero, we discover that it is composed of signs and texts; that it is, in other words, significant. It is rich in moral purpose and meaning, but these can only be read if we take up the correct attitude and call things by their proper names. That is the way to work magic and conjure up spirits. Even the counter-myth of the material world stubbornly insists that matter is deaf, that it knows no spirit, and that we can only address it on its own terms, by using its own proper name, which is 'matter'.

We can see the importance of myths in some philosophical discussions of mind/body interaction hypotheses (such as the hypothesis advanced by Popper and Eccles, 1977). It is argued that any specific structure or force which explains the mind's causal interaction with the brain must be material (e.g. Cohen, 1979: 304). Douglas and Keaney comment as follows:

> Cohen reveals here the ontological sleight-of-hand that makes the materialist's position unassailable. In Popper's discussion of materialism he points out that materialism was originally the belief that all of physics was explained by the physical contact of objects extended in space and interacting as cogs in a mechanism. The Newtonian notion of force at a distance violated materialism, but the 'materialists' rallied and incorporated such forces into their ontology. Cohen threatens that if a new phenomenon challenges the ontology of modern materialism, they will rally yet again. God might yet find acceptance by this form of materialism (1984: 27).

The fact is that 'matter' is being used as a proper name for the substance of the universe, a name with mystical connotations, in arguments that would reduce all problems to physics.

Mythologizing, in the sense of attempting to discover the 'essence' and inner significance of nature, is something we do not easily abandon. The 'anti-myth' of science is very recent, as Robert Musil points out in a chapter entitled 'Science smiling into its beard, or first full-dress encounter with Evil'. It was in the sixteenth century that

> people ceased trying, as they had been trying all through two thousand years of religious and philosophic speculation, to penetrate into the Secrets of Nature, and instead contented themselves, in a way that can only be called superficial, with investigations of its surface (1979: 359).

In the social sciences, we have not yet given up our myths or our deep secrets, and it may be that a good case can be made for not giving up mythical attachments to the world. Ideologies, which may be regarded as social theories plus myths, are probably indispensable for social existence, which requires not merely functional-pragmatic knowledge, but also a kind of vision of 'reality' which enables us to find significance in the world. In other words, myth as sacred text, as inner reality, as knowledge of the proper constitution and order of the world (or at least the social world), may be a necessary part of all social theory.

Let us now turn to metaphor and metonymy.

Discussion: metaphor and metonymy

Whereas myth is an attempt to reduce the distance between discourse and its object to zero, thus producing a sacred text in which the 'Secrets of Nature' are revealed, metaphor and metonymy are attempts to construct similarities and new combinations in discourse. Some time ago, Roman Jakobson pointed out that discourse may develop either metaphorically, by exploring similarities, or metonymically, by exploring associations and contiguities (Jakobson and Halle, 1980).

By now we have had several examples of metaphor, but it will be easier to understand if we place it in the context of myth and metonymy. Similarly, we shall understand each figure better in the context of the other figures. Here are two examples of metonymy from Jakobson:

1. In the scene of Anna Karenina's suicide, Tolstoy's attention is focused on the heroine's handbag.

It is clear that the handbag is not intended to be taken as 'similar' to Anna, but as something associated with her. It is a detail, a small thing she carries; and from this we might be lead to other associations. The principle here is contiguity rather than similarity.

Now another example.

2. In a cubist painting 'the object is transformed into a set of synechdoches' (associated parts) (Jakobson and Halle 1980: 92). Many details are presented next to each other, in contiguity. The eye might travel round the head of the subject being painted and represent its journey on a flat surface, so that you see both sides at once.

Now, we may turn to some examples of basic psychoanalytic processes. The metaphorical processes in dreams and symptom formation are identification and symbolism, whereas the metonymical processes are displacement and condensation. In the metaphorical process of identification, a person may confuse his identity with that of another, and begin to act as though he were that other person. This is a defensive act, since it reduces hostility between the self and the other and enables one to deny feelings of separation. It may also enable one to feel more powerful and secure than one is. Contrast this with the metonymical development of displacement and condensation. Condensation occurs when latent elements in a dream are *combined* and fused in the manifest dream. Thus, as in a cubist painting, various elements are arranged or combined in a surprising way. We can easily distinguish between this and metaphor if we use Barthes's example of dressing from his *Elements of Semiology* (1967). When you put on your clothes, you may decide between a teeshirt, a formal long-sleeved shirt, an open-neck shirt, or some other kind of shirt. This selection is based on *similarity* and is metaphorical. Now, what do you *combine* with the shirt you have selected? You decide that a pair of jeans goes with your teeshirt and a pair of sandals with that, the whole being metonymically composed by association. We should remember that a dream (or any other form of communication) may combine metaphor and metonymy, so that we could place it on the continuum between metaphor and metonymy and myth in our triangle.

Here is an example of a dream analysed by Freud in *The Interpretation of Dreams*. The dreamer is a woman.

> I want to give a supper, but I have nothing available except some smoked salmon. I think I will go shopping but I remember that it is Sunday afternoon, when all the shops are closed. I then try to ring up a few caterers, but the telephone is out of order. Accordingly, I have to renounce my desire to give a supper (1938b: 225).

After some probing, a few interesting facts emerge. Her husband is always praising a rather thin lady friend, with the result that the dreamer has become rather jealous. This friend had spoken to her of her desire to become plumper and had asked the patient: 'When are you going to invite us again? You always have such good food'. When we hear that her favourite food was smoked salmon, and that the husband liked full figures, the dream is quite clear. 'Do you think I'm going to invite you to eat your favourite food and become more attractive to my husband?' we can imagine her asking.

What we see here is essentially a series of allusions or displacements, from thin to eating and becoming plump, from becoming plump to becoming attractive. The main principle is that of building up a picture by a series of associations, allusions and details; in other words, the oganization of the dream is metonymical.

Freud's analyses of dreams and symptomatic behaviour are a continual play of metaphor (similarities) and metonymy (associations). In his classic analysis of hysteria – the analysis of Dora – we find the following example.

Dora behaves as though she were the governess Herr K had been interested in – and Herr K is now making proposals to her. Freud says to her:

> To prove to you how deeply impressed you were by the governess's story, let me draw your attention to the repeated occasions upon which you have

identified yourself with her both in your dream and in your conduct. You told your parents what happened – a fact which we have hitherto been unable to account for – just as the governess wrote and told *her* parents. You give me a fortnight's warning, just like a governess. Freud, 1948: 129).

And, it can be added, Dora waited a fortnight (the time characteristic for a person in service) before telling her parents about Herr K's behaviour towards her.

Other features of her behaviour, such as her continual coughing in an attempt to clear the mucus from her throat are interpreted metonymically. Dora knew about fellatio, and her coughing is an attempt to clear her throat of the metonymical sperm which would accompany the act.

As a final example of the distinction between metaphor and metonymy we may cite, following Jakobson, Frazer's division of magic into two great classes. There is contagious magic, in which we might use adjuncts or associations to work our spell, incorporating a person's toenail clippings or scraps of clothing in our rites and incantations. Homeopathic magic, on the other hand, is based on similarity, as when we engage in fertility rites to make plants grow, or eat the flesh of potent beasts to make ourselves potent.

A summary of some of the distinctions between metaphor and metonymy may be convenient at this stage.

Metaphor	*Metonymy*
Similarity	Association
Selection	Combination
Imitative magic	Contagious magic

This list may be extended in ways which would not be appropriate here, but the interested reader might pursue this question in David Lodge's excellent *The Modes of Modern Writing* (1977), where many texts are analysed as metaphorical or metonymical discourses, as well as in Lakoff's *Women, Fire and Other Dangerous Things* (1987).

Our concern here is to show how both metaphor and metonymy have been important in the development of social theory, and in two ways. The first way is that theorists demonstrate metaphor and metonymy in the symptoms and pathologies of social life. We have produced some examples from Freud and we shall produce some examples from Marx. The second important use of these rhetorical moves is in the development of theory itself. Both metaphor and metonymy played an important part in the development of Freud and Marx's thought. The important metaphor in Freud was hypnotism ('psychoanalysis has inherited this estate left by the hypnotists'); the central metaphor in Marx, as has been said repeatedly, was Hegel's dialectic of development; but whereas in Hegel the spirit was primary and the material world secondary, in Marx this relation was reversed. Marx, as everyone says, stood Hegel on his head.

In the remaining part of this chapter, I shall discuss the significance of the metaphor of hypnosis in the development of Freud's thought; the importance of metonymical moves in the development of behaviourism and also of psychoanalysis; and the significance of metonymy in Marxist theory.

Sequence of events

(1) Freud first heard about Anna O's 'talking cure' from Breuer in 1882.
(2) From October 1885 till February 1886 he visited Charcot in Paris. Charcot impressed him as 'the greatest of physicians and a man whose common sense is the order of genius' (Jones, 1961: 122). What is particularly important is that Charcot demonstrated the use of hypnosis to elicit hysterical symptoms in both males and females, dispelling any illusion that hysteria was a female complaint, a disorder of the womb, or an 'imaginary' illness. Charcot established it as a serious nervous disorder, worthy of the attention of reputable physicians and demonstrated unequivocally that hysterical symptoms could be of psychogenic origin, thus confirming what Freud had learnt from Breuer.

It is important to realize how scientific theory is limited by assumptions about what can be the case. If it is an axiom of medicine that psychiatric problems *must* have an organic cause, then, unless an organic cause can be established, the disorder is 'imaginary', simulated, or a moral deficiency. In fact, malingering. Charcot demonstrated the inadequacy of this assumption and opened the way to the study of the psychological cause of neurosis.

Freud continued to use hypnotherapy and electrotherapy in the early years of his practice (the standard treatments were sedation and tonic drugs, hydrotherapy and electrotherapy). He had some good results with hypnotism, but he gave it up for a variety of reasons. The first was that he did not always find it possible to hypnotize patients; the second was that he found it possible to obtain the results he was seeking by free association.
(3) Freud saw an important demonstration of the recovery of forgotten material at Nancy, where he visited Bernheim in 1889, for further training in hypnotic techniques. He was put off by the barking of commands and suggestions at hypnotized patients, but he carried away

with him the important example of a patient who, though at first unable to recall what had happened under hypnosis, was eventually able to recall everything by a process of 'unreflective' recall or free association. This method of unreflective recall became the foundation of psychoanalysis.

We can see the emergence of an important new metaphor of neurosis to replace the organic metaphor. Charcot produces hysterical symptoms by suggestion; Breuer relieves symptoms by letting Anna talk to him about their origin; Bernheim's patient is able to recall what happened under hypnosis by 'unreflective' talking. Hence Freud's suggestion in his 1914 memoir on the history of psychoanalysis (Freud, 1938a) that psychoanalysis had inherited the estate left by the hypnotists.

(4) Freud also remarks in his memoir that on at least three occasions his central hypothesis that neurosis originates in disturbed sexual life was suggested to him, once by Breuer, once by Charcot, and once by the gynaecologist Chrobak, who directed to him a female patient suffering from 'senseless anxiety'. This patient was a virgin after 18 years of marriage. Chrobak's prescription: *'Penis normalis, dosim repetatur'*.

These insights have been current for centuries, but it is 'one thing to express an idea ... in the form of a rapid *aperçu* and quite another to take it seriously and literally to lead it through all opposing details ...' (Freud, 1938a: 938). What matters is the whole picture, the working through of the metaphor into theory, and its application to a stubborn and unyielding reality.

Metonymical discourse and the development of psychological theory

Metaphor is what strikes us immediately in the development of theory, yet new combinations should be equally important. Here, rather briefly, and more extensively in the section on Marxism, I hope to indicate some of the ways in which metonymical shifts have developed theory. Our first two examples are synechdoche (substituting part for whole), a special form of metonymy.

The first great metonymical change in modern psychology was to treat mind and spirit as thinking substances or *res cogitans* (Descartes). Thinking is *one* of the features of mind, but it came to usurp the whole. This was a symptom of the divorce of body and soul, spirit and matter, human and animal, in Western thought. It was found long before Descartes, but he brought it to finality in our philosophical tradition.

The second great example of metonymy in psychology was the substitution of *response* for behaviour, though curiously enough this occurred in the name of *behaviourism*. Though some forms of behaviour are responses, it is a mistake to treat all forms of behaviour as though they were, since to behave is to act, and to act is to do something for a reason, with certain intentions. Responses are certainly found, but they are adjuncts or accompaniments of behaviour. How did this change of name come about? It was an attempt to escape the trap of Cartesian mind, that separate and intangible essence, and to treat behaviour as a natural phenomenon, on the model of the reflex arc. Reflexes have stimuli, and stimuli can be found, some of the time, in the real world; and even when stimuli were not apparent, they were surely there for the psychologist to find. This metonymy was useful since it sharpened the focus of psychology, but it was a symptom of the divorce of mind and body in Western thought.

Yet another metonymical change was the shift from causal to intentional explanation in psychoanalysis. Though we may point to Freud's continued attempts to find the causes of psychological disturbance, the fundamental change after Freud was to admit the legitimacy of 'explanation by meaning' and hence the possible utility of 'talking cures'. The point is simply that the 'meaning' of the disturbed behaviour had previously been ignored, regarded as secondary and epiphenomenal. It was a mere adjunct or accompaniment (if noticed) of what was really significant – the physical causes of the symptom which had to be treated by physical means. Freud's move was to focus on the adjunct, but this could only be accomplished by postulating that the connection between the symptomatic expression and the true meaning of the act had been suppressed. Hence, there must be an apparatus for obscuring and repressing connections. The implications of this move have not yet been exhausted, since we may search for the causes of that suppression in either the social relation in which the patient is placed – treating the patient as merely one element in such a system – or we may search for the causes in the personal dynamics of the patient. The two kinds of search led to the postulation of rather different processes and rather different programmes of treatment. The first is psychoanalysis, the second is a 'socioanalysis' in which we attempt to uncover the social mechanisms of displaced meaning.

Metonymical discourse and social theory

We may look at Marx's theory of human consciousness as an example of a significant change of form in sociology, and then at the way in which he studies those displacements which occur under conditions of capitalism. This has led to the formulation of theories about the 'social unconscious', as a process which leads to displaced expressions and experiences and to the suppression of the links between them and their true meaning. Of course, there are problems in discovering 'true' meaning, especially in so variable a form as social existence, but the various transformations of meaning in context have been the major preoccupation of social theorists for the last 50 or more years.

First, the displacement which lays the foundation for Marx's theory is the well-known postulate that we should look to the relations of production, or the ensemble of social relations, to understand human beings, rather than inside them for a 'human essence'. Thus, human consciousness and human *being* are social products, and to change the nature of being human we should change the ensemble of social relations. There is a tendency to enshrine the values and ideas of the dominant class as human universals, a tendency which is not necessarily due to deliberate manipulations so much as propagation of what seems to be indisputably true. Provided that we do not restrict our concept of 'ensemble of social relations' to a concentration on 'relations and forces of production', this postulate can be a useful foundation for a social theory, though it needs to be expanded and filled in before we can regard it as even remotely satisfactory science. Nevertheless, let us see what Marx made of it.

Fetishism and social alienation

A fetish is an inanimate object which is worshipped or irrationally reverenced for its powers. It might be an amulet, a relic, a pearl, a piece of gold, or money. It might be any token or sign in which meaning and power appear to be concentrated, as though they were inherent in the object itself rather than in the system of social relations which confers meaning and power on objects.

In worshipping or reverencing such objects, we are in danger of substituting them for the relation in which they have their validity. Often we are aware that they are merely adjuncts of the reality that we respect, but equally often we lose sight of this reality and treat the fetish as though it were the reality.

The contribution to which I shall draw attention here is to be found in Marx's *Capital*, as well as in other writings by him. The reason for drawing attention to it is that Marx discusses some of the social reasons for displacement, showing us that displacement is no idle figure of speech, but a product of social structure. It is not only discourse but real relations of production, of power and of investment, that contribute to displacements of thought and reason, even if they do not completely explain them. Here is one significant displacement: 'Gold and silver, when serving as money, did not represent a social relation between producers, but were natural objects with strange social properties' (Marx, 1967: 83). Commodities are human products, yet they seem to have independent values.

> A commodity is therefore a mysterious thing, simply because in it the social character of men's labour appears to them as an objective character stamped upon the product of that labour; because the relation of the producers to the sum total of their own labour is presented to them as a social relation, existing not between themselves, but between the products of their labour (1967: 72).

We get an inversion: 'material relations between persons and social relations between things' (1967: 73), and 'the productions of the human brain appear as independent beings endowed with life, and entering into relation both with one another and the human race' (1967: 72).

Articles have a use-value, but their price is determined 'by the human labour spent in their production' (1967: 74). However, price may seem related to intrinsic or natural value, particularly when the exchange of values of products has been stable for some time.

The intrinsic or natural value of certain commodities (apart from their use-value) such as gold, diamonds, pearls, fabrics, fine furniture, or other objects, is what Marx calls 'fetishism'.

The point is that value has been displaced from the labour of people to the objects they produce, and the condition of these people – their hours of work, their pay, their education, their value as people – is now regulated by the apparently impersonal exchange of commodities. Furthermore, we might come to believe that this is a natural and unalterable state of affairs, like the law of gravity, simply because we do not understand that this is peculiar to certain modes of production.

The explanation of this inversion of subject and predicate, of the object and its attributes, occupied Marx in various ways and places throughout his life. How is it that we find private property – an attribute or adjunct of human beings under certain conditions – dominating the human condition? How is it that we find human liberty identified with the protection of the property of those who own the means of production? How is it that we protect the product of human labour and not the labourer? Whereas the law punished the smallest theft with the most violent penalties, very little protection was given to the men, women and children who produced the goods that were exchanged in society.

Where 'free competition' is externalized as a natural or normative state of affairs, people become the subjects of apparently inevitable economic relations, and the social links between persons are presented as something external to them, something with the inevitability and naturalness of laws of physics. Individual persons become the adjuncts or attributes of a process of production. The only way for them to participate is to sell their labour under the conditions of capitalism (or of whatever system of social production is dominant). 'Money', 'commodities', 'law', 'capital', 'labour', express social relations of which persons are attributes. There is, as we have said, an inversion of subject and predicate.

How can we account for this phenomenon, in which an attribute of human activity becomes the substantive subject, and persons become attributes? The answer lies in the process of alienation, according to Marx (adapting a concept from Hegel). Consider these forms of alienation:

- Workers sell time and labour to whoever can pay for them and are alienated from their own *work*.
- The goods they produce (and often work is organized so that they produce no more than a component of a finished article) are not their own; workers are alienated from the *products* of their work.
- In the production line workers are alienated from their own *bodies* as they go through the same motions for months or years.
- Workers are alienated from *each other* as they compete for jobs, positions, wages.
- The propertied classes, though subject to alienation, see it as the *source of their power*, whereas the proletariat are ruined by it.

Persons do not create themselves and the conditions of their lives under capitalism; this power belongs to capital – as a social mode of production. Of course, we should observe that this is true of any mode of production, since it is a fundamental premise of Marxism that as we produce objects we also produce our relations with other people: As we transform the natural world, we transform ourselves.

Perhaps we can extract a general proposition from Marx's work: Whatever is reified as the true nature of man at any given time is an attribute or adjunct of the ensemble of social relations at that time.

The point is that we focus on local versions of the nature of man in our discussions of politics, education, marriage, morality and economics for two great classes of reasons. The first is that we are products of the ensemble of social relations which we are continually producing and reproducing. We are often convinced, therefore, of the truth of our statements. The second is that particular versions of the 'true nature of man' may serve our class interests. We perpetuate a form of alienation with which we are comfortable. At the same time, others may be ruined by the processes which we represent as absolute truths. This is the root of class conflict and the source of change in society.

Metonymy and the myths to which it often gives rise are seen to be the products of both alienation and imperfect understanding. Marx's account of the process cannot be complete, since it was designed to show that particular forms of understanding – mainly bourgeois economics under capitalism – are the result of displacement. When we ignore the capitalist mode of production, take it for granted, or regard it as right, then we focus our attention on its attributes as though they were the substantive problem of political economy, namely:

- the 'natural' economic order is free enterprise and free competition;
- the interests of the dominant class are universal rights;
- labour is a commodity;
- the human worker is a unit of labour;
- justice is law; and
- the value of an article is its price.

Much of this is now commonplace, just as the findings of Freud are commonplace. Perhaps what is not trivial, though, is the fact of displacement: we continually shift our attention from the substantive problem to some attribute with which we are more comfortable. There is many a regime in which the rhetoric of justice and the preservation of law and order is used to distract attention from acts of violence and savage repression; acts which, if perpetrated by any set of pirates, thieves or brigands, would lead to an immediate demand for their arrest and execution. 'Law and Order' are then metonymical substitutes for 'violent repression'.

This is no place for a general critique of Marxism. What I wish to draw attention to is his contribution to our understanding of displacement. He showed that under capitalism there is a particular kind of displacement of affect, understanding and judgement and he explained this displacement by describing forms of alienation. For some this alienation is comfortable (the propertied classes); for others it is ruinous (the proletariat). Nevertheless, both are subject to it, though in complementary ways.

Conclusion

Can we say that it is 'rational' to use one form of discourse rather than another, in the sense of preferring metaphor to metonymy, or both to myth? I hope it is clear that 'rationality' is a judgement which must be made on other grounds. Mythical discourse is largely frowned upon today, yet it is an essential component of 'rational' solutions to social and psychological problems.

Each rhetorical manoeuvre is a way of opening up new possibilities to the intelligence. Or, to put it another way, these rhetorical manoeuvres *are* the gropings of intelligence, sometimes successful (in the sense that they solve problems), sometimes unsuccessful.

In the next chapter we shall examine attempts to advance from truisms to axioms in the construction of scientific knowledge.

6 | The fulcrum of reason: truism/axiom/tautology

Though we may open up a field of knowledge by conjecturing new images or metaphors, these are only preliminary steps. Our insights should lead us to clear axioms, hypotheses or 'laws of nature' which can direct inquiry with greater precision. The kinds of laws that we state show subtle transitions from truisms, to corrigible laws, or to axioms which cannot be corrected piecemeal without undoing the fabric of current science.

Let us start with some simple definitions.

Definitions

According to the *Oxford English Dictionary*, a truism is 'a self-evident truth, especially one of slight importance'. The significant thing here is the phrase 'of slight importance'. Truisms are obvious. Though they may be 'true', they are the kinds of truth we greet with a yawn. They do not enable us to solve problems. We would hesitate to build a science on truisms, unless we wished to tell people what they already know. We escape from truisms by abstracting essential features of our picture of reality, and sometimes by inventing new pictures. Then we have axioms.

An axiom is 'a self-evident proposition', like a truism, but it is not trivial, since it can be the basis of scientific problem-solving. It is 'self-evident' only in the sense that, in a given research tradition, it accords with metaphysical presuppositions, with a picture of reality, with arguments which are already current but have not been resolved. When an axiom is changed, we have a shift in our picture of reality. Sometimes an axiom is so well established that we may think of it as a tautology; that is, the results of experiments *must* be in accordance with the axiom. Such axioms are the conservation of mass-energy and the second law of thermodynamics. To treat a law or an axiom as a tautology is a strategic decision; it is to deny, for the time being, that the law is at risk in experiments.

Some examples of truisms and axioms

To crystallize our thoughts, let us look at some examples of truisms, axioms or tautologies, and empirical generalizations or laws. In general, an empirical generalization should be very precise and well established to become a 'law'. Most of the laws that I shall consider are neither – with the exception of the Weber–Fechner law.

Truisms

- We do the things we like to do
- We do things we are rewarded for doing
- We avoid doing things we are punished for doing
- What do cats dream of? – mice!
- Survival of the fittest.

The general feature of such truisms is that they do not surprise us, are too loosely stated, and do not form the foundations of new knowledge. Certainly, they do not provide a base for the problem-solving activities which are characteristic of science.

Axioms

- Conscious being is intentional (Brentano)
- Dreams are wish-fulfilments (Freud)
- Mental operations are interiorized and generalized actions (Piaget)
- Ideology serves class interests (Marx)
- Behaviour is maintained by reinforcements (Skinner)

We shall return to a consideration of axioms after a brief look at their relation to laws.

In general, we may say that a law is a well-established statement of regular predictable relations among empirical variables. The examples we have given are typical of much of psychology and biology in that they are not particularly precise and that they are only relatively well-established. There are precise laws, of course, but they tend not to be at the cutting edge of theoretical advance – though they may be of considerable practical importance. An example is Fechner's law, which states that sensation is proportional to the logarithm of the stimulus.

$$J = k \log R$$

(where J is judged magnitude, k is a constant, and R is stimulus magnitude).

There is a different psychophysical law, Steven's power law, which states that judged magnitude is proportional to the physical magnitude raised to a power

$J = k\,R^P$ (Stevens's notation changed to match Fechner's)

(where J is judged magnitude, k is a constant, and R is stimulus magnitude).

These laws have different functions; but both are empirical, both are relatively well-established, and both could be refined and improved piecemeal without disturbing our fundamental picture of the working of mind. This applies equally to the other empirical generalizations or laws stated above.

It is not my intention to maintain that there are absolute differences between truisms, empirical laws, definitions and axioms. In working science, they often shade into each other and the differences are marked only at the extremes. Axioms are then laws which seem to be part of the very frame of nature, but this is simply because they are part of the very frame of a particular theory or conception of reality. In other words, they are *conceptual* devices, and changing them is a matter of changing our picture of the fundamental working of the world. When they are deep, they are part of what Popper (1976) calls a 'metaphysical research programme' because of the difficulty or even impossibility of refuting them.

Darwinism is, in Popper's (1976) view, an example of such a metaphysical research programme; it is 'a possible framework for testable scientific theories' (1976: 168) rather than a theory. He states it as follows:

> Let there be a world, a framework of limited constancy, in which there are entities of limited variability. Then some of the entities produced by variation (those which 'fit' into the conditions of the framework) may 'survive', while others (those which clash with the conditions) may be eliminated (1976: 168).

Given this logic, there seems to be nothing else that could happen. We are indeed stating a self-evident truth, or axiom, on which a science may be built, provided we are ingenious in drawing out its implications. Fundamental axioms of this kind are of the greatest importance in science and their achievement is singularly difficult. We repeatedly attempt to establish such secure visions of the 'true' nature of reality, because it is only within such visions that really important work can be done.

We may decide, though, *not* to treat natural selection as a tautology – that is, as an axiom which the data of empirical studies must confirm. Popper changed his mind about the tautological status of Darwin's theory in a 1977 lecture at Darwin College, Cambridge (Popper, 1987). The important manoeuvre is to decide that *not* everything can be explained by natural selection. By abandoning the view that evolution by natural selection is universal, we reinstate it as a statement that is up for testing (though it is so deeply embedded in the research programme of modern biology that it would be difficult to dislodge). The decision is strategic. It is a question of what is at risk in particular empirical studies – the data or the theory.

In psychology and the social sciences, there have been several attempts to establish such approaches, and several of them were presented in Chapter 3, when we sketched a variety of theories. It is worth drawing some of these (and a few more) together:

- Intentionality is conserved under repression (Freud)
- Behaviour is proportional to reinforcement (Herrnstein)
- Existence precedes essence (Sartre)
- Mind is a function of social organization (Luria)
- No learning is possible without prior hypotheses (Chomsky) ('you have to have a set of prejudices in advance for induction to take place')
- Intrapersonal or psychological processes are preceded by interpersonal or social processes (Vygotsky)
- Mind is a set of functions of behaviour (Taylor)
- To know something is to act on it; or 'cognitive operations' (Piaget)
- Culture is the continuation of evolution by other means; changes in gene frequencies and in cultural mind-inducing artefacts (culturgens such as language, reading, arithmetic) reciprocally influence each other (Lumsden and Wilson).

Are these axioms, metaphysical research programmes, empirical laws, or working assumptions? It is not always clear, in the creation of science, what kind of tool we are using. Each of these, I should suppose, starts as both a metaphysical research programme and as a working assumption (which the investigator is often prepared to call a 'conclusion' or 'finding' or 'discovery'. If we take the statement that 'Mind is a function of social organization', what is its status? It arises within the general framework of Marxism (though it could quite easily have arisen within other movements). It is a weak empirical generalization, since the variables are too vaguely specified and prediction is hardly possible, given the form of the statement. It is largely a commitment to search for the social organizations (which may or may not be specified in Marxist terms; that is, as classes, relations of production, base and superstructure) which 'produce' mind. How they do it, we cannot tell. It is an approach, with a strong commitment to a materialist metaphysic and to what Sève calls the 'excentration of the human essence' (after Marx's *Theses on Feuerbach*). How could it become an axiom? When we discover ways of drawing it out so as to state problems in a precise and interesting way, to tackle these problems by fruitful methods, and to understand clearly what kinds of variables are referred to, the 'approach' becomes a research programme organized around core axioms. Till then, it may be a dogma which excludes alternative views of problems without compensating gains in problem-solving power.

What I hope to have achieved is the perception that we have a set of terms on a continuum, best understood by contrast. They change status as inquiry and problem-solving proceeds; an 'approach' or a 'metaphysical research programme' may become sufficiently precise to be formulated as an axiom or tautology on which a science is built. Though there is flux in their status, we do well to bear in mind these important distinctions.

1. A 'metaphysical research programme' forms part of the framework of inquiry.
2. An axiom defines the nature of reality in a scientific theory.
3. An empirical law or generalization states relations between variables in such a way that they are predictable. Empirical laws can, in general, be corrected piecemeal whereas axioms cannot be.

What I propose to do now is to examine three axioms – the law of relative effect, the wish-fulfilment theory of dreams, and the theory of evolution by natural selection – in order to gain a more exact impression of the way they function. I shall then ask the question: How do tautologies change? Are they corrigible? Obviously, they must be corrigible at the level of working science, since we have seen many changes in non-empirical laws in the last century, one example being the change from the law of conservation of matter to the conservation of mass–energy.

Now let us turn to the law of relative effect. Though this law was never accepted by all Skinnerians, the strategies to maintain it are of general interest. They show the continual struggle to stabilize theory in a sea of refractory data.

The law of relative effect as an axiom

It is a truism that we do those things we are rewarded for doing, but in order to make this truism part of problem-solving science, it has to be restated. In its present form, it is trivial. Let us look at the way in which this truism – known to people for millennia – has been reformulated in behaviourist theory as an axiom or tautology or non-empirical law.

Behaviour is defined by using a set of three terms (in Skinnerian behaviourism):

$$S_D : R : S_R$$

These are discriminative stimulus (S_D), operant (R), and reinforcing stimulus (S_R). Every behaviour must be studied in the context of both its antecedents and consequences, in other words, and what we find is that the probability of particular behaviours can be systematically controlled by manipulating consequences. The set of three terms is called a 'contingency of reinforcement'. Once we have shown that behaviour is best understood in a contingency of reinforcement, we may generalize our problem to consider more than one behaviour at a time. In other words, we now have a behavioural field, in which several things are possible at once. Which of the possible things will actually happen?

Consider the following simple case. A pigeon is working a familiar environment for food and it has already mastered the responses which will be reinforced – it can peck a key to the right and a key to the left. Now, let us suppose that reinforcements are not delivered at the same rate for pecks to the two keys. What will the pigeon do? Apparently, it divides its pecks in direct proportion to the reinforcements, even though it need not do this to succeed in obtaining all the reinforcements available. In general, the proportion of responses equal the proportion of rewards (Herrnstein, 1970).

The proportion of responses of any given type, B_1, in the total set of responses, is given by the ratio of B_1 added to the sum of all the responses which are being reinforced.

$$\frac{B_1}{B_1 + B_2 \ldots B_n}$$

Similarly, the ratio of reinforcement is

$$\frac{R_1}{R_1 + R_2 \ldots R_n}$$

Then

$$\frac{B_1}{B_1 + B_z \ldots B_n} = \frac{R_1}{R_1 + R_z \ldots R_n}$$

The law of relative effect applies to ideal cases, just as the laws of physics and chemistry refer to ideal cases. It is easy to introduce complications by varying the relative difficulty of competing responses, or mixing reinforcements of food and water. These introduce complications which are analogous to the complications obstructing the application of the idealizations of science to engineering problems. In the same way, the 'behavioural engineer' will have to realize that there are many competing contingencies of reinforcement in most life situations.

What are the significant implications of the law of relative effect? First, in order to know what effect a reinforcement will have upon a behaviour, it is essential to know what other behaviours are being reinforced. Teachers in a classroom may be ineffective in controlling behaviour, not so much because they have nothing interesting to say as because they have not succeeded in eliminating reinforcements for other behaviours which disrupt the class. As a corollary, if all other reinforcers are eliminated, responding to a relatively weak reinforcer may rise markedly and give the impression that its absolute value has increased.

The equation given above may be rewritten in the convenient form:

$$R = k \frac{(r)}{r + re}$$

where R is the rate of responding, k is the maximum possible response rate, r is the reinforcement contingent on responding, and re is extraneous reinforcement for competing responses (Herrnstein, 1970). This means, as before, that any given rate of contingent reinforcement may produce high or low response rates depending on the presence of entraneous reinforcements for other responses.

The equation yields a hyperbola (Figure 1), the two axes of which represent rate of responding (R) and rate of contingent reinforcement (r).

When this equation is applied to data on human responding we may be able to account for almost all the variance in certain cases (McDowell and Kessel, 1979). The particular data to which this equation was applied was a series of button-pressing studies for money on variable-interval schedules of reinforcement.

A clinically interesting application of the equation is to the case of an otherwise normal 11-year-old boy whose self-injurious scratching was reinforced by contingent reprimands. Scratch rates and contingent

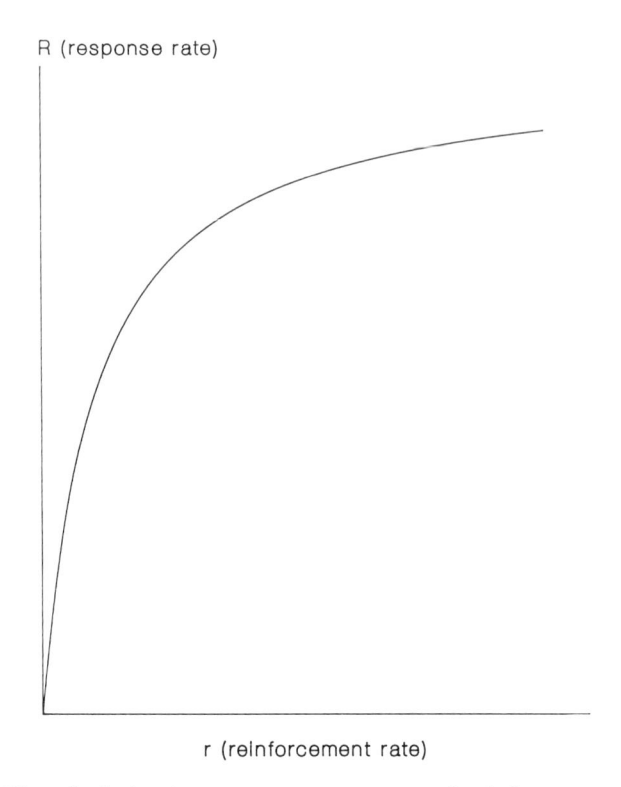

Figure 1 Plot of relation between response rate and reinforcement rate

reprimand rates were observed while the family watched television, prior to treatment, and these data were fitted to the equation described above. The resulting fit accounted for 99.67% of the data (McDowell, 1981). Many further examples of curve-fitting with equal success are reported by McDowell (1982), to data obtained by various researchers.

The equations of relative effect suggest that, to reduce a problem behaviour, we may attempt four different interventions:

(i) Extinction (withdraw contingent reinforcements)
(ii) Punishment (punishments are contingent on behaviour)
(iii) Reinforce concurrent or competing behaviour
(iv) Increase the rate of free or non-contingent reinforcement (re)

How will (iv) reduce the frequency of problem behaviour (R)? We may suppose that, if the organism does not need to do anything to be reinforced, it will simply do less than it did before. This may be the way that satiation or 'unconditional positive regard' works (as McDowell suggests in his 1982 paper).

Conversely, to increase a desirable behaviour, we may attempt the following interventions:

(i) Increase the rate of contingent reinforcement for that behaviour
(ii) Decrease the rate of reinforcements for concurrent behaviour
(iii) Decrease the rate of free or non-contingent reinforcements.

What is the advantage of the hyperbolic equation over the first equation given here? The obvious advantage is that it makes it unnecessary to determine all the separate competing contingencies of reinforcement before applying it. We may estimate the total value of extraneous reinforcements (re) and treat them as a parameter of the equation.

These are the basic field equations of behaviourism, and we see in them the promise of the behavioural engineering Skinner wrote about: 'Teaching is the arrangement of contingencies of reinforcement which expedite learning' (1969: 15); 'Political action is a matter of manipulating contingencies of reinforcement' (1969: 20); and of utopian writers: 'Whether they have known it or not ... they have been concerned with the contingencies under which men live' (1969: 20).

From these statements and from the examples above, it is clear that the law of relative effect is very much concerned with empirical results. But is it an empirical law? Or is it a tautology? And how would we know?

An empirical law, to repeat, is a law which can be corrected piecemeal, whereas an axiom cannot be without affecting our conception of the whole of our subject. Imagine piecemeal correction to the laws of the conservation of matter, or of thermodynamics. Imagine attempting 'slight modifications' to Newtonian laws of motion, or to the 'hypothesis' of evolution by natural selection (to which I shall return)! The point is simply this, as Rachlin (1971) observes: 'Where the first law of thermodynamics is apparently disconfirmed, engineers and physicists assume that they have overlooked some source of energy and they set about finding it' (1971: 251).

Rachlin gives an example from personal experience of working with the law of relative effect (or 'matching law', as it is sometimes called): 'The more our results approximated (Equations of the Matching Law), the surer we were that we had eliminated or balanced extraneous reinforcers in the situation' (1971: 251). He suggests, then, that future investigations should concentrate 'on the manipulations necessary to confirm the law, rather than on whether the law is true'.

He proposes that the law *must be true* if there is any truth or consistency in the theory of reinforcement. It is a definition of the behavioural field. In order to make it true we would manipulate our methods of measuring quantity of reinforcement. For example, we draw a distinction between scheduled and obtained reinforcements, since organisms may not respond to what is scheduled but only to what they actually obtain. Furthermore, organisms may not consume all the reinforcements they obtain, and we may attempt (in any given experiment) to measure actual consumption in order to find the right values to insert into our equation. The point is, as we gradually begin to realize, that the equations above refer to reinforcement *values*, and it is always an empirical problem to determine these so that they fit the equation.

As long as we are intent on preserving a particular approach to the problems of choice in a field of reinforcements, we may decide that the axioms have to be preserved. They are, in that sense, tautologies. The data have to fit the axioms, not the axioms the data. What happens, though, when we try to compare two approaches which start from different axioms? This is the position 17 years later, when the two approaches of matching and maximizing are taken to the problem of choice (Rachlin et al., 1988). The matching approach is that animals allocate time proportionately to obtained reinforcers; the maximizing approach is that animals simply attempt to maximize the overall rate of reinforcement. As before, in complex schedules and choices, the data may be fitted to the preferred approach. Rachlin *et al.* refer to 'occult reinforcers or occult choices' (1988: 122) in obscure cases. There are also baffling findings (from the point of view of the matching law): when animals are on standard concurrent schedules of food versus water reinforcement, responses are inversely proportional to the rate of reinforcement. This is the reverse of what the matching law predicts. However, if we think of the animal as attempting to get an adequate supply of the scarcer reinforcement, there is no mystery. If food is abundant, spend more time trying to obtain water! The scarcer the water the more time the animal should spend trying to obtain it. This is the reverse of matching, which predicts that more time is spent where there is more reinforcer. On the other hand, we can manipulate the data by arguing that the *value* of the scarcer reinforcer is greater. The value of water (or food) increases as its supply declines. Hence, matching could still be occurring. But now we are becoming 'occult'. Rachlin *et al.* draw back from this attempt to preserve matching at all costs; and conclude that matching and maximizing are useful in different problems. 'The time has come, therefore, to recognize that neither is a fundamental law of human nature and to view both principles for what they are – useful tools by which the structure and function of behavior may be examined' (1988: 122).

What this shows is that the status of a 'tool', an 'axiom', or even a 'tautology' is continually changing, according to the claims we are making. This is partly rhetoric – we wish to persuade others of our claims – and partly research strategy. We wish to know what to hold on to and what to abandon when confronted by refractory data. Should the data or the theory be regarded as 'hard'? In the present case, attachment to the matching law is clearly weakening, even among those who previously believed it. It is no longer a 'tautology' (1971); it is merely a tool. Perhaps the 'merely' should be erased, since tools are useful in working a mass of data. Perhaps a fair conclusion is that we choose axioms in such a way as to stabilize the field of inquiry for the time being. This is what we meant by the term 'fulcrum of reason' in the heading to this chapter.

How do axioms change?

Axioms change (1) because we find we cannot apply them to solve interesting problems which ought to be within their domain; (2) because competing theories, resting on different axioms, do better; and (3) because we find them conceptually troublesome. We may see how these kinds of difficulties threaten the law of relative effect, without finally disposing of it.

The first kind of difficulty, then, arises out of a failure to solve problems which we think we ought to be able to solve. An interesting insight may be obtained by reading the debate between Herrnstein and Skinner in the *American Psychologist* of August and December, 1977. Among the problems raised by Herrnstein are (i) the very large differences in susceptibility to conditioning displayed by various responses, leading us to wonder how many behaviours do, in fact, covary with reinforcement as demanded by the fundamental axioms; and (ii) the fact that stimulus and response classes cannot be fractured arbitrarily but have their own organism-specific susceptibility to conditioning. He draws attention to an important difference between 'innate susceptibility to reinforcement' and 'innate behavior' (1977b: 1011). An innate susceptibility to a particular kind of reinforcement can be used to reinforce various forms of behaviour, but it is not necessary to suppose that innate behaviour must be reinforced to be maintained. An opportunity to stalk a bird may be used as a reinforcer for other behaviour in a cat, but it is not necessary to postulate reinforcers for stalking.

Skinner's reply is that his laws apply to conditioned behaviour, not to reflex or released behaviour. 'Phylogeny and ontogeny are friendly rivals and neither one always wins' (1977: 1009). 'Self-reinforcement' of the kind Herrnstein suggests is not within the scope of the theory of operant conditioning. When we attempt to account for an eel which successfully migrates from a European river to the Sargasso Sea for the first time, we are talking about a behaviour which is the end product of a different process to that of conditioning. 'It is an unnecessary bit of environmentalism to appeal to self-reinforcement in the individual eel to explain the strength of behavior that is due to natural selection.'

Herrnstein (1977b) replies that, rather than add a new category of behaviour (phylogenic behaviour), one ought to assimilate it to what is known and apply the law of effect to it as well as to operant behaviour. Citing James, he argues that 'each creature is reinforced by its own ways' (1977b: 1015).

The advantage of this is to save the law of effect. Skinner appears in these articles as a cautious scientist who (i) admits the significance of species-specific behaviour and their contingencies; and (ii) limits his theory to conditioned behaviours.

We said that axioms may be undermined when theories which do not contain them solve problems more effectively than the theories which do. The principal competitor of behaviourist theories is a class of theories which we may call 'cognitive', in which the dominant concept is 'validation of a construct or hypothesis' rather than reinforcement. To the extent that such theories are successful, reinforcement theories (and the law of effect) will either become unnecessary or be focused on the maintenance of the class of ontogenic, conditioned behaviour. The definition of its scope will become increasingly important. The law of relative effect will be seen, not as a general law of behaviour, but as a law applying to a very restricted sub-set of behaviours – a sub-set which may become vanishingly small. Alternatively, it may be retained as a rule of thumb for the investigation of conditioned behaviour.

Finally, there are conceptual problems. Skinner attempted, in his account of *Verbal Behavior*, to extend the concept of reinforcement to the learning of language. In other places, he attempts to account for the advancement of scientific theory by arguing that scientists are 'reinforced' by natural and social contingencies. The various relations of logic and of hypothesis-testing, such as 'implied', 'entailed', 'inferred', 'deduced', 'induced', 'generalized' and so forth are reduced to the unanalysed concept of a 'contingency of reinforcement'. This is conceptually inadequate for a general theory of behaviour.

Let us turn to our second example, which is the axiom that dreams are wish-fulfilments. It is an axiom which has to be understood in the context of Freud's theory of conscious/unconscious mind, and of the conflict between ego, superego and id.

The axiom of wish-fulfilment in dreams

We may commence by looking at two examples in which Freud demonstrates that a wish can be detected in every dream (except in nightmares, where the defence mechanisms of censorship have been overwhelmed).

Here, to illustrate the point, is the dream of a married lady who hears that her contemporary, Elise L, has only just become engaged.

> She was at the back of the theatre with her husband. One side of the stalls was completely empty. Her husband told her that Elise L and her fiance had wanted to go too, but had only been able to get bad seats – three for one florin 50 kreuzers – and of course they could not take them. She thought it would really not have done any harm if they had (1974: 153).

Note the contradiction between the empty stalls and the fact that only bad seats could be obtained. There are many details to be analysed, but we shall concentrate on one. The dreamer had been anxious to see the play, so anxious that she booked her seats early enough to have to pay a booking fee. Yet when they went, there were plenty of seats available. This metaphor represents her anxiety to get married; she had been in too much of a hurry. She might have waited, like her friend Elise, and still succeeded. Emotion is displaced from her regret at having married too early to her regret at having purchased tickets too early. The image of the theatre is a displaced image of her marriage. Many other details can be found in Freud's analysis, but the essential point is the concealed wish: she wishes that she had not been in such a hurry to get married.

Here is another example, one which illustrates the primitive syntax, the elliptical nature and symbolism of dreams.

> His uncle was smoking a cigarette although it was Saturday.
> A woman was caressing and fondling him (the dreamer) as though he were her child (Freud, 1974: 221).

Freud's interpretation is that the dreamer is saying: 'If my uncle, that pious man, were to smoke a cigarette on a Saturday (the Jewish Sabbath), then I might let myself be cuddled by my mother.'

Freud's conception of the dream is part of an entire picture of the relation between id, superego and ego, the language of the unconscious, the processes of defence and censorship, and the development of personality. 'Wishes' are the impulses which we do not acknowledge, but which can emerge in sleep, when repression of 'the older and more primitive methods of working' is not as effective as in waking. Dreams serve the ego by protecting sleep, and they do this by weaving interfering material into an image which simultaneously satisfies repressed instinctual urges in the form of an 'hallucinated fulfilment of a wish' (1973: 48) and seems harmless to the ego.

Once more, the decision to treat the wish-fulfilment axiom as a tautology is purely strategic. It implies that a failure to detect a wish is simply an example of a failure of interpretation on the part of the analyst. Since the rules of interpretation are so loose, we cannot prescribe a procedure, but we may indicate tactics. Ask the patient to free-associate. Look for examples of condensation, displacement, symbolization, inversion of affect. Remember that the unconscious has no negatives. After all, can one provide a set of rules for understanding wit or a cartoon or sentence?

What sorts of things might upset this tautology? In general, if we found that other approaches to dreams solved significant problems, by showing that dreams

(i) solve problems (Breger)
(ii) rehearse instinctive actions (Jouvet)
(iii) consolidate learning (Foulkes)
(iv) get rid of undesirable learning (Crick)

then we would have to question the wish-fulfilment theory. Problems which are successfully solved by competing theories are significant challenges to other theories.

Evolution by natural selection as an axiom

This will be our last example of an axiom and the way in which it can be spelt out as problem-solving science. The 'metaphysical research programme' of evolution by natural selection rests on (i) the production of variety; and (ii) differences in survival rates of different varieties. The biological form of the theory studies the mechanisms which produce variety, the genetic transmission of that variety, reproduction rates, and selection processes.

Here I shall refer to only two problems, in order to show how fruitful the rigorous development of the principle of evolution by natural selection may be. The first is its application to altruism, apparently the most intractable of problems for such a tautology, and the second is its application to the evolution of stable strategies which are not optimal for a species.

(i) Altruism

How does altruism evolve if the first mutation which produces altruistic behaviour exposes the carrier to a greater than average risk? The answer must be that altruism either does not decrease the individual's chances of survival or that it increases the chances of survival of genes of the same type, in other words, the individual token may disappear, but the type multiplies.

If we take a first possible version of altruism, which is co-operation with others for a common advantage, there seems to be no problem. All stand to benefit, on the average. But there are more challenging forms of altruism which seem to challenge the view that 'the gene is the basic unit of selfishness' (Dawkins, 1978: 38).

Consider these cases of altruism. In the first, a bird gives a warning cry when a predator is spotted. Isn't this suicidal? If it were, it would be quickly extinguished, since suicide ends the line and eliminates the gene responsible for it. We must, therefore either abandon the theory of evolution by natural selection or find the advantage *to the individual* in uttering a warning call. Possibly the call attracts the predator's attention to the last bird to freeze and not to the bird uttering the call. This is the more plausible since alarm signals are acoustically designed to be difficult to locate.

A second case of altruism is that of the bee losing its life in stinging an intruder. This is difficult to explain until we remember that the majority of individuals in a colony of social insects are sterile workers. No replicators are lost when they die. They protect the gene line which resides in the queen.

Social insects separate the functions of caring and bearing and it is therefore possible for astonishing degrees of self-abnegation to evolve. Males in the hives are identical twins (they have only one set of chromosomes, derived from the mother) and females are nearly identical (they have identical sperm cells from the father, whereas the probability that they have any given gene from the mother is half: giving a total relatedness of $1.00 + 0.05 = 0.75$). This high degree of relatedness means that altruistic behaviour by all except the queen will maximize the survival rate of the family genes.

(ii) The evolution of stable strategies

One of the more difficult things to understand is why a balance of strategies may evolve which is well below optimum. After all, in the 'Panglossian' world of adaptation theory, shouldn't everything eventually turn out for the best in the 'best of possible worlds' (Gould and Lewontin (1979) level the accusation). Things are far from being at their best, as we all know; the fossil record is littered with the remains of extinct lines. Maynard Smith, in particular, has applied games theory to the study of evolutionary stable strategies which are far from optimal.

Here is an example from Maynard Smith (1979) at the Royal Society Symposium on Evolutionary Theory. Suppose two strategies, hawk (H) and dove (D). Hawks 'fight until victory or defeat'; doves 'display but retreat before being hurt if one's opponent escalates'. The changes in fitness when two animals meet are expressed as a payoff matrix as shown in Table 1.

Table 1. Payoff matrix for contests between hawk (H) and dove (D). (The payoffs are to the player adopting the strategy on the left against one adopting the strategy above.)

	H	D
H	−5	+10
D	0	+ 5

(From Maynard Smith, 1979: 476.)

When hawk meets hawk the payoff is negative (−5). They fight, exhaust and possibly kill each other. On the other hand, when hawk meets dove, the payoff to hawk is very rewarding (+10). A dove meeting a hawk simply retreats, after an initial display (0). In a contest of doves, dove sometimes wins and sometimes loses, but does not lose very much (+5).

Given such a battle, we may ask: 'What would an evolutionary stable strategy be?' Suppose, in a population of doves, a hawk mutant arose. With a payoff of +10, the mutation would spread rapidly, but as it spread, there would be an increased probability of meeting another hawk, leading to a payoff of −5. Some mixture of strategies will evolve, in which every individual plays hawk some proportion of the time, and dove for the remainder, or in which there is a determinate distribution of hawks and doves in the population. For the particular numerical values given above, H and D would be equally frequent.

Assume all players are hawk and dove with a probability of 0.5. Then a hawk move will meet another hawk 50% of the time and a dove 50%. The average payoff for a hawk move is $(0.5 \times (-5)) + (0.5 \times 10)$, or $+2.5$. Similarly, a dove will encounter a dove response half the time and a hawk response half the time. The average payoff is $(0.5 \times 0) + (0.5 \times 5) = +2.5$. The mathematics of evolutionary stable strategics may be found in Maynard Smith (1974).

There are many implications of this approach, but among the more important, for our discussion here, are the following: (1) The stable strategy is not necessarily optimal for the species. Dove meets dove would be best. This is not a Panglossian 'best of all possible worlds'. (2) Stable strategies can be derived from individual advantages and do not depend on 'group selection'.

There is no best solution for survival under all circumstances. Optimum strategies must be advanced for particular circumstances. To look ahead for a moment, this is equally true whether we are talking about genetically produced behaviour or behaviourally produced behaviour: Why is it, given human rationality, that we can't escape from such traps? This follows from the thesis that contestants signal information about their size and fighting ability but not about their intentions. Suppose a contestant were to signal its intentions. Very soon, a 'lying' mutant would arise – say, a dove that announced hawkish intentions – and be favoured by selection. But soon, everyone would be lying, or lying a certain proportion of the time (Maynard Smith, 1979).

Given the fact that everyone may be lying, we have to rely on signals about actual strength and fighting ability in our opponents. Hence, we continually escalate our powers of destruction. Would it pay to reduce them and to signal relative impotence? It might, if it were already obvious that we could not meet a hawk move. Then we would be well off spending our resources on other things. A difficulty is, of course, that there is seldom only one opponent to consider. We might wish to signal our strength to some of the contestants and not to others.

Difficulties with the axiom of evolution by natural selection

These examples have been given to show how problem-solving developments and applications are necessary to convince us of the 'truth' or value of an axiom. At any rate, we are convinced that we have got hold of a problem-solving principle of the first importance. Given this fact, is there anyone who would question it?

The main difficulty is raised by those who argue that evolutionary change is determined to a much larger extent by the total architecture of the organism than by the selection of independent characters. 'Organisms are integrated entities, not collections of discrete objects' (Gould and Lewontin, 1979: 585). They propose that 'organisms must be analysed as integrated wholes' (1979: 585). When an organism is sufficiently complex (and most organisms are very complex indeed), its 'architecture', and its structure, play a more important role in determining future evolution than random mutations do. There may be cascade effects, with one change effecting another and yet another, so that many variations are brought about by these internal structural causes rather than by imitation and natural selection.

This is a distinct possibility. In fact, given the complexity of organisms, linkage must in most cases be a determining factor in change. When we look at the 'reversible figure' of the gene/organism and see only the colony of co-adapted genes, we lose sight of the properties of the organism. When, however, we see the organism and lose sight of the genes, we become aware of architecture, of integration, or remarkable structure. At the level of the gene, we see distinct traits, more or less independently modifiable though subject to natural selection. When we look at the whole organism we are aware of the extraordinary degree of carefully programmed construction that is essential for its production.

The danger of the adaptionist or natural selection programme is that it becomes a dogma which is blindly applied. Gould and Lewontin cite large numbers of cases in which the failure of one adaptionist account leads to another (1979: 586–7). Thus, the Eskimo face was at one time regarded as well-engineered to withstand cold, then as well-engineered to chew.

Horns are regarded as either weapons against predators or as symbols for intra-specific competition among males. Variations in the colour of snails, even in the same environment, must be adaptive, though we can't see how.

The difficulty with the 'adaptionist programme' is that a lack of evidence does not lead to its rejection. This is the familiar (and legitimate) complaint of those who are confronted by scientific tautologies. A tautology marks that stage, in the development of a science, when the puzzle is defined. It is a great achievement to establish a tautology, and a great nuisance to attempt to overthrow it.

My conclusion, on the basis of the arguments presented here, is that we shall probably have to give up the claim that evolution by natural selection is the *only* kind of evolution there is. We shall have to admit that, in complex organisms, much change is determined by the structure of the organisms, by cascade effects which we do not understand very well.

The discrete trait approach and the adaptionist programme have served well, but perhaps the most interesting questions of the future will be found in other approaches. Darwin himself believed that selection was only one mechanism among several, so that broadening one's approach to evolution would, in fact, be a return to the source.

Conclusion

We aim at axioms because they define problem spaces more effectively than most intellectual tools do. As elements of a scientific research tradition, they should not be understood in isolation, though. They form part of an intellectual toolkit which consists of metaphysical commitments, methods, rules, applications, specific theories and hypotheses, and metaphors. Though they can change, like any other tool in science, the surrender of an important axiom is not easy; it means that some large domain of problems will have to be solved in a different way.

7 | Problem-solving and the evolution of theory

Problem-solving is the characteristic and essential feature of science, as we learn from Popper, Kuhn, Lakatos, Feyerabend and Laudan; and this view is shared by active scientists. Medawar (1967) describes science in the phrase 'the art of the soluble' and says that scientists who tackle problems they can't solve can only hope for 'the kindly contempt earned by the utopian politician' (1967: 7). Not only must problems be solved, though; they must be solved in competition with others. All credit goes to the winner of the race. Like athletes, scientists try to be first, though the arena of competition is different in the two cases. This implies that there is no fixed or stationary standard by which the adequacy of performance can be judged, since the standard is continually revised by the latest achievement. Latour and Woolgar (1979) tell us in their interesting study of laboratory life how the standard can be raised to eliminate the opposition, who may withdraw because they don't have the money, the equipment, the talent or the 'guts'. Schally, one of the protagonists in the 'laboratory life' drama, is cited: 'The key factor is not the money, it's the will ... The brutal force of putting in 60 hours a week for a year to get one million fragments' (1979: 118). His team had to collect millions of hypothalamuses to obtain enough of the hormone, TRF, in which they were interested. This was made necessary by their own announcement that the goal of their team was not merely to isolate TRF but to collect enough of it to determine its molecular structure. The effect of this was to reduce the field of competition, since the risk of failure and the sheer arduousness of the task were vastly increased. Latour and Woolgar speculate that it is probably relevant that the main competitors (Schally and Guillemin) were immigrants (1979: 119). Schally dismissed a possible rival as 'Establishment ... he never had to do anything' (1979: 119).

These accounts alert us to the complexity of any account of the ways in which problems are defined and focused. Our stories could equally well be about the personalities of the competitors, social demands, crises, the intellectual climate, or clashes between research traditions. How should we decide which factors are important – the 'internal' history of the tradition, concentrating on the ways in which ideas, practices and problems are modified within a particular scientific community pursuing truth as it sees it and resisting worldly temptation; or the 'external' history of the tradition, which shows temptations, demands and political forces impinging upon the work of science? Wouldn't it be rather foolish to decide that the whole account was to be either one or the other? As a matter of convenience, one might focus on one set of factors, rather than another, but it cannot be a decision of principle, unless one has some quite foolish principles to assert.

How should one investigate the factors which influence the evolution of a scientific tradition? One way, if one is that fortunate, is to find a theory or two to test against the facts of evolution. This is the way which satisfies us best, because it seems more rigorous. Another way, for those who are Low Church Investigators (without the incense or the splendid ceremonial appurtenances of science at its most inspiring) is to draw up a shopping list of factors which should be considered in examining the history of a tradition. Sometimes the theories are merely shopping lists, and the shopping lists have the accents of theory, but we soon grow accustomed to pretentiousness. The value of good shopping lists should not be underestimated, because they can be used to remind theorists who are about to cry that they have made all their purchases that there are still items which may be needed.

Let us look at these approaches to the evolution of traditions. On the one hand, we test theories against facts; on the other, we construct cases by going through our checklist of things to be borne in mind.

Theories and historical facts

Examples of theories of scientific change which might be tested against historical facts are those of Kuhn, Laudan and Lakatos. One of the first problems we face is knowing what they say and how what one says differs from what another says.

Theorists may differ sharply from each other even when they seem to be saying the same thing, and may be saying the same thing when they appear to be saying different things. Each theorist likes to wear a different vocabulary. There are many illustrations of this (and some will follow in the next three chapters), but Feyerabend's (1981) remarks on Laudan may show what we mean. It is the old problem that what is new is not true and what is true is not new. There is nothing novel in Laudan's claims to be focusing on the problem-solving capacities of science (Popper had done this), on the importance of conceptual problems (virtually everyone had done this) or on the importance of traditions (Lakatos had done this, using the term programme). What Laudan had done was to invent some new vocabulary and to proclaim a difference. In this book, a fair amount of use of Kuhn, Laudan and Lakatos has been made, without respecting their differences overmuch. Kuhn's concept of a *disciplinary matrix* is treated as a set of resources in a tradition. The distinction between *traditions* (or programmes) and *theories* has been adopted from both Laudan and Lakatos. The focus on *problem-solving* is shared by all.

It is, therefore, interesting to examine an attempt to state each of these theories in such a way that they can offer competing accounts of historical facts. If they are indeed in substantive competition, then we have been careless in assimilating the one to the other. (This is not to deny that one vocabulary rather than another may be victorious in the end.)

The attempt I wish to consider is one which addresses the facts of the history of learning theory from the perspectives of Kuhn, Lakatos and Laudan (Gholson and Barker, 1985). What they attempt to do is, first, to define each approach in such a way as to distinguish it from the others; and, second, to test each approach against the known historical facts. Their definitions of the approaches are as follows:

Kuhn's approach is said to rest on the assumptions that paradigms are incommensurable; research programmes defeat each other in scientific revolutions; and there is no continuity in content from one paradigm to the next. Since this is a caricature of Kuhn's views based on his early work, they call this approach 'Kuhnian'. The later concept of the disciplinary matrix makes it difficult to believe in hermetically sealed paradigms. However, it is valid to describe a position (whether we call it Kuhnian or something else) with sufficient clarity to make it a candidate for testing.

Lakatos's approach rests on the following assumptions, according to Gholson and Barker. Preference for one research programme rather than another is a rational choice; programmes are progressive or degenerative, depending on whether they solve critical new problems or accumulate anomalies; problems may be empirical or theoretical; each programme consists of core commitments and a protective belt of auxiliary hypotheses which may be sacrificed without abandoning the programme; and as theories mature, a common reason for replacing them is experimental failure. Has Lakatos been successfully distinguished from Kuhn? Certainly, from the approach called 'Kuhnian', with its incommensurable and sealed paradigms; but every feature of Lakatos's approach can be matched in Kuhn's approach, though the emphasis may be different. It has been said repeatedly that showing up non-rational factors in changing theories or paradigms is hardly the same as saying that rational choices are not made. At the frontier, scientists do take risks in betting on competing theories. Presumably, if anyone knew a completely foolproof way to bet they would adopt it. If one waits till nearly the end of the race, one can be (almost) sure who is going to win, but it's too late to bet.

Laudan's approach is said to rest on the following assumptions. Research traditions consist of a family of theories with a common ontology and methodology, which both change as the tradition evolves; and conceptual factors are as important as experimental success or failure in appraising a theory. It is hard indeed to distinguish in a substantive way between research programmes, research traditions, and paradigms (Feyerabend, 1981). It is also hard to see that conceptual factors do not play an equally large role in all three approaches, but let us for the moment suspend judgement and simply take it that three approaches have been distinguished. How do these three approaches explain episodes in the history of psychology?

The strategy adopted by Gholson and Barker is to show that Lakatos's approach fits the facts of history, in both physics and psychology, better than Kuhn's approach. Having done this, they attempt to show that Laudan's approach is an improvement on Lakatos's. The conclusion, therefore, is that Laudan gives the best fit to the historical facts.

First, why do they believe that Lakatos is preferable to Kuhn? They argue that there was considerable 'experimental commensurability' between cognitive and conditioning programmes of research, as shown by conflict and interchange in the mid-1930s (Gholson and Barker, 1985: 761). Second, cognitive psychologists adopted several elements from mathematical learning theorists, such as Markov chains. However, though the Lakatosian account is better than the Kuhnian (if we assume that the approaches of learning theorists and cognitivists represent different paradigms which nevertheless interacted), there are still deficiencies, since the core commitments of learning theorists 'underwent a constant evolution between about 1950 and 1965' and learning theorists also adopted core commitments from the cognitive programme (1985: 761). Core commitments are not supposed to change or exchange, according to their version of the Lakatosian approach. As an example of a changing core commitment, they cite mediation theorists (such as Kendler, 1979) who surrendered the view that all learning is a form of conditioning in favour of the view that there are two processes – learning by conditioning and learning by hypothesis testing, the former being more common in younger children. (Nowadays, when we postulate hypothesis testing and operating principles as essential for the acquisition of grammar in the first two years of infancy, even this would be greeted with scepticism (Slobin, 1979).) This shows, of course, what purists have always feared. Eclectics are everywhere, borrowing wherever they see a good idea, without any respect for purity of form or tradition.

These difficulties and the way in which Laudan's approach apparently solves them, lead Gholson and Barker to prefer Laudan to Lakatos. Laudan does not postulate core processes, though he does postulate that traditions have a distinguishing ontology and a methodology. To cite him:

> A research tradition is a set of general assumptions about the entities and processes in a domain of study, and about the appropriate methods to be used for investigating the problems and constructing the theories in that domain (1977: 81).

It is not clear what the difference is between Laudan's ontology and Lakatos's 'core'. One could regard a change from conditioning to hypothesis testing as a change in either ontology or core, since (referring to ontology), the change is a change in the very nature of the process of learning, or (referring to core) the change refers to the basic processes which are central to the theory, relatively immune to refutation, and yet are part of the theory used in making predictions.

Yet another reason for preferring Laudan's account to Lakatos's (according to Gholson and Barker) is that 'conceptual factors' play a relatively important part in theory appraisal in Laudan but not in Lakatos. As examples of such conceptual factors they cite circularity in definitions of reinforcement and the lack of precision in Piaget's theory, in particular the vagueness of concepts such as equilibration, assimilation and organization (Gholson and Barker, 1985: 765). Conceptual solutions may lead us to adopt a theory; conceptual failure may lead us to abandon it. This is hardly novel. All the approaches to science which are under discussion admit the significance of conceptual factors. After all, we are talking theory and not recipes for cooking eggs. Conceptual clarity, elegance, rigour, and other theoretical virtues are among the essential 'values' of science (in Kuhn's vocabulary). We may illustrate by citing instances in which theorists have maintained a theory against current empirical evidence, because of its virtues.

> It seems that if one is working from the point of view of getting beauty into one's equations, and if one has a really sound insight, one is on a sure line of progress. If there is not complete agreement between the results of one's work and experiment, one should not allow oneself to be too discouraged (Dirac, cited in Brush, 1976).

Circular definitions and vague concepts on the one hand, and sound insight and beauty in one's equations on the other, must be part of every appraisal of theory. Experimental models, axioms, laws, metaphysical assumptions, ideal cognitive objects, and values *are* the conceptual factors in a theory and we don't need a separate category for the latter. Since science consists of both concepts and practices (or methods), it is hardly surprising that concepts and practices are important in the evaluation of a theory.

Nor does the view that theories are rationally compared distinguish any one approach from the other. Kuhn, Popper, Lakatos, Laudan and many others give instances of rational comparisons; yet all conclude that such comparisons are not simple. When should one trust 'facts' and when should one trust theory? Appraisal depends on where the facts come from – who did the experiments and what were they trying to show? – as well as the conviction that some things cohere to form a good picture or deep insight. As was said earlier, up to a certain stage, neither resistance to the evidence nor conversion are entirely rational. Young scientists, ambitious scientists, scientists with a contempt for the 'establishment' may challenge a theory or a tradition on relatively flimsy evidence. They may be prepared for risks. Needless to say, their gamble does not always pay off, and they may never be heard of again. This is not 'irrational'. It is a decision to back a possible winner before everyone else has spotted it. In art, entrepreneurial work, speculating on the stock exchange, and even in science, there are risks to be taken because the truth cannot be known in advance. There is, in all of them, a direct relationship between the level of risk and potential reward. Scientists are well aware of this, as we see from personal accounts (Evans, 1976; Siegel and Zeigler, 1976).

Suppose we look again at the data in Gholson and Barker, but this time we treat each tradition as a matrix of resources – or disciplinary matrix. This enables us to discuss the kinds of change which occur in a complex way, without positing discontinuities. Even when a revolution has occurred, we shall often find that the matrix of resources has not changed completely. In any case, subtle comparisons are possible and we avoid oversimplification.

Thus, in looking at the changes in learning theory we find changes in all the dimensions of the matrix. Mathematical learning theory changes the symbolic generalizations of learning theory by introducing complex new concepts such as stimulus sampling and Markov chains. New metaphors are introduced as hypotheses come to supplement conditioning. The range of exemplary solutions is extended with the application of learning theory to clinical problems. Behaviour modification introduces a wide range of models which are linked, by analogy, to laboratory models of operant and classical conditioning. Mathematical theorizing leads to changes in value. There is increasingly complex speculation in the work of Hull, Estes, Suppes, and others about intervening processes. The 'ideal cognitive object' of the learning theorist becomes an increasingly complex connection machine.

All of these are resources as well as problems. When we examine any real cluster of theories in a tradition, we see that few of them match in all features of the matrix, though all of them will have some of the identifying features. A cluster of theories is, in fact, a fuzzy concept which we continually attempt to grasp by identifying its prototypes. This leads to a stereotyped view of what a tradition is, but is an inevitable consequence of our tendency to understand complex arrays by forming 'ideal cognitive models' of them (Lakoff, 1987; Rosch, 1973; 1978).

We may attempt strict definition of behaviorism (let us say) as a system which reduces all explanations to s (stimulus) and r (response) elements (Fodor, 1968), but when we trace the evolution of behaviourism into cognitive behaviourism, there are many moments of indecision about the applicability of such a strict criterion. The evolution of species implies the abolition of species (as strictly demarcated entities). The alternative often seems to be extremely loose definitions of behaviourism. Danziger (1987), in an essay on 'investigative practices' suggests that there may be a strict use of the term ('specific set of doctrines propagated by men like Watson and Skinner') and a loose sense of the term ('commitment to the general idea of psychology as a practically useful science of human performance'). One may then speak of the burgeoning of the 'behaviourist perspective'.

When one turns to Skinner to see whether he (as a core behaviourist) agrees with Fodor's definition, we find that he says: 'I do not consider myself an S–R psychologist' (Evans, 1976: 85). He continues the interview: 'Behavior is very fluid, it isn't made up of lots of little responses packed together.' And, when you are trying to account for the rate of emission of behaviour, 'some of the influences will reasonably be described as stimuli, and some will not'.

Prototypes are reference points when we are trying to identify a category and describe its ideal structure. What Kuhn's concept of disciplinary matrix does is to give a general way of describing the features on which exemplars can vary to discover the 'family resemblance' of theories. The strategy for attacking a cluster of theories is to attack the prototype theory, but because of this matrix structure of the cluster, we should not expect a neat ending.

Harré (1986: 201) adds to our understanding of the ways in which traditions are structured by the ideal cognitive model (or ideal cognitive 'object', as he calls it). He also uses the term 'theory-family' rather than tradition, but we may disregard these superficial differences and concentrate on the following: a tradition is recognized by the ideal cognitive model which it develops and exploits in understanding the world. Each ideal cognitive model is the union of (a) an 'analytical analogue or model' which is used to give order to perceptual experiences, and (b) a 'source analogue or model' which is used to explain how these perceptual experiences are produced. These analogues correspond to metaphors in Kuhn's approach, though Harré argues that metaphors are not up to the task of explanation, since they collapse into similarity, whereas what is needed is the logic of analogy. In other words, what is needed is a similarity of relations between elements rather than a simple similarity of elements. An example of a successful analogy is the analogue of breeding which Darwin used to develop the theory of evolution by natural selection. As Harré tells us, Darwin might have looked at the English countryside with religion or aesthetics in mind, and picked up evidence of God's bounty or of the picturesque. (Nature imitating Art, perhaps?) Instead, he looked at it as a country gentleman, and picked up evidence of breeding and bloodlines. With the analogue of breeding in mind, he constructs the following pair of relations (Harré, 1986: 204):

Domestic variation acted on by domestic selection leads to domestic novelty (e.g. new breeds)

Natural variations acted on by [....?....] leads to natural novelty (e.g. new species)

Harré's point about the fruitfulness of analogies is well taken, but there is little difference between them and metaphors, unless one wished to confine metaphors to a comparison between isolated elements rather than between structures of relations. It is clear from our earlier discussion that successful metaphors create conceptual structure and that this conceptual structure has a logic (including analogy) which can enable us to understand the problems we are studying. There is a danger in the multiplication of terms. 'Tradition' and 'metaphor' are by now familiar; what we should do is add to our understanding of these rather than add fresh terms. What Harré does, in his vigorous discussion, is to increase our understanding of the structure of the implications of successful metaphor.

The Darwinian analogy has also been used to create an ideal cognitive model to account for the selection of behaviour. Consider the following:

Domestic variation acted on by domestic selection leads to domestic variety

Behavioural variation acted upon by reinforcements leads to novel forms of behaviour.

Skinner has exploited the power of this analogy to create a science of behaviour. He has created experimental models of behavioural selection which have been persuasive for many decades, in spite of major difficulties of the kind discussed in an earlier chapter ('The fulcrum of reason'). These difficulties have concerned the circularity of the definition of reinforcement and the relation between ontogeny and phylogeny; in particular, the question arose whether there could be general laws of reinforcement or laws of learning, given that different species of animals are prepared by their evolutionary history to learn different things about the world. (This will also be discussed later in the present chapter, when considering the impact of Garcia on learning theory.) The problem here arose from an over-ambitious attempt to go beyond the demonstration of behavioural selection by consequence to the conclusions that (a) all behavioural patterns arise by such selection; and (b) all selections occur in the same way and exhibit the same responsiveness to schedules of reinforcement. This would be rather like proceeding from the general argument that evolution occurs by natural selection to the conclusion that all forms of natural selection have a common property, just as all behavioural selectors have a common property – that of being 'reinforcers'. This leads us to search for what it is that they all do to the organism. Natural selection occurs in an immense variety of ways; it simply refers to various processes by which some variants are eliminated and others favoured. Similarly, behavioural selection refers to an undefined set of factors which eliminate some behaviours and favour others. Some selectors may be information which confirms or disconfirms hypotheses; other selectors may be foods which satisfy hunger; other selectors may be pain or relief from pain. Each may be an event in a different functional system, with little in common. We will learn much by using them to understand the ways in which different functional systems operate, rather than by attempting to discover a common property of reinforcement.

What I intend to do now is to extend the Darwinian analogy to the evolution of theory, bearing in mind the dangers of looking for a common factor in the selection process. I shall accept that selectors operate in a variety of ways. All that they have in common is their effect on the survival of theory variants. They do not account for the ways in which these variants arise, nor are they normative in some ideal way; they simply act on variants once these have arisen. Norms may be established and *may* operate in leading us to prefer one theory to another. One such normative description of the way science ought to work is Popper's (1963) conjecture and refutation, though as a description of what actually happens, it is not always correct.

When we look at the factors which select theories, norms of scientific practice can be possible candidates but no more. We may accept or reject a theory because it meets norms, but just as often we change our norms when a theory solves interesting problems. An example of the survival of theory against the norms of evidence and argument is the case of psychoanalysis, which has been subjected to severe critiques and yet continues to flourish and adapt. (For a recent and telling assault see Eysenck's (1986) *Decline and Fall of the Freudian Empire*.)

For the present, let us revert to the shopping list (or does 'checklist' sound better?) approach to historical influences on theory.

Checklists and the evolution of theory

The more we look at the activity of science, in which hypothesis competes against hypothesis and theory against theory, the more we begin to suspect that an evolutionary account of the growth of knowledge is necessary. We take the source analogy of Darwinian evolution and extend it yet again.

> Theoretical variation acted on by social selection leads to novel theories.

A general schema for an evolutionary epistemology (or theory of knowledge) contains '(a) mechanisms for introducing variation; (b) consistent selection processes; and (c) mechanisms for preserving and propagating the selected variations' (Campbell, 1974: 421). From this point of view, a research tradition is a system biased by its history to solve certain problems and not others.

The reason for the rapid advance of the problem-solving capacity of natural sciences is that scientists are trained to introduce theoretical variations, to test them empirically, and to preserve and propagate those innovations which survive whatever tests have been proposed. This is distinct from belief systems (often disguised as knowledge systems) in which propositions are tested against our wishes and hopes. They may become better and better at fulfilling these as long as we can keep the real world at bay. The form of rationality in science – conjecture and empirical selection – has itself been subjected to selection in competition with other forms of rationality, among them: demonstrative rationality, in which propositions are demonstrated by deduction from a priori truths; revealed truths; textual exegesis; truth by consensus or conformity; truth by wish-fulfilment, aesthetic preference; or waiting for patterns of nature to reveal themselves as opposed to experimental intervention to speed up the process of selection. Since those societies which have adopted scientific rationality have, on the whole, been able to produce knowledge-based technologies which have increased their power, wealth, comfort, and understanding of the world relative to those which have not, these methods of solving problems have spread rapidly. Furthermore, as with any complex human practice which has utility, the qualities essential to its pursuit (such as openness to new ideas, rigour, curiosity, willingness to question what is accepted, willingness to submit ideas to the test of experiment and observation, and honesty) are cultivated as virtues by active practitioners.

We might also spend time on taxonomy and classify traditions and theories according to their ideal cognitive objects (as Harré suggests) and models of rationality (of the kinds given above). This taxonomic exercise would be comparable in many ways to the great biological taxonomies, indicating both lines of descent and similarity. This confusion of purposes is, incidentally, a feature of biological taxonomics, where different classifications can result from attempts to group by line of descent or by current similarities in form and function. The former mode of classification is advanced by cladists and the latter by pheneticists. The cladistic approach apparently results in some peculiar reclassifications, such as the abolition of the categories of zebra and fish. Gould (1983) tells us that there is no such thing as a fish, since some (such as the lungfish) are more closely related to terrestrial animals than they are to other fish.

Why should we want a taxonomy – or several taxonomies – of theory? For the same reason that biologists do. When one writes evolutionary history, one attempts to discover both line of descent and similarities in form and function.

What I wish to concentrate on here, though, are the processes of selection which might eliminate some theories and enable others to spread rapidly. 'Internal' models of these processes pay attention to the rational selective processes and norms within each tradition. But one thing we have learnt from the study of evolution is that selection may occur in many surprising ways. This is where the shopping list is useful, though not exhaustive. One way to become aware of outside influences on selection is to think of theories as methods of investigation; then we immediately realize how offensive they may be to those with other views. The result is a long list of 'external' influences on theory change. What would our shopping list look like? One way of organizing it is as follows, going from external selectors to internal selectors, from those which are 'historical accidents' to those which seem to be truly part of the very practice of science.

Selection factors in the evolution of theories
Political movements
Climate of thought; zeitgeist
Professional opportunities
Demonstrations of legitimacy
Institutional power structures
Psychodynamics of leadership
Strategies of competition
Methods of inquiry; disciplinary norms

From a theoretical perspective this must seem to be a truly laughable list, but then a study of the ecology of theories must seem to be a laughable undertaking to the purist, interested only in ideas. What I wish to emphasize, though, is that it is not enough for systems which survive (whether they be theories or organisms) to meet some fixed standard of excellence or fitness. They survive in competition with other systems in a particular social environment, and this competition can take the most diverse forms. This does not slight tests of scientific virtue imposed within the scientific community. It is these tests which make scientific theories so apt to survive and to serve both our need to understand the world and to solve practical problems.

Let us now turn to some of the evidence which each of the entries in our list might lead us to pick off the shelf.

Political movements

It is difficult to estimate the effects of political suppression (or promotion) on the long-term development of science. Overt suppression would seem to be less effective than ideological conversion, which makes scientists willing and even eager to serve the prevailing political system. Thus, overt suppression of Vygotsky's ideas in the Soviet Union has not prevented their reappearance and popularity half a century later; whereas Vygotsky's conversion to Marxism and his attempts to create a truly Marxist psychology have had a persistent effect (see Wertsch, 1985 for recent testimony to this). As Zinchenko and Davydov tell us in their preface to Wertsch, Vygotsky announced 'I don't want to discover the nature of mind by patching together a lot of quotations. I want to find out how science has to be built, to approach the study of mind having learnt the whole of Marx's method' (1985: ix). The synthesis appears to have been fruitful and we can probably look forward to many years of interesting work in this tradition. It seems, therefore, that political suppression can have little long-term effect on the history of science. This is the optimistic view, since we should not take it for granted that political conditions always change in such a way that the continuation of work is possible. At the very least, work may be slowed down.

An equally notorious example of political suppression dates from the same time, when the publication of Luria's researches in Uzbekistan (1931 and 1932) was largely prevented. He was interested in studying changes in the thought processes of people being introduced to 'higher and more complex forms of economic life and the raising of the general cultural level' (Luria, 1979: 213). Possibly the ranking of cultures was, at the time, against official interpretations of Marxist doctrine; possibly there was some bureaucratic anxiety under Stalin. Was it or was it not acceptable to attribute improvements in psychological functioning (abstract classifications, self-criticism, better reasoning) to greater literacy? The result was the almost complete suppression of this work until 1968, when the publication of a brief article revealed that the political climate had begun to change. A monograph followed on *Cognitive Development* (1976) in which his views on the historical formation of mental processes was set forth. One of the key findings was that traditional Uzbekis were not susceptible to classical visual illusions, such as the Muller-Lyer, and Luria interpreted this as support for his view that gestalten are not permanent characteristics of the mind but are culturally and historically variable.

Once more, the ending of the story is a happy one, but the effects on young scientists attempting to learn about psychology were probably considerable. There were many warnings in Luria's career, culminating in his dismissal from the Institute of Neurosurgery in 1950. Pavlov's work became the model and Luria 'had to state that his work on aphasia and the restoration of brain function was deeply flawed because of his failure to apply Pavlovian teaching' (Cole, 1979: 219–20). Luria learnt to write his papers in Pavlovian language, perhaps hoping that readers would penetrate the disguise. 'Sadly, in the 1950s many young Soviet psychologists could not make the translation, nor could I' (Cole, 1979: 221).

I think it is clear that studies of political influence on scientific development would be valuable. The allocations of funds altering the reward structure, ideological conversion, and direct terror or suppression are among the means the state can use.

Climate of thought

Each period has its set of assumptions about what is possible, decent or sane. In the nineteenth century, *progressive* theories could rank people and societies from savage to civilized. A climate of racist thought accompanied and probably facilitated European domination of the globe. In the late twentieth century, such theories would be regarded as not merely wrong but immoral. Cross-cultural theorists work against a background of relativism (Stein, 1986), or at least of anti-antirelativism (Geertz, 1984). Decorum hangs heavy over indications of possible indecency. At its most banal, relativism may be parodied as the view that 'People do what they do ... pretty much because that's what they do' (Hippler, 1984: 434). The West has to compensate, though, for its past by idealizing the Third World (even as its economic policies continue to crush it).

> Among relativists, guilt feelings are transformed via projection into accusation of others who are ethnocentric. At a more primitive level, the relativist symbolizes his inner splits through a dualistic system that portrays the modern West as evil and the primitive as innocent (Stein, 1986: 169).

This, of course, is relativism at its worst. At its best, it is a moral injunction against ethnocentrism and arrogance. The world is indeed a complex place! Relativism may be used to justify keeping the Third World as it is (underdeveloped – a zoo and an ethnology museum) or to excoriate Western arrogance. On the whole, though, decentration is a good thing. It leads scientists to question the authority and validity of their own points of view.

This process of decentration (against a background of relativism) has led to fierce criticism of tests linking intelligence and race in particular, and intelligence and heredity in general, focusing on the work of Jensen (1969, 1980) in recent times. The nature of these links is discussed in Scarr (1980) and dramatically debated in Eysenck and Kamin (1981). The relevant point here is that whereas the climate of opinion was hospitable to demonstrations of links between race and intelligence in the early years of the century, it has now changed in such a way that most scientists either avoid such studies or interpret results in such a way as to reject previous findings of a strong relationship. Racial discrimination and racist science are no longer acceptable (though racist practices may still be common enough). The study of race may flourish under certain political imperatives and cultural assumptions, but under others would be strongly discouraged.

In other fields, social interests have also selected certain scientific achievements for pre-eminence. Latour (1988), in an essay on the 'pasteurization of France', describes the way in which the hygienist movement took up Pasteur's discoveries. His investigation of the invisible agents of illness strengthened their campaign against dirt, leading them to dramatize and magnify his achievements (which were great) in comparison with those of Koch and Jenner. One should note, though, that Pasteur was not only an exemplary scientist but also a national hero at the time of the Franco-Prussian war. This might have had more to do with his national pre-eminence than the efforts of the hygienists.

A remarkable attempt to impose scientific conformity is the *Seville Declaration on Violence* adopted at the business meeting of the American Anthropological Association in 1986. The Declaration solemnly lists five 'scientifically incorrect' propositions in its condemnation of 'a number of alleged biological findings that have been used even by some in our disciplines, to justify violence and war' (Fox, 1989: 58). Among the dangerous scientific theories is the theory of evolution. The Declaration has a deadly, inquisitorial rhythm, with each paragraph beginning: 'It is scientifically incorrect to say that ...'. Certainly, many of those who voted for it appear to have been terrified out of their wits. How else to explain their support for such propositions as:

> It is scientifically incorrect to say that in the course of human evolution there has been a selection for aggressive behaviour more than for other kinds of behaviour (How to quantify 'more'?).
>
> It is scientifically incorrect to say that humans have a 'violent brain' (straw man!).
>
> It is scientifically incorrect to say that war is caused by 'instinct' or any other single motivation.

What the Declaration does is to make psychobiological research more difficult by promoting a new consensus. There is an uneasy divide between 'explaining' and 'justifying' war. If one advances the hypothesis that there are biological factors which contribute to violence, is one justifying violence? Apparently one is, by contributing to 'an atmosphere of pessimism'.

The most important objection to the Declaration is that 'no position can be declared correct or incorrect by fiat... One dreads to think what would have happened to the sciences if a list of "incorrect" positions had been drawn up in, say, 1910 and subsequent research had been guided by that list' (Fox, 1989: 63).

And think of the awful pessimism caused by Darwin in 1859. Should he have been allowed to publish?

Professional opportunities

It is hardly surprising that those scientific movements which meet the requirements of administrators, managers, or others in power will flourish. We see this most strikingly in war or in preparation for war, but there are many other examples.

In many countries and especially in the European colonies, managers wished to select the most productive workers in a largely illiterate workforce. Obviously, those who made a profession of helping them to do this would enjoy their support. In South Africa, to give one example, psychologists (particularly at the National Institute for Personnel Research) were able to make a significant contribution to the selection of 'bossboys' on the mines (Louw, 1986), and to the composition of teams for improved productivity (Mauer and Lawrence, 1988). Many of these tests were exported and used in Commonwealth countries. As far back as the 1st Carnegie Commission to investigate the 'poor white' problem, psychologists had established their professional claims, particularly in the field of vocational guidance. They were recognized as experts to be consulted in education, industry and clinical practice. By 1974, this recognition had led to the establishment of a professional register for psychologists, the effect of which was to grant them a new monopoly in the application of psychological knowledge to practical problems. However, the direction of influence is never one way. Professional demands begin to shape the knowledge base from the earliest times.

This has been demonstrated fairly clearly by Danziger's (1987) study of the modification of investigative practice to meet professional demands in the USA and Germany. In order to meet the needs of educational administrators and the military, group tests and testing techniques were developed to a high level of sophistication. Professional prestige was purchased at the cost of 'a severe constriction of disciplinary aims. The developmental psychology of men like Baldwin and Hull, which could have a prescriptive significance for education, was now replaced by practices that limited themselves to the sorting of individuals' (1987: 21). The prestige of group investigations led to the downgrading of individual case studies as unscientific; and this downgrading became part of the attack on theories which were founded on an intensive study of single individuals.

There is a potential conflict between those who sort large numbers of individuals on the basis of group tests and those who attempt to understand particular persons in order to help them as individuals. This conflict is a product of methodological imperialism: each develops its own investigative practices and attempts to impose these on the other.

The symptom of this is the debate about nomothetic versus idiographic science, or clinical versus statistical methods (Allport, 1937, 1965; Kelly, 1955; Meehl, 1954).

A good case study of this conflict is given by Van Strien and Dehue (1985). Some of pressures on psychological practice and theory may be summarized.

1. Practitioners (in the Netherlands and elsewhere) responded differently to different clients. To industry, they offered psychometrics; to individuals in search of cure or enlightenment they offered holistic understanding of the person.
2. The large influx of students and the growth of the research industry after World War II changed the balance between clinical practitioners and academics. The academics had to train numbers of students, find publishable research topics, and gain scientific recognition, all of which tasks could be most easily undertaken in the dominant psychometric research tradition.
3. This was consolidated by major Dutch academic theorists who replaced the 'subjective and authoritarian style' of intuition by testable predictions of psychometric instruments, which appeared to be transparent and 'democratic'. This eclipsed the phenomenological–existential tradition (and other holistic clinical practices). Intuition was restricted to the 'context of discovery', but excluded from the 'context of demonstration' or proof.
4. However, the failure of the psychometric approach (for clinical practice) became increasingly evident. It could tell little about the complex dynamics and point of view of the individual. In spite of this, the view persisted that the psychometric approach was superior (though of little value) and the clinical approach was inferior (though more useful).
5. The result was a split between 'official' methodological rules as taught in the universities and the rules of practice.

It is hardly surprising, therefore, that clinicians even in the USA rate journal articles and books with empirical findings bottom of the list of useful information (Kupfersmid, 1988). The paradoxical situation arises that the methodology which is least useful to clinicians was approved by academics looking after their own research industry, and the methodology most useful to clinicians was dismissed by academics. As recently as 1980 the clinical practitioner was being advised in the Netherlands to wait for group testing methods to deliver the goods (Van Strien and Dehue, 1985: 15).

Taylor (1958) had vigorously attacked the shallow conceptualization of theoretical problems which led to this kind of science, in a paper aptly entitled 'experimental design: A cloak for intellectual sterility'. He asks the rhetorical question: Would Newton have discovered the laws of motion by correlating data from many solar systems? General laws are able to predict differences as well as similarities; merely lumping together different cases will conceal relations. Can we hope to discover general laws of human psychology by pooling data from many people who, as often as not, construe the situation differently? We simultaneously reject the view that people are identical and pool the results obtained from them. Why do we do this? The professional opportunities cited above suggest at least part of the answer. There was a demand for sorting techniques; those psychologists who supplied them became dominant in the profession and while their dominion lasted they imposed their views on others. The formidable techniques they developed became the true ideology of psychology, so that even when it did not answer questions, the dissatisfied felt that the fault must lie in themselves. Yet it was the usual imperial overreach. What was good for some was thought to be good for all.

Demonstrations of legitimacy

A practice is legitimate if it is positively valued in a particular 'reference system' (Van Strien and Dehue, 1985), or by a particular client or audience. Reference systems may be (1) other members of the discipline; (2) members of other academic disciplines; (3) specific clients; and (4) 'society at large'.

Attempts to show that a practice or theory is legitimate will depend very much on the demands which arise within these different reference systems. Those within a discipline will demand that a novel practice or theory satisfy disciplinary norms and standards of proof. Members of rival disciplines will be anxious not to be displaced. Specific clients will demand that their needs be met. And what of 'society at large'?

When large-scale changes in the balance of political power occur, new publics make their voices heard. It is then that we become most aware of attempts to establish the value or legitimacy of a discipline. These attempts may have significant effects on the way in which that discipline develops or withers away. We may illustrate by referring to the anxieties of psychologists in South Africa. The question which they cannot avoid asking is: How do their activities look to revolutionaries? Will they be supported after massive political change? Does psychology have any specific role to play in the fight against apartheid? In order to examine these questions, a number of young psychologists in Durban, Cape Town and Johannesburg founded a journal, *Psychology in Society*, which 'aims to critically explore and present ideas on the nature of psychology in apartheid and capitalist society', according to the editorial statement on the cover of the journal. The struggle to establish legitimacy can become fierce, as we see from discussions in the journal. Who will play the leading role in the political struggle and who will dictate the content and methods of psychology in a period of transition? One response to the situation was to establish courses in community psychology which would reach out to 'the community' or 'the people'. But this has not been unchallenged, as we can see from a hostile article in *Psychology and Society*:

> Community psychology is a 'red hering'. . . . Certain foxy psychologists . . . know that the herring will enable them to appear relevant while simultaneously keeping open the 'passage' to Australia and the Americas. It is not only individuals who benefit from such a tactic, but also departments who continue to theorize and teach within the mainstream individual paradigm while allocating a few junior staff members to hoist the community flag' (Seedat et al., 1988: 51).

The authors believe that 'lifting one of the masks' of the pretenders is a start, though they lamely confess that it is more difficult 'to develop a psychology that will take cognisance of the psychological processes of oppression and liberation' (1988: 51) than to expose failure. The difficulty in this game is that once we appeal to hidden motives we call for a general confession. The critics should be made to confess with those they criticize. To lift the masks of others is also a way of ingratiating oneself with 'the oppressed' and of keeping the 'passage' open to 'Australia and the Americas'. Cycles of denunciation are a source of gratification; they carry the obligation, if they are to be taken seriously, to propose a psychology which can be subjected to the same criticism. The cycle of denunciation, disguised as methodology, is clearly described in Kozulin's (1984) *Psychology in Utopia*.

One attempt at liberation psychology uses Frantz Fanon as a role model. His psychology of liberation speak directly to students who are members of oppressed groups as well as to students who are among the oppressors. There is, first, the psychology of power. Many Blacks identify with their white oppressors just as the inmates of concentration camps identify with their guards (Bettelheim, 1943). One response to inferiority is to become more like one's oppressors; another is to move against them. In *Black Skin White Masks* (1970; orig. 1952) Fanon describes the process of identification with the oppressor, whereas in later works, such as *The Wretched of the Earth* (1967; orig. 1961), he describes the process of identification against the oppressor. The two books complement each other to form the nucleus of a psychology of liberation. In the former, 'the Negro is comparison ... continually preoccupied with self-evaluation and with the ego-ideal' (Fanon, 1970: 149) – that is, with the image of white superiority. The child who identifies with white heroes wishes to be white. This inner whiteness is possible until he is in contact with whites; then he is black. Fanon cites a novel (*Je suis Martiniquaise*) in which the heroine submits completely to her white lover. Her passionate submission to whiteness, her desire to be filled with whiteness, is a futile attempt to magically transform herself. In another novel, Jean Veneuse pursues the life of intellect, accumulates 'an impressive reading list', and falls in love with a white woman in France. He is accepted because he is not 'really black'. He has a white mind! Of course, he cannot believe it; he needs repeated assurance. He is an Othello waiting to be betrayed. The magic of possession can never work because it remains external. 'When my restless hands caress these white breasts, they grasp white civilization and dignity and make them mine' (Fanon, 1970: 46). As long as he identifies with an aggressor who merely uses him, he is caught in a contradiction. The answer, Fanon believed, was revolution and the assertion of a new identity which would not be self-contradictory. Should there be an ethnic or racist revolution? Or, on the contrary, should it be a revolution based on Marxist theory, in which one class replaces another? What is the political and social significance of this revolution to be, if it is to give content to a new social identity which is free of internal contradictions? This is the theme of critical works on Fanon by Bulhan (1985) and especially McCullogh (1985).

Perhaps this is enough to indicate why the work of Fanon is of particular interest in post-colonial society, and why psychologists have used it in attempts to construct a psychology which might be both illuminating and legitimate in Third World contexts. It confronts the facts of social identity and power in a way that few psychologies do. It grows out of a specific historical context, that of colonialism. It links psychological well-being to the act of liberation.

For this reason it is not surprising that psychologists at the University of Cape Town (and almost certainly at other universities in South Africa and elsewhere) found their students responsive to courses which discussed Fanon's contributions. Several South African postgraduates have gone to Boston to study under Bulhan, the noted Fanon scholar, and may well carry this work further.

A crisis in which a discipline must justify its value is an opportunity which may lead to new advances; or it may lead merely to recriminations if there is no foundation on which to build. South African psychologists concerned with liberation have shown greater skill in 'unmasking' and criticizing each other than in building; but their efforts make one thing clear: the development of knowledge is not isolated from other social processes. Those who practise a profession must continually bear in mind the demands made by their different publics.

Institutional power structures

Scientific work occurs within institutional power structures of one sort or another. Universities make or do not make appointments; journals publish or do not publish articles; funding agencies allocate or do not allocate funds. Within each of these institutions, some individuals have more power than others.

Case studies may be revealing. One of the most complete is the study by Lubek and Apfelbaum (1987) on suppression of the 'Garcia Effect' in the main APA journals. Fortunately, there were other journals in which Garcia could publish his findings, but the case raises questions about the openness of journals to strikingly novel work which challenges the received assumptions of those who control publication.

First, what was the 'Garcia Effect'? Garcia and Koelling (1966) found that rats presented with a saccharin solution or 'bright noisy' water (when they licked a water tube a light flashed and a clicker clicked), followed after a long interval by stomach upset caused by radiation, would learn to avoid the taste but not the light-sound combination. Yet in a complementary experiment, when the saccharin flavour or the 'bright noisy' water were followed by electric shock, the rats learnt to avoid the 'bright noisy' water but not the flavour. The consequences of this experiment, if confirmed, were difficult to assimilate to established learning theory.

> Thus, the occurrence of learning appeared to depend not upon what cues were used – that would have been understandable – or what consequences were used – that would have been understandable – but upon the specific relationship between cues and consequences. This was incomprehensible (Bolles, 1975: 249).

A well-established (or at least widely believed) principle of the learning theory challenged by Garcia was *equipotentiality*, or the principle that it should be more or less equally easy to link all discriminable cues to all effective reinforcers. What was being suggested here was that the process of learning depended on highly specialized functional systems.

The contrast between the traditional view of learning and Garcia's view is as follows:

> From the evolutionary view, the rat is a biassed learning machine designed by natural selection to form certain CS–US associations rapidly but not others. From a traditional learning viewpoint, the rat was an unbiassed learner able to make any association in accordance with the general principles of contiguity, effect, and similarity (Garcia, cited in Lubek and Apfelbaum, 1987: 68).

Not only did the 'Garcia Effect' undermine the principle of equipotentiality, it also undermined the principle that reinforcement had to follow response immediately and frequently in order to establish a link. In Garcia's experiments rats had learnt to avoid flavours which were followed an hour or more later by radiation sickness. From an evolutionary perspective, this makes perfect sense. Animals would not have survived if they had not learnt the most important things about the environment with great speed, while ignoring other relations. The S–R paradigm (like modern cognitive psychology) is biologically empty and therefore not informative about the behaviour of real organisms. The work of ethologists had already shown the value of linking learning to biology, but it took a long time for this to penetrate the American learning theory establishment. The important new principles are: (a) study the functional systems or modules of the nervous system; and (b) adopt an evolutionary approach to these systems.

The story of Garcia's exclusion from the major APA journals, dominated as they were by persons trained in traditional animal learning theory, may be summarized as follows: In the early part of his career, up to 1965, Garcia was able to place his articles in the mainstream APA journals. After this, they were consistently rejected and had to be published elsewhere. Even when he received the APA Distinguished Scientific Contribution Award, the published version of his address ('only the *second* to appear in an APA journal authored or co-authored by Garcia during the previous eighteen years' (1987: 60)) was edited to remove passages satirizing learning theory. In this period of exclusion he had made a significant impact on American science, being one of the few psychologists elected to the National Academy of Science. Rejections of his work included several *ad hominem* remarks. One reviewer suggested that a manuscript 'would not have been acceptable even as a term paper in his learning class' (1987: 79). Another wrote: 'Those findings are no more likely than bird shit in a cuckoo clock' (Seligman and Hager, 1972: 84).

Had the APA journals been the only ones in which to publish,

Garcia's work might have been overlooked and forgotten; and given the competition for research grants and research positions, he might not have been able to continue his work. We do not know whether other researchers have yielded to the pressure to conform, but it is likely.

It is easy enough to understand why a group of scientists should attempt to suppress the work of those who undermine their position. There is, perhaps, a strong conviction that the underminers are simply wrong. Then, it is rational (within limits) to protect one's investment in a particular theory. Loss of a theory may lead to loss of prestige and academic power in a field in which one has achieved eminence. It may mean surrendering the field to advocates of the new theory and accepting that one's lifework is based on error.

Sometimes the position may be saved (for the established tradition) by assimilation. This is made difficult when the new work uses terms and concepts which have been explicitly rejected by the established tradition. Lubek and Apfelbaum describe this as an 'epistemological breakaway' (1987: 68). It was this that made Garcia difficult to assimilate after 1965.

In addition to conflicts within disciplines, there are also conflicts between disciplines searching for power. In the first chapter, I referred to Danziger's (1979a, b) comparative studies of American and German psychology, in which he suggested that philosophy had a strong influence on psychology in Germany (due to its established position in the German universities) and a relatively weak influence in the United States of America. This relationship of domination was even stronger in France than in Germany. According to Piaget (1972: 27),

> the implicit permanent principles of the French university authorities are that psychology is part of philosophy, that every philosopher is fit to teach psychology, but that the converse is not true; that there is no question of an agregation in psychology, since the agreges in philosophy know everything.

One result of this was that 'during more than 50 years (up to the appointment of Fraisse, who has at last been given the opportunity), the psychological laboratory of the Sorbonne was a peripheral institution' (1972: 27–8).

In their struggles with each other, persons working within one tradition may attempt to show that they are indispensable for solving the problems of another tradition. This is what Piaget has undertaken in his work on genetic epistemology, or the development of logic and knowledge in childhood. In his book *Insights and Illusions of Philosophy*, from which I have quoted above, Piaget continues his attempt to show that philosophers cannot do without psychological facts in formulating theories of emotion, motivation, or knowledge. (Strategies of competition will be discussed in greater detail in the following chapter.)

Psychodynamics of leadership

If a tradition is to be actively developed, followers must be recruited, trained, and given the means to work. Since some innovators are better at this than others, it will be a factor in the dissemination of their ideas. The formation of knowledge tribes is well-known in psychology and in all the social sciences, where there are Marxians, Freudians, Nietzcheans, Foucaltians, Lacanians and others. Followers regularly recite the founding father's words and are angry with heretics.

Why this intense tribal life in social theory and criticism? Why the unending polemics and cries of misinterpretation? Perhaps one can suggest a rule. The smaller the probability of deciding an issue, the greater the need for a founding father to whose text an appeal can be made.

Donald Campbell examines a case in psychology – the case of the missing tribe. What, he asked, happened to Tolman's tribe? When we compare two learning theorists, Tolman and Spence, we observe that Spence's students worked on his theory whereas Tolman's students did not. The puzzle is: 'Why were Tolman's students the least loyal when, of all the learning theories of the 1930s, Tolman's can now be seen to have been clearly the best?' (Campbell, 1979: 187). Tolman was a cognitive learning theorist at a time when-learning theories were synonymous with conditioning. Also, Campbell cites data which show Tolman to have been a 'charismatic' leader and a 'source of intellectual ferment' on the Berkeley campus. He was the most 'personally beloved' of the various theorists compared. In the profession of psychology he was respected and his contributions were acknowledged, since he succeeded Hull as president of the American Psychological Association in 1937 and published in its principal journals.

When Spence and Tolman are systematically compared, we find that Spence was much more strongly convinced of the value of his own position, took himself much more seriously, expected a much stronger commitment to his approach, was more authoritarian, aggressive and strong-willed, was much less willing to accept criticism or to allow students autonomy of choice in research problems, and was much less open-minded or humorous.

Tolman's style, on the other hand, was humorous and self-deprecatory.

In Campbell's words, 'he welcomed his students as equal-status fellow explorers. . . . Had it been preceded by the careful reading and examination of *Purposive Behavior*, it might have worked. But it was not, and was instead very poor pedagogy' (1979: 190). The effect was that Tolman failed to convince his students to devote their research to his theory.

Concluding remarks

Knowledge tribes may form more readily under some conditions than under others. Campbell compares two rituals for testing beliefs. The first kind of ritual is one in which the ability of the participants to affect the outcome is reduced as far as possible, whereas the second kind of ritual depends largely on insight and interpretation. The more important interpretation becomes, the more prevalent will be tribal life constructed on the text of some oracle and set of disciples.

Consider the first kind of ritual, of which the scientific experiment is the model. By careful design the experiment is intended to remove the results 'out of the control of one's own hopes and wishes' (Campbell, 1979: 198). This is the ambition of the objective experimenter; it is a procedure which distinguishes the empirical approach to knowledge. Yet its roots go deep into our intellectual history. Apparently caribou hunters would place a shoulder blade of the caribou in the fire and read the cracks according to strict rules in order to decide on the direction of the hunt. The rules were intended to eliminate interpretation as far as possible.

An even better example of the objective procedure in a non-scientific tradition is that in which the Azande consult the poison oracle. The original description is by Evans Pritchard, but I am following Jahoda's (1982) account. When a prince commanded that the oracle be consulted, the result had the force of law, yet the manner of consultation apparently prevented interference by those who conducted the consultation. The poison, which was brought all the way from what was then the Belgian Congo, was carefully tested. Jahoda states that 'it is possible to show that in certain respects the Azande thought about their oracles in much the same way as psychologists think about tests and questionnaires' (1982: 178). First, the poison was tested to see whether it could discriminate, by being administered to a number of fowls. If it killed them all it was said to be 'foolish'; if it killed none, it was said to be 'weak'. The ideal poison would kill only some of the fowls. Jahoda compares this to the psychologist asking: Is this test discriminating? Second, questions were put to the oracle in pairs to see whether a consistent answer was given. Thus, if the death of a fowl indicated that the accused had committed adultery, a second question might be put in such a way that the survival of a fowl indicated guilt. In test jargon, this is the criterion of reliability. Third, impossible events are presented to the oracle to test for false responses. Thus: 'If I shall go up to the sky and spear the moon, or bring back the sun, poison oracle kill the fowl' (1982: 179). If the oracle makes false responses, it also reveals that sorcery is being employed to interfere with the oracle. In other words, the test is biased.

One can read these precautions in consulting the oracle as an attempt to get at the truth, uninfluenced by the hopes and fears of the participants. The result is an empirical test, very similar to the tests employed by psychologists attempting to obtain the truth from subjects who may mislead them. As in all experiments, every precaution is of no avail if the experimenter is not scrupulously honest.

Then there is the second kind of ritual, which depends upon insight and interpretation, possibly by inspired persons. Shamans and priests are required to read the secret messages of sacred texts, auspices, sacrifices and other portents. Mystery is at the centre of such rites.

To the extent that knowledge is tested in the first way, personalities play a diminished part in convincing followers of the truth of a proposition. To the extent that knowledge is tested in the second way, by interpreting and reinterpreting texts, the personality of the founder will remain important. Rites of the first kind are intended to reduce both mystery and authority. Rites of the second kind increase them. As we have seen from the cases of Garcia and of Tolman and Spence, personal interest and authority can never be dismissed entirely, but rites of the first kind reduce their importance. There are no surviving tribes of Spence, Tolman or Garcia. Their writings are disappointingly barren of mystery and authority. On the other hand, the tribes of Jung and Freud, or Marx and Foucault, are likely to be with us for many a year. Rich in mystery, authority and inspiration, they are seers and priests for modern times.

8 | Problem-solving and strategies of competition

This chapter continues the checklist of selectors which influence the evolution of knowledge. If the matter seems to sprawl a little, it is because the problem is ungainly; and regretfully the sprawl will continue into the next chapter, which apparently concerns 'values'. Yet values are what we call upon most in attempting to promote theories we favour and demote theories we oppose. However, the discussion will get entirely out of order if I anticipate what is to happen in the next chapter before stating what is to happen in this.

What we shall see, in looking at strategies of competition, is that there is little truth in the notion that scientists in different traditions are not interested in each other's work. They are very wary of each other, and pretending to be 'not interested' is one of the strategies of a game which is played with considerable robustness. Perhaps Garcia was treated with exceptional roughness, but every psychologist will have received rejection slips in which he is told that he is 'naive' or 'ill-informed' or whatever happens to come most easily to the pen of the anonymous reviewer. As a rule, these are casual and unsystematic blows. It is only when one speaks the language of the enemy, as Garcia did in his 'epistemological breakaway' (discussed in the previous chapter) that the blows become systematic. By thinking of the rat as a 'biassed learner' (with an evolutionary history), and by borrowing cognitive terms such as 'hypothesis', he showed that he had joined the enemy against behaviourism.

Many strategies have been mentioned already. Here I shall collect some of them and give them labels.

Isolation

The first strategy is to ignore the opposition, as one might if one were living in a comfortable paradigm. In the early stages of a theory, isolation from attack and from an unbearable weight of contradictory evidence and argument may be necessary (Holland, 1977); at a later stage theorists may cite only those within the tradition because they believe that they are an elite, or are the only ones with insight (Lemaine et al., 1976). Psychoanalysts cite each other, radical behaviourists cite other radical behaviourists; personal construct psychologists tend to cite personal construct psychologists (Neimeyer, 1985). Nothing could be more natural, since each is concerned with peculiar problems which are best debated with those in the same tradition. This is 'paradigm' behaviour as we expect it; yet it is only one of the strategies open to workers in a tradition. One must always be careful that workers in a rival tradition have not solved the kind of problem one has claimed for oneself in such a definitive way that there is nothing left to do.

Misrepresentation

A common strategy is to misrepresent the opposition and then deal very roughly with that misrepresentation. George Kelly, to give an example, created a highly distinctive and imaginative theory – personal construct psychology – which he made even more distinctive by contrasting it with a caricature of psychoanalysis as the view that you are the victim of your own infancy. He rejected 'hydraulic' and push–pull theories of motivation which postulated forces such as instincts, motives or drives which impelled persons to move in particular ways. For him, the problem was the channelling or directing of processes by a system of constructs which enabled persons to anticipate events. The process of sharpening the contrast between his theory and other theories was a necessary manoeuvre, particularly when his theory was novel. This process of misrepresentation is not necessarily malicious, since it may result from an imperfect assimilation of an alien position to one which is better understood. There have been attempts to assimilate personal construct psychology to both the existential position and the cognitive position (Bruner, 1956).

Sometimes the caricature is quite crude. I have already referred to Fanon's work on colonial identity as a model for a liberation psychology. Much of the misrepresentation that accompanies this process can be seen to serve the function of separation, or identifying *against* the oppressive burden of European domination (Devereux, 1967). In a recent contribution to a conference on *Psychology and Apartheid*, Bulhan (1989) drew a telling caricature of Eurocentric psychology and proceeded to deal it some savage blows, before proceeding to construct an Afrocentric psychology. What is Eurocentric psychology, according to Bulhan? Its major characteristic is that it is solipsistic. It starts from the assumption that 'the "self" – which really translates into "the European self" – is the source of "truth" about humanity' (1989: 2–3). Europe is the centre of the world (even the world is divided into 'first', 'second' and 'third' worlds). This is the kind of narcissistic vision which, in an individual patient, would lead to hospitalization; instead, it has been translated into domination at all levels: cultural, economic, military. Even in 'multi-racial' groups the Europeans see themselves as 'the embodiment of good and beauty' and occupy the first place and largest space – 'extending elbows, arms and legs' (1989: 4). The task of reconstruction in psychology is to free ourselves from solipsism, both in psychological theory and in everyday behaviour. How is this to be done? It can only be achieved if we construct non-Eurocentric psychology 'in Black America, Latin America, Asia, and even in the so-called "centers" of the world' (1989: 4). One such attempt would be an Afrocentric psychology. The great danger in such a construction is to replace one form of solipsism with another; to attempt to replace one kind of domination with another kind. Instead, we should look for universal principles. We should, in Piagetian language, decentre. Bulhan maintains that African folk psychology is *'systematic* and *relational'* in that explanations of illness are 'molar rather than analytic and relational rather than intrapsychic' (1989: 5). These should be the foundations of an Afrocentric psychology. Though he does not elaborate, he invites his South African audience to construct such a psychology in order to liberate people from 'internalized and institutionalized oppression' (1989: 5). He rejects the view that such a psychology can be imported. Furthermore, such a psychology should be used not merely to interpret reality but to change it.

Like all good caricatures, this one resembles the truth in wicked ways. We can recognize the bloated assumption of primacy in much European psychological thought. This becomes most obvious in cross-cultural psychology and anthropology, in which 'primitives' and 'primitive' mentality are compared unfavourably to 'modern' persons and 'civilized' mentality on almost every instrument of mental measurement. Yet the early arrogance has given way to cultural relativism (even if this is often the sheep's clothing in which the Eurocentric wolf prowls, looking for confirmation of narrowly conceived theories). To be more particular, approaches such as radical behaviourism do not start from the individual but from contingencies of reinforcement, or relations and systems. Marxist theory is also not individualist. The fundamental axiom of a Marxist psychology is the sixth thesis of Feuerbach, which states: 'The human ... is no abstraction inherent in each individual. In its reality it is the ensemble of social relations' (Marx, 1975: 427). This is what Sève (1974: 529) calls the 'excentration of the human essence', or the 'Copernican revolution' in psychology. He contrasts this with 'human relations' theories which are ahistorical and presuppose *human being* prior to social relations. This is a 'fetishism of the individual' and it corresponds to commodity fetishism, attributing to individuals or objects powers which we should attribute to social relations. 'Consciousness is from the very beginning a social product' (Marx, cited in Sève, 1975: 72).

On the basis of this systemic and relational approach, Soviet psychologists such as Vygotsky and Luria developed a Marxist approach to developmental and cognitive psychology. Thus, Luria's guiding hypothesis in his study of the cultural and social foundations of cognitive psychology was that

> higher cognitive activities remain socio-historical in nature, and that the structure of mental activity – not just the specific content but also the general forms basic to all cognitive processes – change in the course of historical development (Luria, 1976: 8).

These two examples, that of radical behaviourism and Marxist psychology, illustrate both the complexity of 'Eurocentric' or 'Western' psychology (it's difficult to know where it begins and ends, or which theories should be included or excluded) and its diversity. (It is often forgotten that Marx was a nineteenth-century German philosopher, as 'Western' or 'European' as they come (Kolakowski, 1978).) Does Bulhan's paper have a point, then? Certainly, many theories have been used to further imperialism or domination. We need only think of the use of measures of intelligence to demonstrate the inferiority of 'natives' in almost every part of the globe or the 'imbecility' of immigrants to the USA (Sarason and Doris, 1969). Or of work on ethno-psychiatry demonstrating that the Algerian is 'violent by heredity' (Porot), and that the black African shows 'neurological immaturity' (Gallois), as well as 'lack of aptitude for synthesis ... caused by the underemployment of the brain's frontal lobes' (Carothers) (cited in McCullogh, 1985: 18–21). Yet, equally, the concepts which Fanon used were drawn from dynamic psychology (Adler, Freud), existentialism and Marxism. We need intellectual tools with which to work. What is often wrong is the attitude and the purpose of the persons who use these tools.

The point of Bulhan's paper is that it ridicules a psychology of self-aggrandizement, a psychology of excessive individualism and self-actualization. In this, he is not alone, but he places it in the context of a movement to establish a new pole, a new vantage point from which to understand and criticize. This is Afrocentric psychology. If the dialectic ends here, then we shall merely have moved from one centre to another. What Bulhan hopes to achieve is decentration, which is a mobile system of reasoning in which we understand how individuality and individual processes are relative to collectivity and collective process. The person achieves, by decentration, the capacity to take up a variety of perspectives and to relate these to each other (as Piaget tells us). He is like the child who walks round a mountain or a building and relates the different perspectives to each other, stands in one place and knows what the scenery would look like from another place.

Misrepresentation is, therefore, a start to the process of establishing and defending a new perspective. We need first to make people unhappy with their present position if we wish to persuade them to move. Or, if they are attacking us, we demolish the base from which they attack. But this can only be the start. Finally, as with the child who knows what the building looks like from a point at which he is not standing, or that balancing a lever requires adjusting both distance from the fulcrum *and/or* weight, we need theories which are neither Eurocentric nor Afrocentric. (Perhaps a sign of liberal delusion?) Till then, misrepresentation and caricature will be part of the process by which we are driven to search for new theory and protect it.

Raising the bid

Yet another strategy of competition is raising the bid, or redefining the aim of an investigation in such a way as to discredit the achievements of rivals. This goes to the very heart of science, since it demands more and more of investigation. One is reminded of Douglas Adams (in *The Hitchhikers Guide to the Galaxy*): As soon as we have understood the universe it will disappear and be replaced by something infinitely more complicated. Scientists are engaged in an activity of the same kind. As soon as anyone understands the universe, or a piece of it, the rest attempt to replace it with a puzzle which is more difficult. We have already seen an example of this in the way in which Schally raised the standard by declaring that the goal of his group was to determine the structure of the substance TRF, rather than merely to isolate it and determine its physiological activity.

In psychology, a brilliant and dramatic example of this was Chomsky's (1967; original 1959) review of Skinner's *Verbal Behavior*. It swept aside general accounts of complex behaviour and replaced it with a new goal: Determine the exact system of rules which the child has to learn to become linguistically competent. Broad categories such as tact and mand are not sufficient, nor are broad categorizations of feedback as reinforcement of explanatory value for the new psychology of language. It is not so much that a certain kind of explanation (as in terms of contingencies of reinforcement) was never of any value at all (Chomsky speaks favourably of Skinner's laboratory work on the role of intermittent reinforcements in shaping the behaviour of animals), as that the goalposts have been shifted and some of the players are still attempting to score in the old goal area. Chomsky examines Skinner's use of terms such as 'stimulus', 'control', 'response' and 'strength' and comes to the conclusion that they are merely 'paraphrases for the popular vocabulary commonly used to describe behaviour' (1967: 152). One example may illustrate the way in which he criticizes Skinner's functional analysis. He considers the term 'mand'. First, there is Skinner's definition of a mand as 'a verbal operant in which the response is reinforced by a characteristic consequence and is therefore under the functional control of relevant conditions of deprivation or aversive stimulation' (cited in Chomsky, 1967: 160). Chomsky then looks at some examples:

> In the case of the mand *Pass the Salt*, the word 'deprivation' is not out of place, though it appears to be of little use for functional analysis. Suppose, however, that the speaker says *Give me the book*, *Take me for a ride*, or *Let me fix it*. What kinds of deprivation can be associated with these mands? How do we determine or measure the relevant deprivation? I think we must conclude in this case, as before, either that the notion 'deprivation' is relevant at most to a minute fragment of verbal behaviour, or else that the statement 'X is under Y-deprivation' is just an odd paraphrase for 'X wants Y', bearing a misleading and unjustifiable connotation of objectivity (1967: 161).

The immediate goal of the psycholinguist must be to find ways of characterizing language as it occurs in human development and performance, perhaps borrowing from linguists who see their task as constructing a grammar which determines the structure of sentences. The long-term goal of the psycholinguist must be to understand the way in which children are biologically prepared to discover the structure of language and to use it. How do they generate novel sentences? How do they understand novel sentences? How do they acquire, within a short time, practical mastery of a system which linguists have struggled to understand for so many centuries?

Chomsky has maintained in many places that no general theory of learning is capable of explaining the acquisition of language. This is a view which we find increasingly persuasive. It may be that we have to speak of 'intelligences' and 'learning theories' for the acquisition of different kinds of knowledge. The structure of mind may be modular rather than unitary (Gardner, 1983, 1985).

Chomsky has used his tactic of raising the bid to brilliant effect in his debates with both learning theorists and Piagetians. Frequently, he defines the problem to be solved in such a way that the approaches of his rivals are shown to be inadequate. He then shows the need for a new kind of approach to the problem. Here is a typical performance, drawn from his debate with Piaget at Royamont (Piatelli-Palmerini, 1980).

The question Chomsky asks is: How could a child learn a language with hidden rules unless there were a strong disposition to form a grammatical theory of the correct kind? Take these examples:

1. The man is here → Is the man here?
2. The man will leave → Will the man leave?

How is the interrogative formed? One hypothesis (H_1) might be: Select the first instance of is, will, etc., and transpose it to the beginning of the sentence. A second hypothesis (H_2) might be: Select the first instance of is, will, etc., after the first noun phrase.

We see that H_2 is correct and H_1 is wrong as soon as we proceed to more complex sentences. Applying H_1 in the following pairs we get

3. The man who is here is tall → Is the man who here is tall?
4. The man who is tall will leave → Is the man who tall will leave?

Applying H_2 we get

5. The man who is here is tall → Is the man who is here tall?
6. The man who is tall will leave → Will the man who is tall leave?

It appears from data of this kind that we all learn to recognize grammatical structures such as *noun phrase* without any explicit grammatical instruction. How is this possible? Chomsky suggests that the structure-dependence of rules is a property of the initial state of the language learner 'The child need not consider H_1: It is ruled out by properties of his initial mental state' (1980: 40). Fodor and Chomsky, in their debate with Piaget, refer to the 'tautology' (or 'self-evident truth') that the acquisition of knowledge presupposes concepts in the mind which precede observation.

This, then, is the general form of the argument that Chomsky uses. The objections to this kind of argument are:

1. If something as specific as H_2 were part of the hereditary capacity of the child, we might expect to find specific genetic defects relating to rules of language. Perhaps we have not found them because we have not looked hard enough.
2. The rule might not be an initial state property but rather a discovery based on other initial state properties. Or, as Papert (1980: 95) puts it, 'everything has a developmental history through which it emerges from other, very different things' and these are *not* 'any discrete part of the adult mind' in miniature.
3. In general, 'how else?' arguments are weak and are no substitute for a direct demonstration of how a postulated generative structure might work.

In spite of these objections, the linguists had decisively increased the difficulty of the problem to be solved and knocked most of the behaviourists out of the field. One of the counter-strategies was an attempt to teach sign-language to chimpanzees (Gardner and Gardner, 1975), as well as attempts to teach a variety of simplified 'languages' (Premack, 1971), especially for communicating with computers (Rumbaugh, 1977). There are many reasons for this interest, but one is obviously the wish to create an experimental model to show that conditioning principles are adequate to teaching a language. If this could be shown, then no special learning device (LAD or LAS) is required to learn a language and general principles of learning will do.

The results have been very largely negative (Seidenberg and Petitto, 1979; Terrace, 1979). Though chimpanzees (and other apes) can symbolize, can produce simple sequences of signs after elaborate training, and can understand simple sequences, there is increasing doubt as to whether they combine more than two morphemes or learn any rules at all in sign language. Certainly, they can be trained to observe a strict sequence of signs under computer control, but the structure of the 'language' is very simple and there is no indication of duality, or the existence of both the phoneme and the morpheme levels of language structure. These complex matters are brilliantly discussed by Roger Brown (1986); what concerns us here is that attempts to teach sign language to apes merely confirm the view that we need to investigate *special learning structures* for species-specific forms of learning.

The intervention of Chomsky was *one* of the factors in the move to complex computer models of cognitive processes and to ethology. More generally, we can see that an upward redefinition of standards is an important manoeuvre both in the competition of science and in the evolution of scientific knowledge.

Lessons in methodology

It is often necessary to teach psychologists in rival traditions how to do their work. Learning theorists may be dismayed by the lack of rigour among ethologists (as they were in the 1950s) and urge them to return from the field to the laboratory and from the herring gull to the rat; or they may challenge the sloppy habits, both conceptual and empirical, of psychoanalysts. The methodologist of the tradition is like the party ideologue, deciding on permissible terms, concepts and data. Are mentalistic explanations to be allowed? Is it possible to include intra-organismic constructs, or hypotheses about mental machinery? Is it possible to run experiments with only one subject? Do numerical data have a higher status than qualitative data? Some methodological rules are of a very high order of abstraction, and are all the more frightening for that. Others are more like rules of procedure, which tell one how to avoid contaminating the evidence with one's own hopes and wishes. These are the rules of experimental design, and they are a very useful body of rules, listing such objections to a set of observations as that there are no tests for reliability, that sampling is biased, or that the person who made the observation knew what the observation was intended to confirm or refute. These rules of evidence are both important and often neglected. Yet it may be difficult to know how many observations to make and what distinctions are relevant to these observations. Is it important, in developing Piagetian theory, to conduct cross-cultural studies? It would appear to be important (Dasen and Heron, 1980), but even then it is not clear exactly which cultural differences are crucial, or how they are crucial to theory. In fact, there is a continual interplay between theory and observation in deciding both what theory should account for and what further observations need to be made.

Let us return to the kinds of abstract methodological rules that are brought to bear in criticizing a tradition, and use as our example the rules used in criticizing psychoanalysis. This set of rules, well represented in the writings of Eysenck and Wilson (1973), Farrell (1981), Kline (1977), and Popper (1963), contains the following:

- Psychoanalytic theory is too vague to be falsifiable and is therefore not a scientific theory.
- Most of the evidence for psychoanalysis comes from the psycho-analytic method, which is open to distortion and selective reporting. Other methodological problems are poor sampling and a failure to consider alternative explanations.
- Since psychoanalytic theory is not sufficiently determinate to enable

us to make predictions, interpretation is *post hoc*. In addition, contradictory positions are often simultaneously held. Thus, repressed homosexuality is supposed to lead to paranoid delusions and yet paranoids are said to engage in a high rate of homosexual activity.
- The theory speaks only to converts, since only those initiated into the theory and practice of psychoanalysis can make psychoanalytic observations.

These are cogent points, though it may be observed that theories (if they are interesting enough and solve good problems) may be preserved even though not immediately falsifiable. Also, most theories contain false deductions (Lakatos and Musgrave, 1970).

Even weak theories may survive simply because there is no better alternative. Psychoanalytic theory, so the defence might go, is the best we have and it will survive until we have something better. Furthermore, even if specific propositions are abandoned, the psychoanalytic tradition of unmasking and studying the unconscious has irrevocably changed our approach to the meaning of human action. We should also note that the proposition that observers should be trained to make psychoanalytic observation is by no means absurd. Many observations can only be made by trained observers, but this does not necessarily mean that they do not improve on their observations, question their observations, or become dissatisfied with their observations. Nor does it mean that all are equally good observers.

It has often been observed that Mendel was extremely fortunate to obtain the results he obtained in his genetic experiment with peas; it has even been suggested that he cheated or was cheated by a research assistant; since the probability of getting results as close to the predicted values as Mendel did was calculated by Fisher to be less than one in 30 000. When professionals are asked to perform a similar feat, they obtain results that differ significantly from each other. However, when undergraduates sort only the clear cases and place the others in an intermediate category, they obtain good Mendelian results, provided that they are asked to sort the intermediate kernels so as to achieve the closest possible approximation to the expected Mendelian ratio (Root-Bernstein, 1983). We need to learn to observe and to carry out observation, even in relatively simple cases. The problem arises out of the imperfect match of fuzzy biological and psychological data to the ideal categories of theory. And it is often not possible to make data so robust that naive observers will not destroy them.

A more convincing defence of psychoanalysis might be undertaken by examining it more deeply, asking what kind of science it is, what kinds of claims it makes and how these claims might be evaluated. Naturally, the line taken here is only one possible line and is not intended to be the authoritative defence of psychoanalysis! I am chiefly concerned with methodological criticisms and defences.

The truth-claims of psychoanalysis, as Ricoeur (1977) and Sherwood (1969) say, are:

1. Psychoanalysis increases insight by reducing distortion in self-knowledge.
2. Similarly, it increases insight in interpersonal relations.
3. Through psychoanalysis we recover our fantasies as imaginative truths. Fantasies are distorted pictures of lost objects; imagination works on these when they have become symbolic objects. A prototypical demonstration is the psychoanalyst working with the symbols of theory.
4. Psychoanalysis can enable us to give a coherent account of an entire case history, integrated as a narrative. This is achieved by using generalizations which could be present in ordinary explanations – motives such as love, hate, jealousy which are classes of causes; but also by generalizations which were invented by psychoanalysis – such as oral, anal and genital stages, and the patient's peculiar fantasies and relations to objects. This is what Sherwood (1969) calls the *narrative commitment* of psychoanalysis.
5. The *explanatory commitment* of psychoanalysis (Sherwood, 1969) refers to lawlike statements about the vicissitudes of instinct, the formation of the structures such as the super-ego, the processes of distortion, the wish-fulfilment in every dream.

The explanation of any actual event is a long narrative about circumstances, using the generalizations of psychoanalysis. It does not fit into the hypothetico-deductive format. In this, it is like history, which also has its generalizations, is explanatory, and attempts to discover the origins of events in circumstances, but cannot be predictive. We cannot, from a few assumptions and laws, *predict* what will happen, though there have been a few historical theories, of which Marxism is one, which attempt to proceed from explanation to prediction, yet without any success.

When we examine explanations of the narrative type, we can never ask, 'Did it happen exactly this way?' We have always to compare one narrative against another. There is no way of going beyond narrative, of stripping narrative down to the bone of reality and using this as the key in all our judgements of truth (Munz, 1977). We encounter the same problems in psychoanalysis. We have a number of possible narratives about the person as he unfolds his life story. There is no way in which to discover which one is the whole truth (though we may sometimes eliminate a number as false). In this way, narratives may be as falsifiable (in some details) as theories in the natural sciences. But, because of the complexity of the narrative account, because of the many options of tone and incident one can only rarely falsify a narrative as a whole.

Is there any way, then, to evaluate the truth claims of psychoanalysis?

One of the ways in which we evaluate explanatory theories which are not predictive is to examine the extent to which they are generative: are there systems of rules which can be used to produce the events under consideration and show their inner structure, even if these rules do not tell us when such events may occur? A grammatical theory, if adequate, will not only generate well-formed sentences but will indicate their structure. In psychoanalytic theory, we may find the rudiments of such a theory in Freud's analysis of a case of paranoia (Freud, 1948) – the case of Schreber. Freud starts with a 'core proposition' which is transformed into a paranoid structure which contradicts the primal proposition. The proposition is: 'I (a man) love him (a man)'. The first transformation is *defence*, turning the proposition into its opposite. It then becomes 'I hate him'. The second transformation is *projection*, which means that perceptions and feelings come from outside. Then, 'I hate him' becomes 'He hates me'.

There are yet other transformations of the core proposition which correspond to erotomania, jealousy and megalomania, all of which are fully discussed in Freud's analysis of Schreber's case. The function of such rules of transformation of the core proposition is to exhibit the relationship between apparently different surface structures, as in transformational generative grammars; and as in the case of grammar, such theories leave many questions unanswered, such as: why should these transformations occur? A grammatical theory cannot tell us why people speak; nor can a 'metagrammatical' theory of the neurotic transformations of unacceptable propositions tell us why people transform them in this way (Forrester, 1980).

Coherence of the generative type is retrospective. We must be given the structure to be examined; we can then give a general and principled account of the way in which it is produced by rule. Similarly, in psychoanalysis, we must be given the dream, the symptom, the myth; we can then attempt to trace the way in which it is formed according to general principles and following a standard method of investigation (free association, insight).

Even the most ingenious transformations must make some contact with observation, though. Was Paul Schreber a repressed homosexual?

The curious fact is that Freud used the case merely as an illustration of a theory already formed. Beyond his reading of Schreber's memoir, he knew nothing about Schreber's life. Recent biographical investigation adds nothing to the plausibility of Freud's account. Since the theory is concerned almost exclusively with transformations supposed to have taken place inside Paul Schreber's head, Israëls (1988) concludes that new biographical material has nothing to offer that might support or undermine the theory. Hence we arrive at the pessimistic conclusion that it is not possible to falsify Freud's account of Schreber's paranoia.

There is another test of psychoanalysis (as of every theory). Does it make a large range of isolated facts coherent in some interesting way? If the domain of facts is small, the theory may not excite much interest. Psychoanalysis attempts to integrate material from dreams, myths, neuroses, the social psychology of prejudice, the functioning of groups. It may be mistaken, but it is not trivial.

What do we mean by integrating events in an 'interesting' way? If I were to advance the theory that between 20 October and 21 October in any given year, most people spoke at least ten words, the theory would not excite much interest, one way or another, as a theory. A theory must reveal *news*. It must surprise us. Not only should it surprise us, it should systematically surprise us by the kind of things it makes possible. Psychoanalysis surprises us, with its interpretations of what happens. It transforms observations into surprising facts, by which we mean that it gives them new meanings in a systematic way for which we are not prepared by common sense.

In addition to news of this systematic kind and the ability to transform the meaning of events, a theory should discover new ways of transforming the world. We build theories, which are new objects; and in these theories, there are new facts. Transference, counter-transference and resistance are facts which are constituted by theory. We build conceptual machines to engage reality in a new way and to build and uncover new events. A theory is judged by its capacity to build conceptual machines which will do this. Psychoanalysis is, by this criterion, powerful. It enables us to engage the world in unexpected and novel ways to build new theoretical objects.

Another defence of psychoanalysis is to accept the methodological strictures on the 'rules of evidence' and to attempt to meet these standards. One of the most important of these attempts is Bowlby's (1985) study of attachment and separation in infancy. He is impatient with those who are content with psychoanalysis as an interpretative or hermeneutic science, and strongly supports Freud's ambition to found a causal science. The central characteristic of psychoanalysis is that it attempts a developmental account of personality. In doing so, it has confronted the transformation of attachment and loss, and the formation of sub-systems of personality, often in conflict. Most of these *processes*, though not their symbols, are unconscious. We have to discover the significance of the symbols by tracing the unconscious processes. At the level of theory, Freud's biological concepts need revision; and to do this Bowlby borrows from ethology and modern cybernetic theory. Freud relied on a nineteenth century concept of energy, but it is quite clear that activity does not stop only when energy is exhausted. An infant may stop crying when its mother enters the room and start again when the mother leaves. What we see here is not exhaustion, or depletion of energy, but a system of information and control. Bowlby argues that Freud was aware of the need to link his theory to biology and would have welcomed such revision.

At the level of rules of evidence, Bowlby agrees that theories should be falsifiable and attempts to state his hypothesis so that they are. He also agrees that a prospective or predictive approach is necessary, focusing on the pathogen and its sequelae (hence his studies of separation); and from this it follows that he stresses direct observation rather than retrospective reconstruction.

Of course, it is not clear what shape psychoanalysis will take as it is modified in this way, but it does show two major responses in methodological warfare. The first is rebuttal; the second is accommodation, assimilation and development. Both are significant, but for the growth of knowledge the latter response is most fruitful. The isolation of a tradition from external criticism will eventually lead to sterility.

Showing how: 1. Dora's case

A powerful strategy is to solve other people's problems for them. This is generally preceded by a heavy barrage of criticism to soften their defences, but the barrage is usually ineffectual. Let us, for the moment, stay with attacks on psychoanalysis. The attack is on Freud's analysis of the case of Dora – an analysis which he regarded as one of his supreme achievements – and the reasoning is that, if Freud can be shown up in his moment of triumph, then the rest of his work will be dismissed all the more easily. Even better, if he can be shown how the case *should* have been understood, then the way is clear to showing how the rest of the puzzles of psychoanalysis should be understood.

Let us consider the Marxist critique of Freud's analysis of Dora (Lichtman, 1982). Briefly, Dora was a young girl brought to Freud by her

154 RHETORIC AND CHANGE IN RESEARCH TRADITIONS

father, apparently because of her fits of nervous coughing and occasional loss of voice. It turns out that she has been propositioned since the age of 14 by Herr K, a friend of her father's, but that her father does not believe her, or professes not to. He is having an affair with Frau K, Herr K's wife, but he would like Freud to talk Dora out of her belief that there is something more than a friendship between them. Dora believes that she has been handed over to Herr K as the price of his tolerating the relations between her father and his wife.

Freud explains Dora's symptoms in terms of distorted sexuality. The crucial incident is when she is kissed passionately on the mouth by Herr K (he had arranged to meet her alone in his office). Instead of feeling pleasurable excitement, she is violently disgusted and rushes off. Freud observes then that this is 'without question' hysterical. Dora is in love with her father (1948: 69). All her behaviour is to be understood in terms of her wish to get him back. Her cough is a fantasy of committing fellatio with her father, 'putting herself in Frau K's place'.

> Her behaviour obviously went far beyond what would have been appropriate to filial concern. She felt and acted more like a jealous wife – in a way which would have been comprehensible to her mother. By her ultimatum to her father ('either her or me'), by the scenes she used to make, by the suicidal intentions she allowed to transpire, – by all this she was clearly putting herself in her mother's place. (1948: 68).

In general then, Freud explains Dora's symptoms in terms of a fixation with repressed memories, and the conversion of ideas into physical symptoms. What is the Marxist alternative?

First, there is the concentration on external social relations in the family – a concentration which would be shared by many systems theorists today, without leading them to Marxism. Lichtman draws our attention (as others have already done) to Dora's betrayal, to her conviction that she was being treated as an object for barter, and to her father's loss of interest in the treatment when he found that Freud was not attempting to talk Dora out of her belief that there was more than a friendship between him and Frau K.

Second, though, we move on to a Marxist characterization of these social relations. Here our attention is drawn to the following.

1. The reduction of sociopolitical roles to psychiatric categories. Dora's mother suffers a 'housewife's psychosis' of withdrawal and purposelessness. Dora is discovering that if she cannot get her way by strength, she can get her way by illness – by hysteria. These categories of illness disguise the relations of domination which

produce them. The father of the family has or had most of the resources of domination in his hands: he had economic and legal power over other members of the household, as well as social recognition of his role as the responsible figure.
2. By attributing her problem to a fixation on her father and on the Ks, and to her masturbation, while ignoring the lies and deceits to which Dora is subjected as the social status quo is preserved (as represented in the respectability of the household), Freud throws in his lot with those who maintain the existing order. In other words, to recognize the 'structure of real exploitation' – the bourgeois family and the respectability which limits its operations – would involve one in a social critique and not merely in an episode of individual psychotherapy.
3. 'Freud assumes that the prevailing power structure is irrelevant, or that it is justified, or that Dora can transform it by rational, "non-neurotic" means. All three possibilities are mistaken and ideological' (Lichtman, 1982: 156).
4. The structure of the family – atomized, nuclear, competitive, patriarchal (certainly, in the nineteenth century), and yet apparently based on voluntary and rational acceptance of the existing order, mediates between capitalist structure and the growing individual.

This discussion is intended to show the way in which explanations gain in depth as we proceed from the intrapsychic to the social, specifically the sociopolitical level. As we advance from purely phenomenological toward social explanations of action, we find that we change level of explanation.

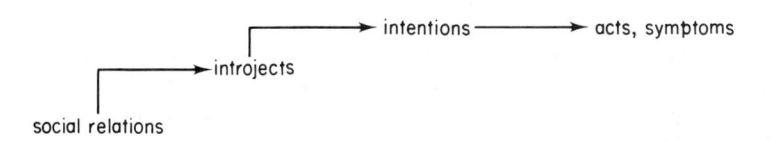

```
                         ┌─────────→ intentions ─────────→ acts, symptoms
              ┌──────────→ introjects
              │
social relations
```

When we question events at the most superficial level, we are content with an intentional account of what people do. However, when we try to explain why they should wish to do what they do, we have to search for deeper generative structures. When we ask why these structures, or introjected representations, have the value and significance which they do have, we are compelled to examine the relation of power and control between them. Why is the family patriarchal? Why is pleasure deferred for so long? Why is it so difficult to leave home and become independent? What determines the ideas that are disseminated and consumed?

A comment on the above might enrich our understanding of the relations between social relations and introjects. Social relations are indeed complex, but one aspect of them is that they are composed of 'social representations' (Farr and Moscovici, 1984), or 'discourses' (e.g. Potter and Wetherell, 1987). We may treat the two concepts as largely synonymous. Both are emotionally charged constructions of knowledge and experience. Both are produced in social groups, as part of the collective human effort to allocate or achieve power, behave correctly and decently, and create meaning. Both persist over time, are often self-contradictory, and contain different 'voices'. There are dominant and subordinate representations and discourses, but they may change places at different times and in different places. Psychoanalysis, for example, was an attempt to change a subordinate discourse (about sexual desire, dreams and hidden impulses) into a dominant discourse, within a particular arena.

What is it that we internalize? It is not helpful to say that we internalize social relations – the concept is too broad – but it makes great sense to say that we assimilate a social representation (emotionally charged as it is) or discourse; and assimilation must always be to our own cognitive structures, since nothing can be internalized 'raw'. The result may be a radical simplification, especially in early childhood, as well as a further emotional charge from the child's own phantasies. These introjects of social representations or discourses (transformed by our capacity to construe) will construct the attitudes, voices and positions that we take up in social relations.

The way forward is to examine development in a wide variety of social structures, while attempting to formulate hypotheses more precisely. A review of cross-cultural studies of psychoanalytic hypothesis is to be found in Kline (1977), as well as in many texts on psychological anthropology (e.g. Bock, 1980; Bourguignon, 1979; Spindler, 1978).

Another attempt at *showing how* is the existentialist critique of Freud's analysis of Dora. This follows the Marxist critique and my comments on the Marxist critique very closely though without specifically invoking social representations. The point is that persons are subject to historically specific disorders, arising out of communications typical of the period, which we may term socioses (van den Berg, 1961). Not only are the sexual hysterias which Freud analysed typical of his time, but we can even detect him collaborating in their production. In Dora's case he makes it clear that he believes her account that these adults, some of whom he knows, had conducted a complicated pattern of deceits and lies. But he accepts *their* attribution of the sexual problem to Dora herself, and sets about convincing her of her guilt with all the manipulative weaponry of psychoanalysis (Maddi, 1974: 99).

The most peculiar feature of the case is that Dora never accepted Freud's interpretation of her symptoms and that she seems to have been cured *after* termination of therapy when she got Frau K to admit the affair with her father and Herr K to admit the attempted seduction. Yet Freud believed that Dora's case was strong evidence for his theory that hysteria was a product of unconscious sexual fantasies! Also, he believed that the best test of his interpretation was that the patient would be cured by accepting it. Yet here the patient resists his interpretation, apparently cures herself, and satisfies Freud that her case is the best possible proof of the sexual origin of hysteria!

Freud himself demonstrates a historical entrapment, a willingness to collaborate with adults in maintaining a disorder so as to confirm his theory.

Showing how: 2. Experimentally induced neuroses and behaviour therapy

I shall omit 'little Albert' (he is always 'little') and proceed straight to the demonstrations of Sears (1944). He takes pity on Freud, as so many have in the last century: 'If Freud had learned his academic prejudices a quarter century later than he did, if Pavlov, Bekhterev, McDougall, and Watson could have influenced him, psychoanalytic theory might have had a very different systematic texture' (1944: 306). He then proposes to 'examine psychoanalytic terms by more conventional scientific logic, and in order to do this they have been translated into behavioral terms' (1944: 306). In the same volume, there are demonstrations of 'experimental behavior disorders in the rat' (by Frank W. Finger), the goat, and the pig (by Liddell). Unfortunately, none of them could be psychoanalysed; does it follow that there were a fair number of disordered animals in the laboratories of America and Russia in the 1930s and 1940s?

Fortunately, behaviourists were at work creating models of behaviour therapy to supplant psychoanalysis. Wolpe and Lazarus (1966) remark that Freud would probably have been a behaviour therapist, given their opportunities and knowledge, and make the dramatic claim that 89.5% of their patients recovered in an uncontrolled study of 210 cases. Since then, claims have tended to be more modest and more specific (Kazdin and Wilson, 1978).

From our point of view, the important characteristic of behaviour modification studies was that they found the centre of the stage occupied by psychoanalysis and mounted a vigorous campaign to show both that psychoanalysis was ineffective and that behaviourist approaches were effective. Since they aimed to occupy the same professional niche as psychoanalysis, the first move was to displace it. It is only recently that therapists have begun to study the possibility that the practice of therapy might benefit from a selection of techniques for different purposes (e.g. Lazarus, 1971).

All of these attempts – Marxist, existentialist and behaviourist – to show how psychoanalysts ought to have done their work, are examples of an im ortant manoeuvre in science. One way to embarrass our rivals is to solve an exemplary problem without explicit reference to them; another is to rub it in by solving their problems better than they could themselves. The effect on the progress of science is emotionally and intellectually invigorating.

Challenge and response

We have seen that raising the bid and finding internal contradictions in rival theories are common methods of weakening them. This is especially so if one's own theory can solve the problems which arise. It sometimes happens, though, that the rivals rise to the challenge and turn a possible defeat into a victory. Yet, once again, we see that theorists are not indifferent to each other, even if they work in different traditions.

In the 1920s, gestalt psychologists presented many apparently insoluble problems to learning theorists, one of the problems being that of *transposition*. In Kohler's experiments, chickens were trained to respond to the darker of two greys. After training, they were presented with a new discrimination task, consisting of the grey to which responses had already been reinforced in the training experiment and a new, darker grey. The chickens responded to the darker grey. In other words, they appeared to have learnt a relationship and not merely a response to a stimulus (Kohler, 1929).

This was one of Kohler's challenges to stimulus-response theory. In 1937 Spence not only met the challenge, but derived the prediction that transposition would only occur within limits.

Spence's solution depends upon two hypothetical processes. The first is the growth of a *gradient of positive stimulus generalization* round the

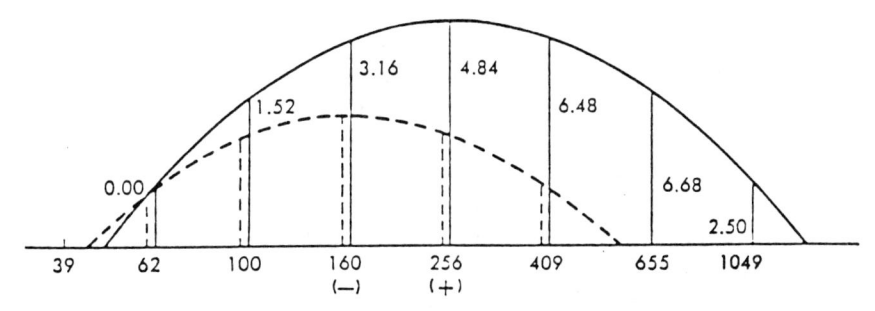

Figure 2 Diagrammatic representation of relations between the hypothetical generalization curves, positive and negative, after training on the stimulus combination 256 (+) and 160 (−). (Adapted from Spence, 1937.)

target stimulus to which responses were reinforced; the second is a *gradient of negative stimulus generalization* round the stimulus to which responses were not reinforced. The probability of response to any new stimulus is the algebraic sum of the generalization curves, positive and negative. This is illustrated in Figure 2. Suppose a training problem in which chimpanzees are reinforced for choosing a square 256 cm^2 and for rejecting a square 160 cm^2. A positive generalization curve, with its maximum strength at 256 cm^2, is produced, and a negative generalization curve, with its maximum strength at 160 cm^2, is produced at the same time. In a transposition problem, the animal will choose whichever stimulus corresponds to the maximum difference between the curves of positive and negative generalization. Thus, in a choice between 256 cm^2 (originally reinforced) and a new stimulus of 409 cm^2, the chimpanzee should choose the new stimulus. In this way, Spence met the gestalt challenge by drawing on concepts of stimulus generalization which were already part of the behaviourists' repertoire.

Even though the sketch was no more than a hypothesis, with no real values for the curves filled in, it preserved the behaviourist position because it was a solution in principle. It also led to a further prediction, that there were transpositions in which the original stimulus would be preferred and the relationship (choose the larger square) would be reversed (e.g. when pairing the original 256 cm^2 with 1049 cm^2). After this, the main task within the tradition appeared to be refinement of theory and finding ways to determine the shape of generalization curves.

What is important, from our point of view, is that the gestalt challenge led to theoretical development in the behaviourist camp. We recognize, yet again, the fact that theorists respond (when they can) to the challenges of those in different traditions as well as in their own.

Conclusion

This concludes the list of strategies in the present chapter, though it is certain that there are many more. The impression we get from looking at these strategies and from the selectors in the previous chapter is that there is an enormous degreee of competition in the development of science, and that this competition is both within and between traditions. A further impression, when we examine the very large number of articles in journals, most of which are barely read (Garfield, 1972), is that there is a prolific seeding of ideas for selection. This enormous seeding of papers provides the variants from which selection can occur. It is as wasteful as all seeding in nature, and as essential. Evolution requires a selection of minute and large variants, and it is often impossible to know in advance which will survive.

Early in the previous chapter the evolutionary concept was extended to the selection of theory variants, and we included among the selectors of theory not only the internal logic or rules of science (which are themselves theory variants produced in a laborious history); but also the various social contexts of knowledge, ranging from the intellectual assumptions of the time and political movements to the fierce competition between theories and traditions. Popper (1963) was among the leading exponents of an evolutionary epistemology, though he was not the first. A good account of the field and Popper's antecedents is given in Campbell (1974). As Popper writes:

> there is no more rational procedure than the method of trial and error – of conjecture and refutation: of boldly proposing theories; of trying our best to show that these are erroneous; and of accepting them tentatively if our critical efforts are unsuccessful (1963: 52).

What changes is that the conjectures become more and more elaborate, guided by past successes, and the attempts at refutation become increasingly systematic as rival traditions pose more and more rigorous tests for each other. What has happened since Popper is that the process of evolution has been described in various ways by Lakatos, Feyerabend, Laudan and Kuhn. What they have in common is much more striking than their differences; and what they have in common is the abandonment of a fixed goal, of a final truth, and of an unchanging concept of reality. All of this follows from an evolutionary epistemology. Values such as 'the real' are signposts, or ways of summarizing an investigative practice and tradition.

The investigative practice and tradition which gives this value its meaning is that of empirical investigation. The rule is that conjectures should be tested, not only by logic, but against empirical facts. That is, in the 'real' world.

The general form of the doctrine of evolutionary epistemology refers to the 'social selection' of theoretical variants. Natural science is a tradition (or a 'kingdom' of knowledge) in which particular emphasis is placed on empirical selection, which is a form of selection in which the enquirer takes pains to avoid influencing the outcomes (see end of previous chapter). This does not eliminate other forms of social selection, but it does give primacy to this one method. It is, once this value is accepted, well-defended against other claims on knowledge, such as that it should serve political ambitions, or deceive the enemy, or be aesthetically pleasing, or confirm a religious belief. The rules of empirical testing were accepted (themselves developing by selection) because they were successful in competition. They enabled those who followed them to discover knowledge which could be discovered in no other way, and their knowledge was both intellectually satisfying and socially powerful. After a slow beginning, as we would expect of the evolution of a new species, there has been an exponential growth in theories tested in this way as whole societies have become dependent on science-based industries. The current success of this species of knowledge should not be interpreted as a final stage, or as the climax of knowledge. It could well be the end; or it could be that other kinds of knowledge will shortly take precedence.

Let us summarize the natural science tradition and its mode of evolution:

Variations in practices and ideas acted upon by empirical selection leads to the development of novel theories.

The identifying characteristic of research traditions in the natural sciences (which may or may not include psychology as a whole or in part) is that they meet empirical tests, by solving empirical problems. This does not mean that they do not solve 'metaphysical' or 'theoretical' or 'conceptual' problems, but that ultimately they go into the arena, like ancient gladiators, to meet facts of nature. Whatever their other successes, they are nothing unless they can succeed here.

And what is an empirical problem? This was addressed at the end of the previous chapter, but let us draw it out into the open once more, not by tight definition but by noting a series of contrasts between 'empirical' and 'other' kinds of knowledge (such as ideology, or religion, or myth).

Empirical tests	*'Other' tests*
Seeker cannot interfere with model	Seeker interprets; influences outcomes by prayer, intercession, etc.
Results indifferent to personal wishes of experimenter	Results influenced by wishes, hopes, etc.
Seeker avoids appeals to authority	Seeker abides by consensus, obeys authority
Seek 'objective' reality	Seek 'subjective' or, constructed reality

Empirical problem-solving shades into ideological problem-solving or ethical problem-solving. All of these depend in matters of fact (Hare, 1981), but they differ in the extent to which authority, the wishes of those proposing the solutions, and fantasies are included. This does not mean that there is ever any final standard by which to judge the accuracy of observations, or that nature ever comes to the observer naked, unaffected by the observer's expectations, conjectures or beliefs. Since conjecture is an essential part of the process, this could not be. Conjecturing is the process by which workers in scientific traditions produce theory variants which enable them to commence new cognitive and practical transactions in the world. These variants, if successful, solve problems in such a way that the results are recognized as 'facts'. Such a recognition is a mark of approval and acceptance. The collective which produces facts will thrive, where these facts are solutions to important problems. ('Importance' is something which I have already commented on several times. It combines judgements of utility, theoretical depth, promise and surprise.) This is another way of saying that some theory variants will, by virtue of their consequences, enjoy a selection advantage and will be reproduced in the minds of the scientific community.

9 Values

It has been repeatedly said that problem-solving is the core of science. Let us look once more at a summary of this position.

> The first and essential acid test for any theory is whether it provides acceptable answers to interesting questions: whether, in other words, it provides satisfactory solutions to important problems (Laudan, 1977: 13).

'Acceptable'? 'satisfactory'? 'interesting'? Can't we go beyond that? Laudan's next thesis is that it is more significant to ask whether a theory solves an important problem than whether it is 'true', or 'corroborated', or 'well-constructed' (1977: 14). Perhaps we can understand this best in terms of the rules or quasi-rules of what we have called traditions, theory-families, theory-clusters, or thought collectives. Each of them has a particular image of reality at its core, a vocabulary of elementary concepts, and paradigmatic experiments. When we look back at Spence's solution to Kohler's problem, we see that it preserved the vocabulary of s–r theory by introducing hypothetical processes of unknown intensity and duration. The solution was 'interesting', 'acceptable' and 'satisfactory' for a variety of reasons, not least of which was the anticipation of many years of PhD research! More significant, though, was that it avoided introducing cognitive existents. It preserved the world picture of behaviourist learning theory.

It is always difficult to state the rules of a tradition, as we see when we examine Weinberg's (1976) attempt to state the rules of the 'Galilean' style of research in physics and Chomsky's (1978) proposal to adopt these rules in linguistics. Among the rules (which are *values* applied to judging theoretical attempts) are: Mathematization, deep explanation and theoretical observation, all to be discussed below. When Laudan states that solutions to problems are judged primarily by whether they are 'acceptable answers' to 'interesting problems' and only secondarily by whether they are 'true' or 'corroborated', he is stating, albeit vaguely, some of the values of science, as he sees them. These values change – they are standards of judgement which depend as much on what is possible in a given domain as on what is desirable – and they are as often implicit as explicit.

I shall now give a brief list of some of the values which have been used to judge theories. This list is by no means complete and it is not used consistently; on the contrary, elements in it may be used 'opportunistically' (Feyerabend, 1981) or, we might say, 'strategically' for defending or attacking theories.

Principal values for judging theories
Satisfactory answers to interesting questions
Formal statement theory
Mathematization
Theory is programmable
Deep theory and theoretical observation
Theory-driven research contrasted with utility
Causal explanations/interpretation
Truth
Realism

What I shall do now is to say something about each of these values.

Satisfactory answers to interesting questions

Answers may be satisfactory for a variety of reasons. They may be useful, they may lead to new research and new facts, or they may explain the findings of observation and experiment. This is another way of saying that the rationality of science is judged by the way it solves problems, and we can then compare different traditions according to their success in this task. It is not the absolute level of problem-solving in a tradition that makes it rational to adhere to it, but its comparative level. There is also the important question of the kind of problem that is solved, when we come to choosing. This is why some will be interested in cognitive psychology or artificial intelligence and others in psychodynamics or social psychology.

It appears then to be relatively straightforward to construct a transcultural or even trans-temporal rule in judging rationality; we compare problem-solving success. Yet what does it mean for a scientist to choose a progressive (successful) rather than a degenerating (unsuccessful) programme? Surely, no one would deliberately choose a degenerating rather than a progressive programme or tradition? These characterizations are *post hoc*. Would it not have been rational to adhere to Hullian theory in the 1930s and 1940s? Yet this tradition, which once seemed so promising, is dead. Is it rational to pursue a cognitive psychology which is heavily dependent on computer metaphor for its inspiration? This may have been the smart thing in the 1960s and 1970s, but there are increasing doubts, as we shall see. It is only afterwards that we know what was rational at the time. The Hullian tradition threw up many exciting problems and was strongly progressive. It collapsed mainly because the language of cybernetic machines and computers could do more conveniently and powerfully what Hull's theory had sought to do – populate the organism with hypothetical processes which could make it learn, choose and even reason.

Rational behaviour increases the probability of success, but success does not always follow. Knowing that there are more black than red balls in a bag, we may bet on finding a black when reaching blindly into the bag, but we could easily grab a red one. Theories may be selected for promise, but promise is as often not fulfilled as fulfilled. The individual scientist must take risks, and some are seen (retrospectively) to have had better luck or judgement than others. Argument, comparison and evidence are important in choosing, but in many cases they cannot be decisive. Though some investments are clearly foolish and some are probably wise, there is a large class of investments which can only be judged after the event. These may be great acts of either innovation or folly. We may quote Mill in this connection

> Justification comes with research, it cannot be a precondition of it; nor can one expect it to turn up within a well-defined time interval, as a result of steps that are known in advance (cited in Feyerabend, 1981: 242).

One may spend one's life working in a tradition and eventually come to the conclusion that it would have been better spent at some amusement. We can no more judge individual rationality simply by success or failure than we can judge individual virtue by its reward. What makes the *system* rational on the other hand is that traditions compete and that theories within traditions compete to solve problems, according to the process and the rules that are being discussed. The system of criticism which eliminates as far as possible the wishes and authority of the participants is a rational system, rejecting in the long run those theories which are least successful in solving problems. What is also rational is the prolific seeding of hypotheses (in the form of papers and books) containing a wide range of variants for the selection process to operate on. Finally, it is rational to reserve the greatest fame for those who take the greatest risks by radical innovation. Though it is rational to allocate something to those who consolidate lines which have already been shown to be successful, the few who manage to start new lines must be the most celebrated.

Formal statement of theory

Though a formal statement of theory is admired, the degree to which it is attempted varies greatly. It is obviously a risky thing to do, since the more precisely a theory is stated, the more easily it should be falsified. Yet an appearance of rigour can be a very good tactic if one wishes to build an intellectual empire. The recipe is to establish a theory in a limited domain and then extend it, by implication, to the rest of behaviour. One may even establish one's principles with dogs and pigeons and then explain human behaviour without further elaboration. The precision and power of the earlier work creates a laboratory analogue for those impatient to grasp the many complexities of human beings. Commenting on this tactic, Kozulin notes:

> Only specialists could have become excited at the discovery of the fine mechanism of secretory or sensory-motor activity in dogs. The picture changed drastically when these same mechanisms were proclaimed the only possible way to analyze human mental functions. From the point of view of the social history of science, Pavlov's case was, however, not atypical.... While Skinner taught pigeons, he was merely known to his pigeons and to behavioural specialists, but once he transferred the rules of pigeon training to human society he soon became a celebrity (Kozulin, 1984: 42).

One way of guarding against this is to include a 'range of convenience' or focus in one's theories. As Kelly (1955: 68) observes, every construct (or system of constructs) 'is convenient for the anticipation of a finite range of events only'. It should be one of the tasks of the theorist to determine the scope of his or her theory. If a theory has been developed to explain changes in salivation, it should not be extended to language behaviour without a rigorous inquiry into the difference between the one problem and the other. It is realistic, though, to anticipate that there will always be overextension of theories. Theory abhors an intellectual vacuum.

The value of rigorous theory has been stated many times, but we may take the arguments of J.G. Taylor as typical. Taylor observes that theories must be 'real' (internally consistent) before they can be either true or false, and he claims that few psychological theories are real in this sense. In 'Phantom theories' (1970) he examines a *petitio principii* in one of Bower's experiments. Since infants react differently to different stimuli (in this case motion parallax), Bower concludes that they have perceived the difference. This appears to be commonplace, yet Taylor argues that it depends upon the premise it is attempting to prove, which is that 'the subject can react differentially to degrees of motion parallax if and only if he can perceive the difference in distance that is responsible for the parallastic difference' (1970: 282). The unspoken premise is what Taylor calls the mind-over-body axiom, that all actions of the conscious organism are governed by conscious mind. This seems so resoundingly obvious (even after Freud) that it is apparently not necessary to include it as a formal axiom in a theory. Taylor rejected this common sense point of view and attempted a consistent and formal statement of his theory.

A. *Axioms of behaviour theory*
   Definition: A state of readiness for a given learned response is defined as a state of activity, induced by the conditioned stimulus, in the cerebral links mediating the response. This state of readiness exists whether the response is evoked or not. States of readiness for two or more different responses may exist simultaneously, in which case the organism is in a state of multiple simultaneous readiness.
B. *Axioms relating to consciousness*
   (1) The state of multiple simultaneous readiness that exists at any moment determines the state of consciousness at that moment.
   (2) States of readiness for two responses that are clearly distinguishable from one another determine two different elements of consciousness.
   (3) If two different patterns of stimulation arouse readiness for responses that have common features, the associated elements of consciousness are to that extent alike (1968: 224).

These axioms taken together form a system of formidable complexity. Several implications are immediate and obvious, though. First, the theory fits in with recent trends towards 'connection machines', or computers which work by altering the weights of connections (and have patterns of interaction) rather than with digital computers. Second, the theory does not take it for granted that the actions of the infants are directed by conscious perceptions similar to those of the adult. Nor, indeed, does it take it for granted that the infant consciously perceives anything at all. The reverse is true, since conscious mind is defined as a set of functions of behaviour. This may not be wholly true, since some forms of consciousness may be phylogenetically prepared, but at least we are prevented from taking it as read that discrimination implies perception. Conscious mind becomes a problem for theory. Third, we can understand corrections of perception in the light of a general theory of perception, since mind is a state of *multiple simultaneous readiness* to respond.

In language which comes more easily today, we might say that the processes of perception are analogous to computations in parallel. Taylor (1962) refers to studies which show that when inverting spectacles are worn for a long period, perception of the world is not corrected all at once, but in systems. For example, writing on the page was seen the right way up when more distant objects were still seen as inverted. Taylor corrected his own experience of a phantom limb after an amputation by repeatedly passing his hand through the 'limb' when he became aware of it. The phantom limb is a sub–set of the set of simultaneous readinesses for action which determines the conscious field. Although it is no longer there, connections in the nervous system are still activated. It is necessary to inhibit them by new connections, and this is what passing the objects through the phantom limb does.

Taylor's work was stimulated by many sources. He acknowledged the pioneering work of Hull (1943), who attempted a rigorous system of formal postulate and deduction; and he drew heavily on Ross Ashby's (1952) *Design for a Brain*.

Perhaps Taylor's work, like that of Hull, illustrates the dangers of precision. It was so rigorous and specific in its domain of application that it could be dismissed almost immediately. It was not rich in imagery, metaphors, and surplus meaning. The manners of science – conjecture and refutation – are not a guide to survival, except for the very few. Delphic utterance, a deep ambiguity, and a slippery contempt for testability, are often the proper strategies of survival, as we see from the examples of Freud and Jung. The gurus survive, like genetically flexible beasts prepared to adapt to every eventuality, while the scientists perish. Psychologists need myths. They need, on the one hand, the myth of science; and on the other hand, great big guiding myths to give meaning to their practice. Many examples of Freudian indifference to evidence are given by Eysenck (1986) as well as by Israëls (1988), whose review of the case of Schreber (which Freud used as a basis for his theory of paranoia) led him to conclude that psychoanalytic theories can only be confirmed but never refuted.

This is the pessimistic view. We can take another line, though, which is that theories should be like manuals of strategy. They should indicate a general line of approach, with flexible responses, when the territory is little known; yet they should become increasingly precise as knowledge increases. It is of little value to map out a detailed line of attack when there are too many unknowns. In fact, it is not merely imprudent, it is almost always a recipe for defeat. Formalization should be undertaken with caution, since it may be a way of denying the complexity of the subject, giving it an unmerited appearance of exactness. In spite of these prudent words, though, scientists with bold natures will quite correctly attempt the ultimate prize, which is the equivalent of a Newtonian theory in psychology.

A relatively formal system which will be better known to most readers is Kelly's (1955) theory of personal constructs. It consists of a fundamental postulate and eleven 'corollaries' which are not corollaries but extensions and developments of the position in the fundamental postulate. What is puzzling at first sight is that though the theory has been the framework within which research has been concluded (Bannister and Fransella, 1980), very little fundamental work has been done. There has been little further specification of the corollaries, little attempt to make them more rigorous or capable of making novel predictions. In fact, 97% of empirical studies in personal construct psychology utilize a method, the repertory grid, which Kelly regarded as incidental to his theory (Neimeyer, 1985: 62).

What is wrong? The theory is like a proposal to write a theory rather than a theory. Yet almost everyone has taken the proposals as though they were theory and has gone on from there. In order to show this, consider a few of the corollaries. The first corollary is the construction corollary, and we may as well start there.

- A person anticipates events by construing their replication.

Precisely. But how do persons construe replications of events? One takes this difficult problem for granted in order to write what appears to be a 'law' or an 'axiom' or a 'corollary'. The bull of inquiry follows the cloak of theory and charges in the wrong direction.

The second corollary, which is the individuality corollary, merely tells us that people may construe things in different ways.

The third corollary, or organization corollary, tells us that persons evolve ordinal systems of constructs (constructs are not isolated from each other). Again, the problems are: How do they evolve such systems and how are the systems organized (in detail)? It is rather as though Piaget were to declare that persons evolve logical systems in the course of development and to leave it at that. What is interesting is the nature of these systems, their organization at different ages and for different purposes, their application to concrete problems, and their mode of development.

One could go on like this, but let me skip to the last corollary, or sociality corollary.

- To the extent that one person construes the construction process of another he may play a role in a social process involving the other person.

This is either a truism or a guide to problems which ought to be researched. Once more, what are the factors which enable us to construe another's processes? How do we learn to do this? What cues do we use and what kinds of constructs should we use in understanding another? Wouldn't psychotherapists like to know?

What Kelly has done is to list a series of outstanding research problems in personology and to state them as axioms. The list is a very interesting one indeed, but each item in the list contains a dozen or more subordinate problems. These are not the elementary statements that are essential in theory-building.

Kelly's trap is a good Irish joke: He leads one to believe that the problem is the solution, and he does it with so much wisdom that one begins to suspect he may be right. This may be the right place to confess that Kelly's approach has often come to my aid in thinking about difficult problems (Du Preez, 1980).

In conclusion, a soporific. Formal statement of theory is excellent, but it has many imitations. And where the theory is not an imitation, it is a dangerous thing to construct, leading usually to sudden scientific death.

Is the moral that fame is more usually obtained by mimicry? This is a strange way of confirming a value.

Mathematization

It is a characteristic of modern science, at least since Galileo, that we search for mathematical expressions of reality (Husserl, 1970), and that we search with such conviction that 'often physicists give a higher degree of reality (to the mathematical models) than they accord the ordinary world of sensation' (Chomsky, 1978: 9). Chomsky urges this style, which he calls 'the Galilean style' in the study of language and mind (Botha, 1981).

Some areas of psychology (such as mathematical learning theory, psychophysics and decision theory) are rich in mathematical models, yet few believe that these reveal the inner structure of mind, in the way that physicists such as Dirac apparently believed their mathematics captured the deep reality of matter (Brush, 1976: 81). Possibly this is because mathematics has only recently turned to the organization of symbolic processes and is still more appropriate to understanding the physical than the mental world.

The tribute which psychologists have paid to mathematics has often been a misplaced admiration for numerical data. The institutionalized 'methodological imperative' of statistical research leads to a condition in which 'numerical models function as theoretical models' and 'the structure of the numerical system is taken to *represent* the structure of the empirical system' (Danziger, 1985: 4). We have a strange situation in which aggregate data are used to test propositions about individuals, even although individuals may differ critically from each other in the way in which they construe a situation. We need general laws to predict specific differences, and these are exactly what aggregate data won't give us in many cases. Taylor (1958) asks the rhetorical question: Would we have discovered the laws of motion by correlating data from different solar systems? General laws are meant to predict differences as well as similarities, and merely lumping together different cases will conceal relations as often as they reveal them. In this Taylor was defending Lewin's (1935) distinction between Galilean and Aristotelean modes of thinking. Galilean thought pursues the genotypical structure of the world which underlies the phenotypical variations and similarities; whereas Aristotelean thought classifies phenotypes as surface appearances, rather like questionnaire research.

Psychologies which attempt to discover such universal deep structures, such as psychoanalysis or personal construct psychology or Taylor's own theory of perceptions are true examples of the Galilean style; and this may be more important than any superficial appearance of mathematization.

A theory should be programmable

At first sight this seems to be a perfectly straightforward proposition, even though it may be difficult to write programs for complete processes. Nevertheless, the ambition to put a theory into program format is the same as setting it up in a mathematical formula. The formula is a conceptual machine for giving certain results when we set its variables at particular values. These results can be checked against experimental data. The advantage of the program is simply that variables and manipulations may be numerous.

When we regard the programmed computer purely as a calculating device, there is no reason why it should simulate the physical processes of the organism. It need not be realistic in this sense at all. In practice, though, since the first 'symbol machine' (Newell and Simon, 1961) which solved a problem, there has been the ambition to make computer models match mental processes in as many ways as possible. We may regard this purely as an aid to theorizing, since machines are good (and sometimes misleading) models to think with, in attempting to devise theories as well as to calculate. When we use them purely as calculation devices we are not using them as analogues of mental processes – intercommunicability of program manipulations and mental processes may be low: on the other hand, when we use them to simulate processes, they may be epistemological devices for thinking about the nature of mind. It is then that the architecture of the machine becomes important and we begin wondering whether we should be modelling processes on a connection machine or a digital computer. In the former, there is no program; it consists of large networks of parallel networks, each with an activation value. Adaptation occurs by changing the values and hence patterns of activation.

Though connection machines can be represented on a digital computer, this can only be done to the extent that the connection machine (or the nerve network or whatever) is fully understood. It is always possible that there are properties in the network which we do not suspect and therefore cannot program. It is also possible that some of these properties might emerge if we build a system which not only represents but also imitates or resembles the original. This is rather like building a model of a dam or a harbour to investigate complex dynamic effects which are beyond the range of explicit theory. Shouldn't we, in the same way, build systems which not merely represent processes in the nervous system but also resemble them? For this purpose, massively parallel connection machines might be more informative than a digital computer.

Thus we arrive at a distinction: A model may be of two kinds. The first is a kind of simplification or miniature of the process we wish to investigate. The important thing here is that the model resembles the object of study. Computations have sometimes been thought of in this way, as possible simulacra of mental processes – rather like the minds of robots in science fiction. The second kind of model is the computational device referred to at the beginning of this section. It is a program which represents, by means of symbols and ordered transformations, the processes which are thought to occur in the real thing. There is no physical resemblance, though, between the operations in the programmed machine and the processes in the nervous system. The program does not enact the real process at all – no more than a theory of motion moves.

We sometimes confuse the two versions in psychology. (Hofstadter and Dennett (1981) are still interesting to read on this; Blakemore and Greenfield (1987), pp. 209–292 say more than I ever could; Smolensky (1988) gives a penetrating analysis of the virtues of connectionism.)

Deep theory and theoretical observation

All deep views of the world have required that we interpret observation in order to understand why we see what we see and hear what we hear instead of what common sense suggests we ought to see and hear. Here is Galileo's Tower Problem to show how apparently damaging observations, when properly understood, can be rendered harmless to a theory we wish to protect. This is the problem which faced Galileo, as well as other spinning earth theories.

When a rock is dropped from a tower, it does not strike the earth hundreds of yards to the east of the tower, as it should if the earth were spinning.

Here is Galileo's solution:

Tower, rock and observer share the earth's circular motion and hence this motion is not observed. Only the downward motion of the falling rock is peculiar to it and hence that motion is observed. The example of motions in a carriage and on board a ship are used to persuade us of the correctness of this view.

Galileo distinguished between the sensory basis of observation and observation corrected by theory, introducing what Feyerabend calls the 'relativity principle' (1979: 90), a principle which may be stated as: 'Our senses notice only relative motion'. In this way, Galileo introduced a *new observation language*.

It is difficult to think of an intellectual system with any pretensions at all which does not require theoretically informed observation to resolve contradictions between the system and surface phenomena. Perhaps only the enterprise of questionnaire psychology goes against this view.

- Why do sinners' ways prosper? (Asks the Christian, believing God is good)
- How can infants discriminate between stimuli? (Asks Taylor, believing them incapable of conscious perception)
- How can Dora deny sexual arousal by Herr K? (Asks Freud, believing that any girl of her age would be aroused).

And so forth. Every theory tilts with contradictions, must unhorse them, and must make them swear allegiance.

Theory-driven research contrasted with utility

Kimble (1984) reflects on the scientist/humanist dimension in psychological culture and collects evidence to show that some psychologists attach more value to the utility of knowledge than to its theoretical significance. Those who must justify themselves before a wider public as practitioners are, not surprisingly, less interested in the performance of the rat in the maze than are those who must justify themselves to their colleagues in learning theory.

Impatience with theory is more likely at that state of a discipline's development when its practices have not been revolutionized by fundamental discoveries. In medicine, the discoveries of the 'germ hunters' of the nineteenth century conclusively established the significance of theory for practice, but in psychology there has hardly been such a wave of fundamental innovation.

As we have already seen, when there are professional 'crises' (either marked opportunities or threats), psychologists discover utility in the most extraordinary professional tools (Verhave and van Hoorn, 1984). A good example of this is the way in which psychologists in various traditions have persuaded the armed forces of their usefulness in time of war. Psychoanalysts have been employed to probe the personality of opposition leaders (e.g. Langer's (1972) study of Hitler) and psychometricians, personologists, counsellors and others have been employed at their usual tasks of selection, diagnosis and therapy. The German version of the expansion of psychology in war is given by Geuter (1987). What is striking is not the explicit ideological work done by psychologists in providing theories which justify racism – there are plenty of others to do that – but the emphasis on practical utility which led to the establishment of new posts, new training facilities, new chairs. What is remarkable is not the positive picture of racism but the silent opportunism, the pragmatism of professional expansion, and the absence of protest when Jews were dismissed. Thus, Jaensch is portrayed as something of an exception, though his typological theory in which Jews were classed as 'synaesthesics', a labile and inferior category, fitted into a German tradition of typology (Kretschmer, Spranger, Jaensch). What was opportunistic was Jaensch's redescription of the category to which Jews supposedly belonged. In his 1937 text *Personality*, Allport puts the matter crisply: 'All typologies place boundaries where boundaries do not belong' (1937: 296).

To return to the central point: the value of fundamental theory versus utility (if such a distinction were to be forced upon us). We generally find that the closer we are to writing a conceptual or internal history of a discipline, the more we stress what is fundamental; the more we are concerned with a contextual history, the more we shall have to stress utility. Though constructs have two poles, as Kelly (1955) observed, these two poles are joined in all but the psychologically disturbed. (And perhaps in commentators who get too absorbed by words?) It follows that research is driven by both theoretical innovation and practical utility.

Causal explanation/interpretation

Though natural scientists feel bound to attempt causal explanations of events, many social scientists appear to be more concerned with interpretations of events, or regard interpretation as an indispensable part of causal explanation. Semiotics, or the science of signs, is mainly a matter of interpreting relations between signs, and this would appear to be the model of much social accounting; yet we insert terms which appear to imply causal relations. For example, when we say that Marxism serves the interests of the pedantocracy (academics and teachers, particularly in the social sciences) we imply that interpretation is best served by understanding causal relations. A sketch for an argument about the value of Marxism to the pedantocracy might go as follows:

1. Western academics, because they often feel inferior to figures of the existing economic and political establishment, are drawn to an adversary position.
2. Marxism, which is both jargon-laden and messianic, can be used to attack this establishment and to strengthen academic credentials at the same time.
3. Therefore, academics in the social sciences frequently adopt Marxist postures. Marxism restores their conviction that they have secret knowledge of the inner workings of society.
4. We may add that, in Third World situations, the use of Marxist language has the added benefit of painless identification with revolutionaries. The university Marxist is like the Christian Cardinal, someone who makes a profession of a revolutionary doctrine originally addressed to the poor and dispossessed.
5. Also, social scientists who have a direct interest in redistribution rather than in production find Marxist tools useful for this purpose.

There are many hidden premises in the argument, as in all arguments about belief. Why do some adopt the adversary position and others become apologists for the establishment? What structures perpetuate academic profession and faiths? To what extent does Marxism respond to 'cognitive interests' (a search for truth) rather than 'material interests' (an attempt to enhance one's position).

What is clear, though, is that every attempt at 'unmasking' is an attempt to substitute cause for disinterested reason. Where the speaker advances a logical argument, the critic finds an 'interest' or material cause for a behaviour, as we have in describing the attachment of pedants to Marxism.

An example which is closer to psychology is the understanding of 'culture-bound syndromes', which are enactments of major social conflicts (Littlewood and Lipsedge, 1986). Such syndromes are conservative, in that they dramatize these conflicts without any overt political challenge. They are medicalized, they reduce conflict to an illness. This carefully seals off the potential criticism and allows it to be handled by society's healers. Examples of such 'culture-bound syndromes' are anorexia nervosa, neurasthenia ('housewive's' syndrome), amok, kleptomania. They are parodies of ways of dealing with problems. Anorexia may be a parody of slimming. It may be even more – a parody of the meaninglessness of the nearest thing we offer in our society to a coherent philosophy of the self – the cult of diet and exercise. It may be a comment on the worship of the thin and infantile. It may be atonement for the guilt of living affluently in a world of poverty. It may be the sympton of those who wish to pass once more 'through the eye of a needle' (Warner, 1989: 420).

It may be all of these and much more. What we see here is that understanding the syndrome *apparently* requires a deep understanding of the culture. This is interpretation of a system of signs. It also requires us to understand why those signs are used and how their message is contained. This is causal.

Once more, to understand the situation we need to apply a construct with two poles (not isolated ends). Interpretation and causation shade into each other. The causation of which we speak here is not 'push–pull', but selection. What factors select the kind of message that an illness transmits and select the treatment or containment of this message? The consequences of a message are probably among the factors which control its repeated production.

If we focus on an isolated 'text' or system of signs, we may believe that interpretation is enough; but the moment we introduce 'context' (which will often change our interpretation of text), we will introduce questions about why something happened and how it happened; and some of these questions will be best answered in causal terms. When we interpret a text, we may explain its particular context by referring to markets, or to interests, or to selective mechanisms, such as grants. When we understand a symptom, we may refer to deprivations, or brain damage, or influence processes of various kinds. There is no absolutely clear division between explanation by causes and reasons, between causal explanation and interpretation

Prediction

Every experiment makes predictions in order to test hypotheses, yet it is extraordinarily rare for psychologists (or other social scientists) to be able to predict anything that would not have been predicted by a significant majority of persons of roughly the same culture and level of education. On the one hand, a plethora of prediction; on the other hand, largely failure. Is sexual activity bad for the child? Will ethnically homogeneous groups of workers outperform mixed groups in team tasks? Will a rapist repeat his offence? Will permissive education lead to greater creativity? These are the sorts of questions on which psychologists rarely do better than laypersons. In fact, Gordon *et al.* (1978) found that psychologists rarely did better than laypersons in predicting outcomes in the field of industrial-organizational psychology.

Nevertheless, the imperative to predict is there. It is part of the formal apparatus of the experiment. The moment that any theory enables us to predict (in the sense of manipulate and control as well as merely expect) dramatic results, it will have a decided advantage. Our admiration for such theories is seen in our willingness to apply the theories of Skinner and Pavlov, which make excellent predictions in limited domains of knowledge, to almost every form of behaviour. Overextension is thus a tribute to the value of prediction. And who did not wait (many still do!) for the psychometricians with their mysterious manipulations of superficial data to predict what no one else had known before? After gazing into the crystal ball of a correlation which 'accounts for' perhaps 10% of the variance, the seer proclaims a 'significant' relation between X and Y (say, extroversion and a liking for parties).

If we are modest in our expectations, statistical predictions do have value in recurrent situations when the type of population, the conditions of testing and the criteria of success are held constant. This is frequently not possible. None of this implies, of course, that clinical prediction is any better.

Truth

Theories are cognitive machines for enabling us to carry out virtual manipulations of the world so that the results can be empirically tested.

They are seldom merely pictures of the world, the way a miniature dam might be a 'picture' of a big dam. In order to work, theories should not be self-contradictory and should refer accurately and in detail to certain aspects of the world. Which aspects of the world should be referred to will depend upon the conceptual work we wish to do. In order to understand and predict motion we might leave out all references to the value, colour or emotions of the body being hurled through space. We might also leave out most features of that space, such as the colour of the sky, the weather or the scenery.

A theory is obliged to tell 'nothing but the truth', yet it cannot tell 'the whole truth'. That would take too long. Very well, but *can* it tell 'nothing but the truth'? Since science is a continuing attempt to put together new conceptual machinery for doing new intellectual jobs, there is no way of saying that a new assemblage may not require us to reshape a concept slightly. We may carve the joint or cut the pie in different ways. Yet each of these may be 'true', in the sense that we have checked our reference repeatedly and thoroughly.

This brings us to Harré's (1986) treatment of truth, in which he draws on a lecture by Ellis (1982). To say that something is 'true' is not to offer a final adjudication on its status but to certify that it has passed various tests. We reinterpret the search for truth as a statement about the moral practices of the scientific community. Thus, Popper's principle of 'fallibilism' is a moral principle or a guide to good scientific conduct, leading to maxims such as: 'However much personal investment one has in a theory one should not ignore contrary evidence'; or 'One should seek harder for evidence that would count against a theory than for that which would support it' (Harré, 1986: 90). The words 'true' and 'false' are used to urge us to better investigative practices: Better experiments, better designs, better techniques, better theories. They refer to the moral scrutiny which scientists impose on themselves in arriving at conclusions.

To the extent, then, that traditions prohibit moral scrutiny and questioning, they are not committed to truth. A commitment to scientific truth is not a commitment to what we already know or think we know, since that must always be incomplete, but a commitment to a course of action, viz. to engage in the continual checking of theory against evidence rather than authority.

Conclusion

The values we have described are the virtues of science. They define some part of its moral practice. But why are scientists attached to these virtues and why is science a moral practice? Is that merely incidental? It is quite clear that the morality of science is indispensable to its success. Without the willingness to appeal to evidence rather than authority, or to submit to the rigour of proof, or to search for contrary evidence, or to publish freely and widely, or to compete freely and tolerate other theories, science would not have advanced in its ability to solve problems.

A word of caution is necessary here. Even an ideal society has its delinquents and in science there have been some notorious examples. Cyril Burt has been paraded as one of the worst offenders for allegedly faking his data on the IQs of identical twins reared apart (Hearnshaw, 1979). Recently, Joynson (1989) has reviewed the case against Burt and has come to the conclusion that the verdict should be 'not proven'. Doubtless the debate will continue. There have been offenders in most branches of science, some of whom are mentioned in St James-Roberts (1976). A good example is the discovery of N-rays by Blandot in 1903. After he had announced his 'discovery', many laboratories confirmed his finding before R.W. Wood showed in 1904 that N-rays did not exist. Liam Hudson (1989) makes the point that many pioneers in science were visionaries who bent or selected the facts to fit their theories. (We have already mentioned Freud's use of Schreber's memoirs to illustrate a theory he had before reading them.) Hudson writes that 'those with the psychic energy to drive our disciplines on to previously untrodden ground are no more to be trusted unfailingly to tell the truth than were stout Cortes or Francis Drake' (Hudson, 1989: 1202). What is important, though, is that the visions are usually sifted and tested by the process of ordinary scientific investigation.

From an evolutionary perspective, we can understand the values of science as having been selected because they enable scientists to solve problems. In other words, the values of science are not fortuitous, nor are they mere embellishments; they are part of the problem-solving apparatus of science. Those scientific communities which put them into practice will, in the long run, also be the communities which solve scientific problems. And societies in which such scientific communities flourish will also be societies in which other practices of liberty and democracy flourish. Freedom of thought and totalitarianism are natural enemies. One has only to read a study such as Kozulin's (1984) *Psychology in Utopia* to realize this. The repeated revision of scientific theories to satisfy ideologies is as contrary to scientific freedom as scientific freedom is contrary to the despotism of ideologies.

Scientists continually submit to empirical evidence, or to tests of reality. One of the ultimate values of science is the discovery of nature, or the real world. This is what has driven thousands of scientists for centuries. It is part of the process of decentring from our more immediate concerns, from our own limited point of view. What is the universe really like?

In the next chapter I shall ask: What is realism? What does it imply?

10 The quest for the real

There are two kinds of object in science. The first kind consists of objects we can discover more and more about by improving our technology of observation and manipulation; whereas the second kind consists of objects we can discover more about by understanding our theories better. The first kind of object is a real item in the world, like a heart or a protein molecule; the second kind of object is a real item in a theory, like a centre of gravity or an equator. Better microscopes or other machinery will tell us more about hearts and protein molecules; but can they tell us more about equators or centres of gravity or, for that matter, human rights or justice? The task of science is to open up access to the first kind of reality, to the real items of the world, and to avoid confusing them with the logical constructs or concepts which are an essential part of the language of science.

The difficulty here is clear. One can often see, retrospectively, that a particular object was not an item in the world, or should have been earmarked as an item in the world, but at the time it may not be clear at all. Are objects such as 'self', or 'identity', or 'superego', or 'intention', or 'motive', or 'plan', or 'script' or 'trait', or 'construct' objects of the first kind or the second? Should we plan to open up access to them by new technology or should we clarify their behaviour in our theories? If we adopt the first strategy, then discovering a motive would be like getting hold of a heavenly body, such as the moon, and studying its properties. Our theories might change – we might decide that it is a planet, or a star, or a satellite, or an asteroid, or a gigantic spaceship – but the body would remain a body about which we could discover more and more as we improved our technology. It is an item in the world as well as in somebody's theory. What changes is its conceptual status, not its existence (as Boyd (1979) made clear).

Can we discover psychological objects in this way? Consider attempts such as Schafer's (1976) move to do away with Freud's 'metapsychology', which was Freud's attempt to explain psychological observations by postulating real underlying entities and process. Schafer attempted to strip psychological language down to an 'action language' which would avoid all reification. Thus, he says, 'we should not use such phrases as "a strong ego", "the dynamic unconscious", "the inner world", "libidinal energy", "rigid defense", "an intense emotion", "autonomous ego function", and "instinctual drive"' (1976: 9). Instead, we should use action statements consisting of verbs and adverbs, avoiding names wherever possible. A simple example will have to suffice: instead of saying, 'A change was occurring in his attitude from friendliness to belligerence', we might now say 'He changed from acting friendly to acting belligerently' (1976: 11).

There is much to be said for this. It certainly enables us to avoid making entities of activities, pretending that we know how things are caused when we do not know. If we confine ourselves to action language we will not so easily think of these fictitious entities as propelling us into action, forcing or causing us to behave in particular ways. Action thinking gets us away from the pseudo-explanation of: 'a mechanism of defense wards off the demands or pressures of a repressed impulse' (1976: 14).

The retort to this is that, however much we may wish to return to a pure phenomenology, we shall have to study the processes that enable us to function. Whether we describe these processes as networks, as flow charts, or as computer programs, we shall sooner or later be speculating on their existence as items in the world. Can we propose some rules to avoid simple redescription in pseudo-causal language?

1. An explanatory mechanism cannot be simply a reification of the event it accounts for. It must have surplus properties which enable us to make surprising new discoveries about it. This is another way of saying that we should be able to conceive of hanging onto it as an item in the world even if the particular causal relationship in which we are led to suspect its existence were to fall away.
2. We must state our explanation in such a way that we gain a real understanding of a process which we did not have before. When we describe the structure of a gene, we increase our understanding of the ways in which it is replicated and information is carried. In descriptions of the superego or of defence mechanisms as real items of the world (if that is what they are), we should attempt to explain how they function to produce the effects they do produce. To understand a causal relationship is to understand the mechanism which produces the effect.

This is very easy to declare after the event, but it is not easy, in groping for an understanding of events, to sort one's objects neatly into conceptual and real objects; or (to use the terms which Reichenbach

(1938) introduced and Dennett (1987; 1988 has adopted), into *abstracta* and *concreta* (or *illata*). When solutions to problems present themselves to us, it is not clear whether the objects in them are theoretical fictions or real items in the world, about which various hypotheses may be entertained without affecting their reality. The reason for this confusion is quite simple. As our theories have dealt increasingly with objects which are difficult to observe, so it is increasingly difficult to decide whether these objects are items in the world, waiting to be observed when we have the appropriate technology, or are items in our theory, never to be observed no matter how sophisticated our technology. Or, if located and referred to (as a centre of gravity or a counter-transference might be), never to be understood further except by clarifying the theoretical role of the concept in the discourse of physics or psychology or whatever science we are doing.

The size of the problem becomes evident when we consider Harré's (1986) typology of theories. It is in the third type of theory that it is particularly difficult to decide whether one is confronting a real item in the world or an item in a theory. Consider his theory types.

Type 1 theories are pragmatic and make it possible to predict observable phenomena. Like all theories, they must classify data so that observation is possible, and show how such data are related in logical or mathematical form. Typical theories of this kind are Newtonian kinematics and Skinnerian behaviourism. In kinematics, the precise relations of mass, force, acceleration and velocity are determined. In Skinnerian behaviourism the emission of operant behaviour under schedules of reinforcement is determined. What kinds of experience do theories of this kind refer to? Apparently, to realities we can observe or could be trained to observe with our sensory organs, given the appropriate practices of observation and measurement. Harré calls this domain of experience Realm 1. Theories of type 1 avoid unobservables and 'deeper' realities.

Type 2 theories contain theoretical objects with iconic properties, though these objects have not yet been observed at the time that the theory is formulated. As Harré notes, the vast majority of scientific theories are of this type. What realm of experience do type 2 theories commit us to? Apparently, to both Realm 1 experiences of objects which can be directly perceived, and to a further order of experiences, Realm 2, which consists of objects which can be experienced only when technology has amplified our senses. Viruses, molecules, brain waves and many other objects can be observed only with the right technology. Theories of type 2 postulate real objects and processes which are in principle detectable with technological advances. The most readily available psychological theories of this type are neuro-psychological theories.

Type 3 theories contain non-iconic or 'non-picturable' systems of beings; unobservables which are ideally constituted in mathematical form. Harré cites Einstein's special theory of relativity and quantum field theory as examples of type 3 theories. What realm of experience do type 3 theories commit us to? Apparently, to both Realm 1 and Realm 2 experiences (our observations, both assisted and unassisted by instrumentation), but also to realities beyond experience. Type 3 theories commit us to objects and 'to beings which, if real, could not become phenomena for human observers, however well equipped with devices to amplify and extend the senses. Realm 3 is a domain of beings beyond all possible experience' (1986: 73). Harré lists as examples of the 'denizens' of this realm, 'Quantum states, naked singularities, social structure and Freudian complexes' (1986: 73). What kinds of being are these and why should they be beyond experience? Harré suggests two reasons. The first is that we lack the sensory equipment to observe them. We can't observe magnetic fields of force or curvature in space–time. The second reason is that we have no idea how some of the 'denizens' of Realm 3 might manifest. Could one perceive energy states or social relations?

There is something not quite clear about the denizens of Realm 3. They seem to be non-picturable for different reasons. Some of these may be objects we could find in the world (given the right technology and the right theory), but others appear to be part of the language of the discipline. Yet others may be hybrids. Consider a construct such as a 'rule' in a universal grammar which enables human beings to acquire language. We might hypothesize that we are born with such 'rules' as part of our equipment. Such 'rules' would appear, if they exist, to be denizens of Realm 3, since it is difficult to know how they would be observed. To attempt to discover them would be rather like attempting to discover a new form of electromagnetic life, only rather more difficult.

There is another possibility, though, and that is that there are no such rules in the infant mind. We may be constrained to learn languages the way we do because the human brain functions as it does, in persons interacting with other persons. It is quite possible that conceptual analysis will lead us to conclude (as it has led Harris (1987) and Searle (1987)) that when we describe the brain as possessing a universal grammar we are creating a fiction. Similarly, when a linguist says that a person has internalized a grammar (even though that person may not know the grammar) we may be led to search for it in the person's brain. One step would be to include such a grammar in any program we wrote to simulate behaviour. Thus, our program to stimulate real-time functioning might include such rules as $S \longrightarrow NP + VP$; $NP \longrightarrow N + Art + Adj.$, etc. If we were then to look for these rules in the brain, or in processes corresponding to these rules, we might be committing ourselves to a lifetime of mistaken effort, and there are at least three reasons for supposing this. The first is that the so-called internalized grammar (or system of rules) is merely a reification of our attempts to describe an aspect of the behaviour of people speaking a language. It has no surplus value. If we find an NP in the behaviour, then we put an NP in the head; and so forth. There is no value in this, since it is rather like someone studying embryology and attributing the development of a head, a leg or a nose in the foetus to a miniature head, leg or nose in the fertilized ovum, and perhaps in the genes. The nose is attributed to the nose gene and the head to the head gene. This quite obviously explains nothing. The second reason is that even if people speak 'as if' they know the rules of grammar it doesn't follow that they do; and it follows even less that they have internalized rules which they do not know (Harris, 1987: 511). Considering that there are many possible grammars of every language, it is not clear what the person should internalize. A third reason for avoiding the search for internalized grammars is that it is difficult to imagine what we would search for. In other words, what sort of existent would we be trying to discover? It would certainly be quite different from a 'rule' or a 'grammar', though it might be a biologial mechanism which would enable the person to learn rules or grammars.

Let me summarize here by saying that we learn two kinds of task when we attempt to understand the real world. The first is to improve our access to real items in the world, and this involves the development of EEG machines, electron microscopes, particle accelerators and telescopes, among a vast array of devices. These enable us to *explore* the items we find. The second is to improve the network of concepts by which we relate the properties of what we observe, in a systematic way. These properties are ideally 'calculation-bound' entities, such as centres of gravity, mass, acceleration, equators, lines of latitude, or momentum. By extension, we may speak of identity, grammars, superegos and traits – in fact, many of the 'realities' of psychology – as being of this kind.

Let us now return to the vocabulary for items in the world and items in the language and see what use we can make of it. The former (to remind ourselves) are called *illata* (by extension from *concreta*, which are objects of unaided sensory experience; *illata* are inferred real objects, to be made accessible with the right technology); whereas the latter, *abstracta*, are objects constituted by our ways of talking about the world. Though discourse may lead us to place something in time and space (a pawn, an equator, a centre of gravity, a human right), we discover more about that something by investigating our discourse rather than by improving our technology for observing the pawn, or the centre of gravity, or the human right. We might, of course, learn more about them by observing the discourse and practice of others, if we were strangers to these concepts.

We now turn to Dennett's suggestion that we can learn about the reality of the self by distinguishing between *abstract* and *illata*.

Self and identity

Dennett (1988b) wishes to show that 'self', like 'centre of gravity' is an *abstractum* or theorist's fiction. If 'self' is to be useful as a concept, then it should have a definite explanatory role in psychological talk, just as centre of gravity has in physics. Abstracta may enter into causal statements, such as that a body overbalanced because its centre of gravity moved past its point of balance, yet the centre of gravity is not a material item in the world. It is the resultant of forces in the body which has overbalanced, a notional point at which the mass of the body is concentrated. Similarly, we can use the self as a centre of responsibility, of beliefs and intuitions, to explain a person's actions (Dennett, 1988a: 537). Here, one may point out immediately that not all theoretical systems use the concept of 'self'. Psychoanalysis, precisely because of the contradictions which persons reveal in their intentions and actions, dissolved self into different sub-systems in opposition to each other. In other words, self is not regarded as a well-behaved theoretical concept. Yet Dennett's arguments apply equally to the additional sub-systems identified by psychoanalysts – ego, superego and id. To what extent should we regard these as real items in the world rather than as *abstracta* which have a purely 'combinatorial role' in theory? My suggestion is that their theoretical status is the same as that of the self. Let us therefore continue following Dennett's discussion for the time being.

The difference between fictional objects, such as centre of gravity, and real objects, such as atoms, is that fictional objects do not have properties other than those they have been endowed with by theory (1988b: 1016). It makes no sense to propose a further empirical study of centres of gravity (as I have already said), to see whether they have unexpected properties. Could they be pink, or consist of carbon, or be organized as cellular structures? Centres of gravity (and selves, according to Dennett) have a purely conceptual existence, and it makes no difference if they are embodied (like pawns, or husbands in a particular society). Atoms or molecules, on the other hand, have all sorts of unknown properties to be discovered by empirical inquiry. They have composition and structure of bewildering complexity, which vast machines built at enormous expense may be used to probe. Should we attempt to investigate self in the same way, building apparatus to probe its structure, or is Dennett correct in supposing that once we know the properties that self has been endowed with in psychological theory, there is nothing left to discover, except by conceptual clarification or theoretical labour? The same would apply to many other psychological constructs, such as ego or superego, script and schema. In each case we would improve our understanding of their behaviour by understanding their combinatorial role in theory, not by direct probe of the apparent object. Such empirical work as we might undertake ought to be devoted to understanding the discourse in which they are embedded rather than to attempting to establish their existence as items in the world. Then, we might study the kinds of discourse which we characterize as 'superego' talk, but we would be misguided if we were to attempt to show that superegos exist.

Similarly, rules may be posited in attempts to describe regularities in sentences but not to model brain processes, unless as a first approximation. The same applies, even more strongly, to beliefs. Among the arguments which Dennett produces for this are that

> there can be an infinity of beliefs in a finite brain; between any two beliefs there can be another; the question of exactly when one has acquired a particular belief can have no objective, determinate (interpretation-independent) answer (1988a: 537).

Even stronger arguments against the existence of items such as rules and beliefs as generative mechanisms in the brain were raised above. They have no surplus value. To use them to explain behaviour is rather like positing the 'nose gene' to explain noses. We need other kinds of accounts of how noses and utterances are produced. Similarly, though we attribute all sorts of actions to the self, we can understand it rather as a point of conversion, a necessary fiction, a resultant of processes in the person. If we were to conduct empirical studies, it would be to show how (let us say) 'self' performs different combinatorial roles in different cultures. Do all cultures posit an autonomous self? Do all cultures find it necessary to decompose the self into ego, superego and id? There is no more reason to suppose that 'self' has the same properties in different cultures than to suppose that 'husband' has. We might find very different roles for husbands: in some societies (and periods) they might know their rights – that is, how to behave; in others they might be confused and engage in contradictory discourses. We find the same integrity/confusion in other social entities, such as 'medical doctors'.

Where there is confusion of role and discourse, behaviour is confused and fragmented. This is clearly shown (to give one dramatic example) in the talk of Lifton's (1986) Nazi doctors, alternating between saving life, selections for the gas chambers, exterminating 'life unworthy of life', working with prisoner 'colleagues', and being 'good' Nazis. Bursts of inconsistent talk escape their lips. 'You don't know what it was like'. Compromise and fragmentation reveal layer upon layer of unintegrated discourse.

What sort of agent is the self, given these circumstances? Let us now look at the analogies which Dennett employs in reaching his decision about the kind of existence we should attribute to the self.

The first analogy we are by now excessively familiar with. It is that, just as physicists understand the behaviour of bodies in gravitational fields by referring to centres of gravity, so ordinary persons (and often psychologists) understand the actions of persons (including their own actions) by referring to the self.

The second analogy is that, just as novelists invent fictitious characters to connect events in their stories, so persons invent fictitious selves to connect the events of their lives. The kind of self that is invented will change historically; it will be different in different moods as well as cultures. The self we find may be active or passive, empty or full of reason and motive, strong or weak, connected or disconnected. We reconstruct our past self to make it intelligible or acceptable to the present. We invent a future self to fulfil our wishes or ambitions.

The third analogy is between our revisions and multiple personality disorder. At times, we seem to lose control of the narrative, as in cases of multiple personality disorders such as those recorded in Thigpen and Cleckley (1954) and Osgood et al. (1976). When this happens, life consists of different narratives of different selves. For each life, a different self has to be invented to give coherence to the narrative. The central difference between the condition of multiple personality disorder and the normal condition of confabulation and daydreaming is that of dissociation. Unity is preserved as long as the different selves are in contact with a stable self; this is lost when a bad experience cannot be assimilated to the main narrative of the person's life, and a different narrative is constructed, requiring a different self which is out of touch with the principal self. Different life stories coexist, each with a different self, and in poor communication with each other. The ordinary condition is that selves arise in narratives and daydreams and then disappear, or are revised out of existence. The pathological condition is that these narratives persist and lose contact with each other.

By now we take for granted the modularity of mind, the fact that it is a partially connected system (Ashby, 1952; Gazzaniga, 1983), and the fact that many different and contradictory discourses may coexist in the same mind. This was one of the principal puzzles to which psychoanalysis addressed itself, and one of its principal reasons for rejecting the concept of a unitary self.

In moral discourse, on the other hand, we find it difficult to abandon the responsible self. Though it might be a resultant of many psychological forces, it enters into our causal accounts not only as a 'well-behaved fiction' but also as an entity, a focus of praise or blame. There is nothing illogical in this. Just as 'centre of gravity' enters into causal accounts in physics (the centre of gravity of the object crossed the point of balance and it overturned), so 'self' enters into moral accounts (he placed himself in a situation from which it was virtually impossible to escape with honour).

The lesson of all this, if true, is that 'self', like many terms in psychology, must be understood as a resultant – a way of summarizing the interaction of more fundamental processes.

Concluding comments

Why should realism be one of the guiding values of science, in the sense that scientists make sustained attempts to open up access to the real objects of the world? The first reason is the belief that, if we wish to understand how the world works, we should try to establish what is in it. If we wish to understand heredity (to take an example), we should attempt to establish whether genes really exist and, if they do, how they work. There is no contradiction between the fact that we repeatedly revise our understanding of the objects and mechanisms of the world as we improve both our theories and our techniques of observation and manipulation and the fact that such objects really exist. If we are observing at the limits of our powers, we would expect further observation to correct earlier observation. There is an important distinction between observation and mere 'sensation' (the antiquated view that we simply sort out whatever 'information' the world gives us). Observation is theory-directed and technologically supported. At earlier stages of evolution, the 'theory' is built into our biology and the technology is built into our bodies. Each animal is an observer, or biased learner. It asks its characteristic questions and obtains accurate answers if it is to survive. It does not know the whole truth about the real world, but it must know some of the truth if it is to find food, avoid enemies and gain shelter. At the level of human, cultural evolution, the theory and technology are exosomatic. They exist as artefacts. Each cultural tradition makes us biased learners, asking characteristic questions and obtaining answers to these questions. If we did not, we would not survive. Science makes explicit doctrine of this, as Popper (1963) insisted. Our theories must meet the reality tests to which we expose them. By deliberately exposing them to these tests in systematic programmes of research, we allow them to die in our stead. If we fail to do this, we may find ourselves doing the dying because we cling to falsehood.

There is absolutely no reason to suppose, when we take the evolutionary perspective, that (a) we ever arrive at a final representation, since other creatures or cultures with greater or different powers of observation may quite easily replace us, of that (b) our observations are necessarily false, since if they were so we would not have survived. With due care, our discoveries may be true relative to our powers of observation. This is true of the tick which locates its source of blood by detecting butyric acid (von Uexküll, 1921); the frog which detects bugs by registering contrast, convexity, moving edge and dimming (Lettvin *et al.* 1959); or the alga which detects light for photosynthesis (Wachtershauser, 1984). We survive, and our theories survive, by discovering facts about the real world, and by continually improving on these discoveries. If we did not postulate such representations of the real world, at different levels of complexity, we would be 'left with an inexplicable miracle, a piece of "pre-established harmony"' (Bartley, 1987: 39).

The distinctions that have been drawn in this chapter between different kinds of reality, between *illata* and *abstracta*, tell us how to conduct further investigaton. Should we invest in technology or in a clarification of discourse? Since they direct the effort we make, they help us to design cognitive tools for studying the world.

In the last chapter of this book I shall sketch a reflexive psychology: one that applies to those who study theories and to those who are studied by theories. How could such beings evolve?

Part III

Towards a reflexive psychology

11 | Polyphonic beings

> Polyphonic 1. Mus. Composed or arranged of several voices or parts ... many-voiced.
> *(Shorter Oxford English Dictionary)*

In this, the final chapter, I shall attempt to sketch an approach to psychology. Such an approach, as I have said, should be reflexive, applying to psychologists as well as to the people they theorize about. We should be able to see how the persons described in such a psychology could join together to engage in research, as well as in many other activities, such as exploiting others, fighting for a cause, or telling stories. Our psychology should show the function of the self as a fiction or as a theory.

The foundations of our theory of the polyphonic person are *rhetoric* and *consciousness*. We should first explore the implications of looking at persons as though they were rhetoricians; then we should look at the significance of consciousness for such a view of persons.

The enterprise of looking at persons as though they were rhetoricians is by now well under way (Billig, 1987; Harré, 1980; Jahoda, 1980). By looking at persons as rhetoricians (which subsumes their activities as scientists, politicians, therapists, bureaucrats and self-deceivers who tie themselves and others into rhetorical knots) one may hope to gain insight into the communicative functions of the self. The self is the fiction (or *theory* if fiction seems too flippant) which gives our moral talk its point. As we persuade, imagine alternatives, select one course of action rather than another, adopt a tone of voice, and speak from a position, we are hinting at, or sometimes explicitly referring to, a self which has some relation or another to what is going on. In fact, since each address is an I/you relationship at the very least, there are *selves*, candidly or slyly invited to take up their position in a narrative or theory of some sort. Each conversation is a conspiracy of such imaginings, in which appeal fights indifference, passion encounters irony, and occasionally sympathy encounters sympathy.

Rhetoric occurs in a blaze of consciousness, though this does not imply that we are conscious of all that we do. Consciousness is a scarce resource, allocated most obviously when deliberate choices have to be made. Then we 'pay attention'. From time to time, the decisions we make are contradictory and we tie ourselves into rhetorical knots. Others may be tied up with us. If we are fortunate, other skilled rhetoricians (priests, therapists, parents, friends) will help us untie the knot, or will persuade us to tie the knot in a way that is fashionable at the moment. This is what psychodynamics is about, and this is why I regard psychodynamic theory as a rhetorical theory, in which transference and counter-transference are the processes by which client and therapist threaten each other with particularly dangerous knots.

This is reflexive. The process is, as Devereux (1967) observed in the study of cross-cultural psychology, the one which gives us our basic data, if only we can become aware of it and understand its implications. It reveals to us our sincerity and insincerity, our guilt and shame, our fantasies about each other, and is most marked in the dangerous connections of cross-cultural work, therapy, parenting or loving.

A reflexive approach to psychology should: (a) explore the implications of looking at persons as rhetoricians, and (b) link rhetoric to a theory of consciousness. To summarize our reasons for adopting this position:

1. Persons invent theories as well as act them.
2. Persons are continually at work trying to persuade themselves and others of some position, truth, or view. They tell jokes, stories; they make gestures. They try to impress, overwhelm, project a stance. They hold conferences and political meetings. These are rhetorical occasions and strategies. The rhetorician corresponds to discourse as the agent corresponds to action.
3. Persons tie themselves into rhetorical knots and skilled rhetoricians (therapists and counsellors) are employed to untie these knots. The essence of the process is captured in Finn Tschudi's (1977) paper: 'Honest and loaded questions'.
4. The approach is reflexive. It describes what I am doing as well as what I am referring to.
5. Consciousness must have evolved because it confers a selective advantage, in that it gives its possessors insight into the choices available to themselves and to others. Thus, it is essential to a rhetorical approach; without consciousness we would not conjecture alternatives and (as Popper said) allow our ideas to die in our stead, nor would we conjecture other points of view and be able to coordinate complicated social actions. As Weber observed, an action is social to the extent that it takes into account the motives of other

persons. And as Kelly said, an action is social to the extent that you can construe another person's construing.

How did all this happen? The only sensible position, it seems to me, is evolutionary. Rhetoric and consciousness are what they are because they have conferred an evolutionary advantage on the species. Now let us develop the argument.

The rhetorical self: some stories

We have seen that to be a self is to enact a theory, to believe a theory, or to try out a theory, as in a narrative or an account of one's actions and the actions of others. In trying out a self, the person adopts a voice or an attitude, where voice is 'the speaking consciousness' (Bakhtin, 1981: 434). To become a self is to slip into a certain kind of awareness as well as to talk about that kind of awareness from time to time. Though the experiments of self are conscious, they are only occasionally self-conscious, when we are faced with a question or a failure of performance.

The theory that gives continuity to our experiments in self-hood can be called a *project*, the existential-phenomenological tradition. To understand persons, you try to understand their projects and the selves these imply. These selves may complement or contradict each other. Sometimes, they may be accepted without reflection, as clichés, so that we seem to be external to our own lives, like persons rather indifferently or automatically following a recipe. After all, to make something of a life, to unify it by an interesting project, requires courage, imagination, resources and hard work. Not everyone is up to that. This is one of the reasons why we are fascinated by plays, by fables, by narratives, by case histories, and by all sorts of accounts of people making sense of themselves and their lives. In these we find tools and models for constructing our own selves. This is why we find the historical story of the colonized self as depicted by Fanon (1970) and dramatized by Genet in various plays so interesting. Should the oppressed identify with the colonizer and distance themselves from the 'natives'? Should the oppressed openly identify with 'the people' or 'the masses' and resist identification with their oppressors? Each of these is a different project, a different life, a different self.

In extreme situations which persons are not able to resolve by a simple project, different selves are produced at different times. Lifton (1986) describes the 'doubling' or the 'division of the self into two functioning wholes, so that a part-self acts as an entire self' (1986: 418). This happened in Nazi doctors working in Auschwitz. On the one hand, there is the healing self, given over to the vocation of medicine, and on the other hand there is the killing self, selecting new arrivals for the gas chambers. Lifton describes one doctor ('A human being in SS uniform'): 'His own doubling is evident in his sympathy for Mengele and, at least to some extent, for the most extreme expressions of the Nazi ethos (the image of the Nazis as a "world blessing" and of Jews as the world's "fundamental evil")' (1986: 424).

What is most common, though, is the ways in which people continue to release streams of talk more appropriate to a discarded self, a self which they are trying to forget. 'It speaks in me,' is Fassbinder's image of the stirring of other voices, other selves which we are unable to finish off. As Lifton's talks with Doctor B continued, his submerged self spoke more and more strongly. 'Earlier he had gone quite far toward collaborating with me as a critic of Auschwitz and the Nazis, and thereby expressing his postwar German (non-Nazi) self' (1986: 331). But digging into the past revived the Auschwitz self. He stressed the 'logic' of extermination (given the belief that Jews were the 'fundamental evil'); he expressed some nostalgia for the sense of purpose of those times; he used his talk about Mengele as a vehicle for his own contradictory thoughts about the 'Jewish problem' (1986: 324).

In the course of their duties, the Auschwitz doctors went through an important rite of passage: that of 'selection' or 'ramp duty' whenever new trainloads of prisoners arrived. Doctors took the leading role in selecting who would go to the gas chambers and who would live for the time being. Doctor B had refused. He had not gone all the way in constructing an Auschwitz self, though he had, by his presence and participation in many other activities, gone a long way. It is in crucial acts that we commit ourselves to a theory, to a self of a particular kind. Having crossed some thresholds, we are bound to think of ourselves and be thought of by others as having taken up an irreversible position.

Sometimes we may speak of doubling, but equally often there will appear, to the attentive eye and ear, shades and whispers of half-organized and half-presented selves, never sufficiently coherent to be dignified by a coherent narrative line. These belong to the sub-plot, modulating the main play though barely heard and seldom recognized.

Suppose that you have been invited to lecture in South Africa. How do you present yourself and to whom do you justify yourself? What theory can preserve the continuity of your self when interrogated by different people? What are the symbols which you can move in this game of defending a story about yourself? This defence must preserve you from guilt and shame, both of which eat away your moral substance. You imagine yourself appearing before different judges, and defending yourself or attacking them. Reasonable words, angry words, examples and episodes happen in your imagination. First, there are your more or less liberal academic peers (you construe yourself as a liberal) and their interpretations of your actions. Would it convince them if you had the support of the African National Congress? Should you apply to liberation movements in South Africa to find out what their views are? Later, you write your report and it is published. This is a great help in presenting yourself in a coherent and understandable way to the kinds of persons you respect. In the report, there are edited (not necessarily untrue) accounts of your encounters with spokespersons for the various positions. You found in your contact with a black student group that 'everyone there spoke with respect and self-discipline but without fear', and this contrasts sharply with the voice of official South Africa, the bone-headed lady at the South African consulate in Chicago. (She says: 'But who is Jean-Paul Sartre? Isn't he political?') The validity of identification with the former and of identifying against the latter is demonstrated even in this small detail (and don't we all know these bone-headed officials!). You construe your position for your potential critics (as we all do) so that they can approve. You are a person who does not pretend 'that one can get through life with clean hands. The real question is, what does one do with one's dirty hands?' You explore questions carefully and ask many questions. Yours is (I respond by identifying myself as one of the 'liberal academics' to whom you appear to be speaking) a thoroughly persuasive and decent account. You conclude that what you brought to South Africa was a message of solidarity to those who wish to be part of 'a world of rational analysis and human values, and of a larger world-historical struggle for social justice'. You tell us: 'You are not alone. You are part of a larger world.'

In your account you project various identities: those by whom you wish to be exonerated and accepted as well as those by whom you would be pleased to be condemned. Into this world of other selves you project your own self to construct a moral story. In construing a position from which to act – a series of identifications and projects for achieving these – you use all the theoretical apparatus of folk psychology, which is the psychology most appropriate to explanations of this kind. In the course of this, you populate the world with an almost invisible audience and an edited set of real characters – the ANC spokesperson, the black students, the person who extended the invitation, and the official afraid even of dead philosophers. You develop a theory of a credible self: You are an explorer and fighter who is not afraid to get his hands dirty. You are a person 'committed to reason not in the narrow technocratic sense, but in the full human sense' (Aronson, 1988: 15).

It is skilful performances of this kind that make social action what it is; directing, coordinating, persuading, exploring, condemning, judging. What sort of action do we want and how do we make it possible? As we move from virtual action to real action, so we move from imagined self to committed self. The committed self is the self which explains what happens, which gives coherence and moral meaning to the narrative. We can speak of the committed self as 'character'. You become, as the possibilities diminish, more and more of a character in the story of your own life.

The rhetorical self: cognition

We are condemned to character as the point of what we are doing is gradually revealed to us. Or, if we are active and optimistic, we might say: As we discover the point of what we are doing and become clearer about our own commitments.

To strengthen the case for the rhetorical approach, let us look at the way it understands some of the problems of cognitive psychology. Here I want to follow Billig's (1987) interesting proposals. He observes: 'The view of Isocrates and the Eleatic Stranger, that thinking is like a quiet internal argument, has direct psychological implications. Most immediately, it suggests that psychological and rhetorical theories should be closely linked' (1987: 118).

The 'internal argument' is portrayed most vividly in psychoanalytic and cognitive balance or dissonance theory. It has attracted more attention from psychologists attempting to understand breakdown than from those attempting to understand normal functioning. It has certainly attracted very little attention from cognitive psychologists, who are more concerned with coding and processing than with the possibility of argument. After all, argument plays a very small role in the operations of computers. Psychologists tend to be wedded to the ideas of balance and harmony, of fitting each input into its cognitive slot. In the words of Billig, cognitive psychologists have concentrated on logos and have neglected anti-logos, or disagreement and dissent.

There are, of course, exceptions. Martindale (1984) is a cognitive psychologist (to take an example) who has drawn on the opposition of primary and secondary process thinking in his story of the development of aesthetic traditions. But what of opposing processes at the secondary level? Do we have to go outside this level for creative tension? Kelly (1955) is another psychologist who has built contradiction into his theory. Each construct has two poles which often contradict; and in the process of thinking there are contradictory needs. The first is to reduce anxiety by increasing the goodness of fit between our anticipation of events and real outcomes; the second is to avoid boredom by finding situations where our anticipations are not confirmed. We can postulate (as Devereux (1967) does in looking at the psychodynamics of cross-cultural theory), that science is a method of increasing anxiety (refutation), and of reducing it to manageable proportions (successful conjecture). Inventive scientists enjoy increasing and reducing their anxiety in this way. They avoid boredom by seeking uncertainty and then attempt to conquer that uncertainty, like mountaineers climbing new rock faces.

The particular contradiction which Billig (1987) examines is that between categorization – the central concept of modern congitive psychology – and particularization. Those who read standard texts in cognitive psychology will acknowledge that the typical problem of cognitive psychology is seen as putting a stimulus into a category, since this determines how the person reacts to it. The act of categorization is to treat 'distinguishable events' as equivalent. Equally important, though, is the act of particularization, which is to notice significant differences between equivalent events. (We may note, in passing, that in Kelly's theory, to construe is to impose a grid of similarities *and* differences on the world. Categorization and particularization are equally important, depending as they do on a dynamic interplay of similarity and difference. Also, Piaget refers to the opposing process of assimilation and accommodation.) But, to continue with Billig's account, we note that those who are classified as cognitive psychologists generally emphasize the process of categorization, which reduces the variety of the world to 'usable proportions'. Schemes, frames and scripts are devices for categorizing events. Personal constructs enable us to construe replications of events.

The kind of thinking that is portrayed by emphasizing categorizations is classificatory or 'bureaucratic', of a narrow sort. Billig goes so far as to maintain that 'social psychologists adhering to a cognitive approach sometimes tend to see all thought as being inherently prejudiced, or, at least, they suggest that prejudice arises from the normal processes of categorization, which are assumed to lie at the basis of all thought' (1987: 125). One ought, on the contrary, to realize that prejudiced and unprejudiced persons who are apparently in the same camp can be distinguished from each other by the reasoning they employ to reach their conclusions and by their willingness to continue reasoning about their conclusions. What kind of arguments and evidence are they open to?

Billig concludes that 'according to the logic of categorization theory, tolerance is "strictly speaking" an impossibility, since "all experience has to be mediated by distorting categories or schemata"' (1987: 127).

Billig, as we see, has adopted a standard rhetorician's tactic for upsetting a one-sided picture: 'if a psychological theory concentrates upon a single principle, it often pays to reverse that principle' (1987: 130). The reverse is often as easily maintained as the original. This is not to say that the original is necessarily untrue, or that the reverse is true, but that both are incomplete.

If we reverse the basic assumption of categorization theory, which is that the organism benefits by simplifying the environment, we arrive at something equally true, which is that the organism may benefit by noticing differences. Also, human tolerance is as natural as prejudice, if we adopt the rhetorical position and cultivate it in society. And the assumption that we would be overwhelmed by the cognitive demands of complexity if it were not for categorization can be reversed to the principle that we would be overwhelmed by the task of reintroducing complexity into behaviour mediated by over-simplified schemes. If there are infinite ways of finding events similar, there must be infinite ways of finding them different (1987: 133). Billig's conclusion is remarkably similar to that of Kelly (1955). Categorization and particularization are not two distinct processes. We need to do both. Our cognitive processes do not function only to provide psychological stability and sameness; they also lead to argument and novelty.

Categories are often controversial. They are not always 'givens' or an accepted part of the social furniture. Is South Africa a terrorist state? Are our conflicts race or class conflicts? Does the equation ANC = terrorists = guerillas = freedom fighters hold? In each case some will particularize and some will categorize. Thus, one may be a patriot among dissidents and a dissident among patriots. In each case, one is distinguishing one's self (in true rhetorical spirit) from the prevailing orthodoxy and simplifying categories. Of course, there is also a time to ignore differences and to seek agreement, and that is the other half of the rhetorical task.

Implications of the rhetorical approach

The metaphor of the rhetorician captures many psychological characteristics of persons. The important concept of internal argument suggests a 'society of mind', the possibility of several selves, the capacity to project a large number of identities and positions in conversations. On the one hand, we can detect a seminar of selves – or, to use another image, we can listen to the polyphonic music of selfhood. It is indeed a composition, and not a single voice or a simple unity. The composition conceals the diversity. On the other hand, we present ourselves as a single agent of action and are so regarded by others, except in cases where the dissociation, the multiplicity of selves, is 'pathologically' transparent. To borrow Bakhtin's (1981) phrase, our discourses, both inter- and intrapersonal, are often *'hybrids'*, in which different voices carry different ideologies or positions. An utterance – and, of course, a series of utterances, – may carry its own negation, as when we laugh at what we say, or say it in an absurd way. Only by listening to the inner dialogue – the interpenetrating voices – can we understand what people are saying. In fact, people have always understood this multiplicity of positions. That is how they detect irony and absurdity. They hear the inner mockery at the outward solemnity.

The importance of an internalized 'society of mind' is that we can thereby construe and reconstrue social relations. First, there is the probability that the conversations in which we are engaged from our earliest years create this internal society. We learn to converse with others, then we learn to converse with ourselves, as Vygotsky (1978) said. And, in conversing with ourselves, we take up various positions (as we know from imaginary solutions to difficult moral problems). Internal conversation is a resource for solving personal problems without committing ourselves to action. Once more, we are presented with the opportunity to 'let our theories die in our stead', as Popper says. The prudent person will learn to converse internally in defending and shaping a position. This is not the whole picture, though. The internal conversation must often become external. It is then that the social advantages of voice, position and projected self are even more visible in coordinating action. Conversationally, there can be a collective testing of options, and a collective testing of anticipated outcomes.

Historically, the social construction of self is equally significant. As societies change, so the external conversations (or 'discourses') change, with the result that we change. These conversations, with their many powerful and persuasive voices, speak in us and through us. The reconstruction of the external world is accompanied by its reconstrual. The changing system of identities is accompanied by changing conversations in which the problems of their relation, their utterances and their actions are slowly sorted out. Is one with them or against them? Above them or under them? Conversations of identification, power and authority, of empowerment, prohibition, solidarity and antagonism are conducted among us and within us. To change, we must learn to speak differently, and to learn to speak differently we must speak with others. Support groups, movements and associations are started to strengthen new kinds of talk against the old. And, of course, each new kind of conversation is a struggle, because it may imply radically new relations between radically new selves.

The implications of these internalized conversations between conjectured selves are not difficult to see. They:

1. Enable us to change as social relations change.
2. Since each self is a theory, we may be proactive as well as reactive. By conjecturing alternatives, we may change society.
3. We are not committed to a fixed social order. This view is radically anti-utopian, since utopias are usually designed to prevent change. After all, if you have invented a perfect society, you don't want anyone messing about with it.
4. This approach to the person is thoroughly historical. Persons exist and change in historically changing societies.
5. In the background is the evolutionary question. How did we evolve as conversationalists? Though the selective advantages of the capacity to communicate ideas and to respond to different perspectives seem clear enough, the mechanisms of this evolution are not clear.

Let us now turn to the other essential feature of the rhetorical approach: consciousness and its evolution.

Consciousness

Nicholas Humphrey (1987) approaches the problem of consciousness by asking what difference it makes to an animal if it is conscious. It is this 'difference' (if there is one) on which natural selection will work, making the species either more or less conscious. Humphrey's suggestion is that we take 'insight' literally, and treat consciousness as a sense organ for picturing 'the workings of the brain' (1987: 379). This does not imply that the picture is complete or always accurate, but that it is useful. It gives us information about our inner states which is worth having, just as eye and ear and nose give us information about the outer world which is worth having – without implying that this information is complete or always correct. Nevertheless, we are a lot better off with this information than we would be without it.

Yet what is the use of information about the workings of the brain? This self-knowledge enables us to understand others. It turns us into natural psychologists. The fact that we can interpret others' actions enables us to act as social creatures. In Kelly's (1955) words, we can play a social role in relation to another person to the extent that we can construe their psychological processes. Humphrey's point is that we would not be able to do this if we did not have self-knowledge as a model, just as we would be grossly handicapped in attempts to find our way in the world without vision, touch, smell, hearing and pain receptors.

This view of consciousness – as a sense organ – makes it rather different from Cartesian dualism. We do not regard consciousness as a separate *essence*, but as a separate function.

Barlow (1987) has arrived at a view of consciousness which is similar to Humphrey's; but he enlarges on its social function. He proposes that consciousness is most deeply concerned with communication between persons. Though unconscious communication is possible, whenever we are selecting messages or attempting to persuade or to understand other persons, we are conscious. Even in one's inner talk, one is addressing other persons. Barlow links consciousness to communication to the extent of claiming that a skier who is rehearsing a run before a race is probably 'rehearsing messages from (or to) his trainer, rather than rehearsing the motor actions he will perform' (1987: 368). There is an alternative view, proposed by Popper, that 'consciousness originates with the choices that are left by open behavioral programs' (1987: 151). 'Open behavioral programs' (in contrast with 'closed behavioral programs'), are those in which genetic control of behaviour is indirect, regulated by specific *learning* programs rather than by behaviour programs. In other words, the organism is biased to learn certain facts about its relations with the world, but is left with considerable discretion in mastering details. Popper points to the advantage of trying out moves mentally before they are executed. Symbol systems add to this capacity, but may not be necessary for consciousness, since rudimentary anticipations and choices are likely to accompany the extension of the phenomenal world with the evolution of distance receptors such as eyes and ears (Thinés, 1977). Not all actions are communications. As soon as language develops, the range of options increases rapidly. Symbolic systems make it possible to create a world of knowledge, such as theories and hypotheses, which we can allow 'to die in our stead'.

A new kind of consciousness is created, which we may call *reflective consciousness*. It is this that communication makes possible, since persons can begin to see themselves and their problems as external objects only when symbolic forms are created for them – forms which can be 'laid on the table' and looked at objectively. Persons can both conjecture and exhibit alternative constructions of events. Often, they continue to treat these conjectures as though they were parts of themselves, feeling hurt and offended if they are attacked. (And, of course, attacking the conjectures of others as though they were extensions of their persons.) But the possibility of a discourse is created in which conjectures can be subjected to tests recognized by competent observers. The social forms of arbitration depend on turning forms of communication into 'objects' which we can examine 'neutrally', condemning the 'communicative object' without condemning the person. This is a painfully acquired attitude, but where it is cultivated, astonishing progress in our thinking has occurred.

Thus, consciousness is not a property of the brain itself, says Barlow, but of its communications and interactions with other brains. To this I would add, interactions with the world under 'open behavioral programs'. Consciousness of the kind Barlow is thinking of is reflective consciousness and self-consciousness, both of which probably require some mode of internalization – as in language, or symbols, or models.

These are important insights. We can begin to understand why consciousness might have evolved and what it might do. We can also see how consciousness is extended and made critical or reflective by the use of language.

Rhetoric and consciousness

Our task is now to combine insights into rhetoric and consciousness to form a unified theory of conscious being. Rhetoric refers here to the selection of discourse in social interaction. This is a task of formidable complexity which would be entirely beyond my powers if I did not have J.G. Taylor's (1968) axioms for a conscious organism as a model. I use his system of axioms, with some of the concepts modified, as a basis for my theory of consciousness in persons.

Axioms for a conscious being (adapted from Taylor, 1968):

A. *Axioms relating to communication*
   (1) A state of readiness for discourse is defined as a state of activity in the acquired system for generating that discourse. States of readiness for two or more different discourses may exist simultaneously, in which case the person is in a state of multiple simultaneous readiness.
   (2) A discourse is a learnt communication practice with a limited currency, appropriate only to a restricted set of transactions in a restricted set of social settings.
B. *Axioms relating to consciousness*
   (1) The state of multiple simultaneous readiness that exists at any moment determines the state of consciousness at that moment.
   (2) States of readiness for two discourses that are clearly distinguishable from one another determine two different states of consciousness.

(3) The interpenetration of different discourses produces complex states of consciousness.

Let me now explain some of the features of this set of axioms.

First, why refer to 'a state of multiple simultaneous readiness' (A.1)? This is to indicate that many connections may be active simultaneously, although one system may be selected as the dominant or controlling system. Metaphors, mixed discourses, unexpected changes of tone, the possibility of speaking against what one has just stated with conviction, logos and anti-logos (to use Billig's terms), are explained if we assume multiple states of readiness. We can then understand how a person may start off in one tone of voice, selecting the wrong currency for a company, and (sometimes) recover by switching to an appropriate currency. In a moment, I shall add something on hybrid discourse.

Second, why refer to 'discourse' rather than 'utterance' or 'speech' (A.2)? Potter and Wetherell (1987) tell us that there is no agreed definition of the term discourse, but I am using it in a particular way here to indicate that speech practices have, like money, a circumscribed currency. They can only be exchanged under particular conditions in particular places and for particular purposes. I can't use baby talk or love talk or professional talk wherever I wish and with whomever I wish, unless I intend to be regarded as mad, bad and boorish. There are all sorts of things to be said about discourse, about the authority, power, sphere of influence and validity of each practice, but that would be another book.

Third, what is the implication of the axiom that the state of multiple simultaneous readiness determines states of consciousness (B.1)? This means that the inner dialogue – the contradictions, the point of view from which I am addressing whomever I am addressing in reality or fantasy, the qualifications, the contradictions, and the possible alternative discourses I might employ – will determine my states of consciousness. The implication here is that consciousness is a function of voice against a background of alternatives, and that it arises out of these alternatives.

Fourth, consciousness changes as readiness to discourse changes (b.2). If I speak in a prejudiced or sexist way, I become a particular kind of consciousness. I speak generously, and feel full of love for my fellow human beings. These discourses are evoked by different circumstances, in different places; but since I am always in a state of simultaneous readiness, there need not be a one-to-one correspondence between situation and the discourse I produce.

Fifth (and referring to axiom B.3), there is always the possibility of different discourses interpenetrating. This is a consequence of their simultaneity, of the fact that I am not merely a single consciousness in a unitary state. I am ready to do different things at any given time. In fact, I may master ways of deliberately introducing different voices into my discourse, in order to achieve comment on what I say even as I say it. This has already been referred to as *hybridization*, and is brought to a fine art in writing prose, in making speeches or in cracking jokes. It has also been brought to a fine art by those who excel in paradoxical communication. Here are some simple examples:

'This is a great occasion' (with a grimace).

'James is exactly the person to speak to the Dean, since he's incapable of boredom.'

'You must do your best and work very very hard and grow up very very good if you want to marry a male chauvinist pig' (mother to daughter).

In each of these examples, there are contradictory voices, representing different states of consciousness. First one idea is presented and then an unexpected contrast.

When used with skill, interpenetrating voices may be blended like the instruments of the orchestra (as Bakhtin said of Dostoevsky). When used without awareness, the effect may be confusion, because the speaker may deny an intention to communicate a particular effect. Under axiom B.2, different states of readiness produce different states of consciousness; under B.3, these may interpenetrate. It will sometimes happen that one discourse will be used to countermand or deny the existence of another. It is then the function of the therapist both to make the speaker aware of the different voices and to find ways of dealing with the contradictions between them. Often these voices are learnt at different stages of development; but the most pernicious hybrids may be those learnt in the paradoxical communications so well described by Gregory Bateson in his various publications. (Bateson *et al.*, 1956 is a good enough example; and there are the parallel accounts in Watzlawick *et al.*, 1968, as well as many others in the psychodynamic literature.) It is possible that the discourse which is learnt by those taking part in such dialogues contains instructions for denying part of the discourse. Even without such instructions, we often find ourselves saying: 'I didn't mean to convey that impression' (with more or less sincerity).

Looking back over the axioms, would it not be fair to conclude that, to change persons you merely have to change their ways of talking? Isn't that too easy? What about insincere speech? This is indeed a puzzle. The reply would have to be that a change of consciousness could only follow a change of inner speech as well as of outer speech. In other words, we are referring to *all* states of readiness for discourse and not only those which the person utters. This would be sleight of hand were it not for the fact that these voices can be revealed by psychoanalysis. That, after all, is what the process is about. We are warned, though, not to make easy assumptions about teaching persons some new way of talking in order to change them. This will work only if the new discourse is compatible with the inner dialogue. Now we see also the significance of the axiom B.1, referring to 'multiple simultaneous readiness'. There is not merely one voice waiting to utter one discourse. The person is constituted by dialogue and continues to conduct various dialogues throughout life. To change the person we must strategically intervene, choosing the conversational point of entry and the rhetorical mode most likely to persuade. A good therapist, like a good rhetorician, learns many voices.

Conclusion

In Chapter 3, each tradition was presented by referring to the use it made of elements in a disiplinary matrix consisting of primitive undefined objects, metaphors, exemplars, values and axioms. I can think of no better way to summarize the rhetorical tradition.

Primitive objects:	State of readiness
	Consciousness
Metaphor:	Rhetoric and the rhetorician
Exemplars:	Analysis of voices, or different states of speaking
	Consciousness in hybrid texts and paradoxical communications
Values:	Search for a causal explanation of how dialogue (both internal and external) has evolved
Axioms:	As stated above. Fundamental is that consciousness is a state of multiple simultaneous readiness for discourse. From this it follows that to change persons you must change this state of readiness. Change the inner as well as the outer dialogue.

Is this a complete human psychology? That would be most unlikely, since we make many things besides conversation. It is true that we can decipher the text in war, building, procreation, hunting, agriculture or athletics. They have their rhetorical aspects, but they are more than rhetoric. We can't build or procreate only with symbols, though some have tried. There is also a tendency to say that when we 'construe' a world we 'construct' it, especially among social scientists who have never constructed anything in their lives. To make symbols is important, but it is not the whole of life or the world. The world is not merely a sign.

In order to understand people, we need many metaphors. This is entirely compatible with the metaphor of the rhetorician, proceeding from metaphor to metaphor. Each time we believe that we have found the ultimate metaphor, we shall find that it is merely a net, and that like all nets it is only good for catching some things and not others.

That is exactly as it should be.

Epilogue

Towards the end of Chapter 1 I ask how we can find a way of 'decoding' knowledge. Are we confronted with a set of arbitrary variations, or is there some way in which we can interpret these? This is precisely the problem which Popper looked at in in his 1977 lecture at Darwin College, Cambridge (Popper, 1987); and, of course, it is an analogue of the problem Darwin had looked at a century earlier when he asked how animals and plants were designed.

When we observe animals, we see that they are exquisitely designed to perform certain functions and to know certain things about the world, though for each species these things will be different. Ticks know butyric acid and use it to detect their prey; frogs know bugs because their visual systems incorporate a theory of what a bug is; human infants apparently have some knowledge of what a language is, and this makes it possible for them to learn one (or more). All animals have some knowledge of the world. This must be because they have been designed to know these things in some way or another. The best answer we can come up with is that they have been designed by natural selection

Just as animals are adapted to learn some things about the world, so are cultures. More specifically, research traditions are designed by social selection to learn certain things about the world, and they do this in competition and collaboration with each other. The result is an incalculable explosion of knowledge, yet it cannot result in complete knowledge – a knowledge of everything. This would make no sense at all, since most of it would be entirely useless, serving no purpose. It follows that to understand any culture, we have to understand the selective pressures which operate on the variations that arise. Some of these selective pressures are built into research traditions – this is what the scientific method is about – but many are not. This is why every research tradition has both an internal and an external history. The internal history refers to the deliberate tests of theory; the external history refers to the ecology of theory – the various historical selection pressures which made certain kinds of research prosper and others fail.

Each research tradition has a focus and a range within which it solves problems most effectively. No tradition is at the centre of the world; it is merely we who are at the centre of a tradition. This decentration continues what Darwin started. Traditions are creatures of time. They come and go, like all species. Culture continues evolution by other means, exosomatic adaptation replacing endosomatic adaptation as the principal source of change. Before culture, theories had to be built into the bodies of animals; after culture, theories could be built into their minds – by communicated symbols and artefacts.

We are still trying to absorb the consequences of this view, which amounts to recognizing that knowledge is based on 'groping' (Piaget) – on variation and selection. Yet, if we think of persons plus theories as cognitive machines which are designed to solve certain problems and not others, it is quite clear that theories cannot be arbitrary or baseless. Like the hand or the eye, they are adapted to their tasks. However, like hand and eye, they can always be subjected to further selection. The way to understand theories is not to attempt to justify them from first principles, but to search for the selective processes in which they arise and decay. Knowledge, since it is based on groping, or on making and matching, is both 'unjustified and unjustifiable' (Bartley, 1987); it cannot be shown to be final or derivable from first principles.

Scientific theories grasp realities though, not 'The Real', which fades forever and forever when we move. What is implied by an evolutionary approach to knowledge is, to state only a few things:

1. Cultural variants (memes, to use Dawkins' word) are selected by their reproductive fitness; i.e. how many minds do they colonize?
2. One cultural form is the research tradition. A research tradition is a community in which cultural variants are subjected to agreed tests. Those which survive these tests colonize the minds of members of the community according to the received view of science. Yet there are many 'scandals', when theoretical variants which have not been successful according to approved criteria are nevertheless seen to spread. The major task of those working on the 'natural history' of knowledge is to clarify what the selective processes are. The 'shopping list' of selectors suggested in this book is a small step in this direction.
3. We should study the ecology of a variety of theories and beliefs – magic, homeopathy, nuclear physics, liberation ideologies – in an attempt to see how they evolve. This approach to technosystems is adopted by Marchetti (1985, 1987) with considerable success, viewing each technosystem as a species competing with others. Thus, wood, coal, oil, electricity, nuclear fission/fusion, and the sun are the sources of energy in competing technologies; each spreads rapidly in

a favourable environment, like a species filling a niche, and each is accompanied by a wave of innovation and theory.
4. It is not always clear what the function of a form of knowledge is, or what sustains it. Sometimes our views on what sustains a tradition are wrong, and this may even be an essential condition for their survival. Thus 'false consciousness' or 'repression' may enable particular theories of the world to survive, or to perform functions which they would not be able to perform if they were properly understood. Radical behaviourism, psychoanalysis, and Marxian sociology and social psychology are first steps in the process of demystifying certain theories. What do they do? They study the conditions which sustain a theory or a sympton (we should bear in mind that a symptom is an elementary theory or construction placed upon events) in an attempt to demystify and change that theory. This is an ecological analysis of the conditions under which a theory works, and it is not surprising that theories do not always do what theorists say they are doing. These tasks are often spoken of as hermeneutic or emancipatory tasks, as though they differed in kind from the rest of the theory. Yet they are of a kind which is common in biology, wherever the ecology of species is studied. The task is: Find out what this theory (species) is doing in this context (environment) and how it does it. What are its competitors?
5. Since new variants can always arise, no theory is ever final. This is our final point.

The evolutionary perspective is a research tradition which is being applied to knowledge in an increasingly systematic way (Radnitzky and Bartley, 1987; Wuketits, 1984). In this book, a few steps have been taken towards understanding psychological knowledge in this way.

References

Agassi, J. (1948). The cheapening of science. (Review of Karin D. Knorr-Cetina, *The Manufacture of Knowledge*. Oxford: Pergamon, 1981.) *Inquiry*, 27(1), 166–72.
Allport, G.W. (1937). *Personality: a Psychological Interpretation* (London: Constable).
Allport, G.W. (1965). *Letters from Jenny* (New York: Harcourt Brace).
Althusser, L. (1971). *Lenin and Philosophy* (London: New Left Books).
Aron, R. (1967). *Eighteen Lectures on Industrial Society* (London: Weidenfeld and Nicolson).
Aronson, R. (1988). Fighting with dirty hands. *Times Higher Education Supplement* 14 October, p. 15.
Ash, M.G. and Woodward, W.R. (1987). *Psychology in Twentieth-century Thought and Society* (Cambridge: Cambridge University Press).
Ashby, W.R. (1952). *Design for a Brain* (London: Chapman and Hall).
Bacon, F. (1974). *The Advancement of Learning and New Atlantis*. Edited by Arthur Johnston (Oxford: Clarendon Press).
Bakhtin, M.H. (1981). *The Dialogic Imagination* (Austin: University of Texas Press).
Bannister, D. and Fransella, F. (1980). *Inquiring Man* (2nd edn) (Harmondsworth: Penquin).
Barlow, H. (1987). The biological role of consciousness. In Colin Blakemore and Susan Greenfield (eds) *Mindwaves* (Oxford: Blackwell).
Barthes, R. (1967). *Elements of Semiology* (London: Cape).
Bartley, W.W. (1987). Philosophy of biology versus philosophy of physics. In Gerard Radnitzky and W.W. Bartley, III (eds) *Evolutionary Epistemology, Rationality, and the Sociology of Knowledge* (La Salle, Illinois: Open Court).
Bateson, G., Jackson, D.D., Haley, J. and Weakland, J. (1956). Toward a theory of schizophrenia. *Behavioral Science*, 1, 251–64.
Bazerman, C. (1981). What written knowledge does: three examples of academic discourse. *Philosophy of the Social Sciences*, 11(3), 361–87.
Beardsley, T. (1983). Animals as gamblers. *New Scientist*, 103, 615–18.
Berlin, I. (1963). *Karl Marx; his Life and Environment* (London: Oxford University Press).
Bettelheim, B. (1943). Individual and mass behaviour in extreme situations. *Journal of Abnormal and Social Psychology*, 38, 417–52.
Bhaskar, Roy (1979). *The Possibility of Naturalism; a Philosophical Critique of the Contemporary Human Sciences* (Brighton: The Harvester Press).
Billig, M. (1987). *Arguing and Thinking; a Rhetorical Approach to Social Psychology* (London: Cambridge University Press).
Black, Max (1979). More about metaphor. In A. Ortony (ed.) *Metaphor and Thought* (Cambridge: Cambridge University Press).
Blakemore, C, and Greenfield, S. (eds) (1987). *Mindwaves* (Oxford: Blackwell).

Bock, P.K. (1980). *Continuities in Psychological Anthropology; an Historical Introduction* (San Francisco: W.H. Freeman and Co).
Boden, M.S. (1982). Is equilibration important? – a view from artificial intelligence. *British Journal of Psychology*, 73, 165–73.
Bolles, R.C. (1975). Learning, motivation, and cognition. In W.K. Estes (ed.) *Handbook of Learning and Cognition Processes*, Vol. 1 (Hillsdale, New Jersey: Lawrence Erlbaum).
Boss, M. (1978). *Existential Foundations of Medicine and Psychology* (New York: Jason Aronson).
Botha, R.P. (1981). On the Galilean style of linguistic inquiry. *Stellenbosch Papers in Linguistics*, no. 7.
Bourguignon, Erika (1979). *Psychological Anthropology; an Introduction to Human Nature and Cultural Differences* (New York: Holt, Rinehart and Winston).
Bowlby, J. (1985). *Attachment and Loss* (3 vols) (Harmondsworth: Penguin).
Boyd, R., 1979. Metaphor and theory change. In A. Ortony (ed.) *Metaphor and Thought* (Cambridge, Cambridge University Press).
Brentano, F. (1973). *Psychology from an Empirical Standpoint* (New York: Humanities Press).
Brown, R. (1986). *Social Psychology: the Second Edition* (New York: The Free Press).
Bruner, J.S. (1956). You are your constructs. *Contemporary Psychology*, 1, 355–7.
Bruner, J. (1975). The ontogenesis of speech acts. *The Journal of Child Language*, 2, 1–19.
Brush, S.G. (1976). Fact and fantasy in the history of science. In M.H. Marx and F.E. Goodson (eds) *Theories in Contemporary Psychology* (New York: Macmillan).
Bryant, P. (1974). *Perception and Understanding in Young Children* (London: Methuen).
Bulhan, H.A. (1985). *Fanon and the Psychology of the Oppressed* (Boston: Boston University Press).
Bulhan, H.A. (1989). Afro-centric psychology: perspective and practice. Paper presented to Psychology and Apartheid Conference, University of the Western Cape.
Campbell, D.T. (1974). Evolutionary epistemology. In P.A. Schlipp (ed.) *The Philosophy of Karl Popper* (La Salle: Open Court).
Campbell, D.T. (1979). A tribal model of the social system vehicle carrying scientific knowledge. *Knowledge: Creation, Diffusion, Utilization*, 1, 181–201.
Chomsky, N. (1967). Review of Skinner's *Verbal Behavior*. In L.A. Jakobovitz and M.S. Miron (eds) *Readings in the Psychology of Language* (Englewood Cliffs: Prentice Hall).
Chomsky, N. (1978). A theory of core grammar. *Glot*, 1, 7–26.
Chomsky, N. (1980). On cognitive structures and their development: a reply to Piaget. In M. Piattelli-Palmarini (ed.) *Language and Learning: the Debate between Jean Piaget and Noam Chomsky* (London: Routledge and Kegan Paul).
Cohen, G.A. (1978). *The Marxist Theory of History: a Defence* (Oxford: Oxford University Press).
Cohen, L.J. (1979). Review of *The Self and its Brain* by Karl R. Popper and John C. Eccles. *Mind*, 88, 301–4.
Cole, M. (1979). Epilogue: a portrait of Luria. In A.R. Luria, *The Making of Mind: a Personal Account of Soviet Psychology* (Cambridge, Mass: Harvard University Press).
Danziger, K. (1979a). The positivist repudiation of Wundt. *Journal of the History of the Behavioral Sciences*, 15.

Danziger, K. (1979b). The social origins of modern psychology. In A.R. Buss (ed.) *Psychology in Social Context* (New York: Irvington).
Danziger, K. (1985). The methodological imperative in psychology. *Philosophy of the Social Sciences*, **15**, 1.13.
Danziger, K. (1987). Social context and investigative practice in early twentieth-century psychology. In M.G. Ash and W.R. Woodward (eds) *Psychology in Twentieth-century Thought and Society* (Cambridge: Cambridge University Press).
Dasen, P.R. and Heron, A. (1980). Cross-cultural tests of Piaget's theory. In H.C. Triandis and A. Heron (eds) *Handbook of Cross-Cultural Psychology*, Vol 4 (Boston: Allyn and Bacon).
Dawkins, R. (1978). *The Selfish Gene* (Londn: Granada).
Dennett, D.C. (1981). A cure for the common code? In Ned Block (ed.) *Readings in Philosophical Psychology* (London: Methuen).
Dennett, D. (1987).*The Intentional Stance* (Cambridge, Mass.: MIT Press).
Dennett, D. (1988a). Precis of *The Intentional Stance*. *Behavioral and Brain Sciences*, **11**, 495–546.
Dennett, D. (1988b). Why everyone is a novelist. *Times Literary Supplement*, 16–22 September, p. 1016.
Devereux, G. (1967). *From Anxiety of Method* (Paris and the Hague: Mouton).
Dewey, J. (1950). *Reconstruction in Philosophy* (New York: New American Library).
Donaldson, M. (1982). Conservation: What is the question? *British Journal of Psychology*, **73**, 199–207.
Douglas, R.J. and Keaney, B.P. (1984). Popper and Eccles' interaction thesis examined. In Otto Neumaier (ed.) *Mind, Language and Society*. (Vienna: VWGO).
Du Preez, P. (1980). *The Politics of Identity* (Oxford: Blackwell).
Einstein, A. (1954). The problem of space, ether and the field in physics. In S. Commins and R.N. Linscott (eds) *The Philosophers of Science* (New York: Random House).
Ellis, B. (1982). 'Lectures of truth and reality'. Delivered at Oxford.
Evans, R.I. (1976). *The Making of Psychology* (New York: Knopff).
Eysenck, H.J. (1986). *Decline and Fall of the Freudian Empire* (Harmondsworth: Penguin).
Eysenck, H.J. and Kamin, L. (1981). *Intelligence: The Battle for the Mind* (London: Pan).
Eysenck, H.J. and Wilson, G.D. (1973). *The Experimental Study of Freudian Theories* (London: Methuen).
Fanon, F. (1967). *The Wretched of the Earth* (Harmondsworth: Penguin).
Fanon, F. (1970). *Black Skin White Masks* (London: Paladin).
Farr, R.M. and Moscovici, S. (1984). *Social Representations* (Cambridge: Cambridge University Press).
Farrell,B.A. (1981). *The Standing of Psychoanalysis* (Oxford: Opus).
Feyerabend P.K. (1979). *Against Method. Outline of an Anarchist Theory of Knowledge* (London: Verso).
Feyerabend, P.K. (1981). *Problems of Empiricism* Vol. 2 (Cambridge: Cambridge University Press).
Fodor, J.A. (1968). *Psychological Explanation* (New York: Random House).
Fodor, J. (1976). *The Language of Thought* (Brighton: Harvester).
Fodor, J. (1981). *Representations* (Brighton: Harvester).
Forrester, J. (1980). *Language and the Origins of Psychoanalysis* (London: Macmillan).

Foucault, M. (1972). *The Archaeology of Knowledge* (London: Tavistock).
Fox, R. (1989). Anthropology's auto-da-fe: the Seville declaration. *Encounter*, **73**, 58–64.
Freud, S. (1938a). The history of the psychoanalytic movement. In A.A. Brill (ed.) *The Basic Writings of Sigmund Freud* (New York: Random House).
Freud, S. (1938b). The interpretation of dreams. In A.A. Brill (ed.) *The Basic Writings of Sigmund Freud* (New York: Random House).
Freud, S. (1948). *Collected Papers* (London: Hogarth Press).
Freud, S. (1973). *New Introductory Lectures on Psychoanalysis* (Harmondsworth: Penguin).
Freud, S. (1974). *Introductory Lectures on Psychoanalysis* (Harmondsworth: Penguin).
Garcia, I. and Koelling, R.A. (1966). Relation of cue to consequence in avoidance learning. *Psychonomic Science*, **4**, 123–4.
Gardner, B.T. and Gardner, R.A. (1975). Evidence for sentence constituents in the early utterances of child and chimpanzee. *Journal of Experimental Psychology: General*, **104**, 244–67.
Gardner, H. (1983). *Frames of Mind*. (New York: Basic Books).
Gardner, H. (1985). *The Mind's New Science* (New York: Basic Books).
Garfield, E. (1972). Citation analysis as a tool in journal evaluation. *Science*, **178**, 471–9.
Gazzaniga, M.S. (1983). Right hemisphere language following brain dissection a 20-year perspective. *American Psychologist*, **38**, 525–37.
Geertz, C. (1984). Distinguished lecture: anti ant-relativism. *American Anthropologist*, **86**, 263–78.
Gergen, K.J. (1982). *Toward Transformation in Social Knowledge* (New York: Springer-Verlag).
Geuter, U. (1987). German psychology during the Nazi period. In M.G. Ash and W.R. Woodward (eds) *Psychology in Twentieth-century Thought and Society* (Cambridge: Cambridge University Press).
Gholson, B. and Barker, P. (1985). Kuhn, Lakatos and Laudan: applications in the history of physics and psychology. *American Psychologist*, **40**, 755–69.
Goffman, E. (1968). *Stigma* (Harmondsworth, Penguin).
Goffman, E. (1971). *The Presentation of Self in Everyday Life* (Harmondsworth: Penguin).
Goffman, E. (1975). *Frame Analysis* (Harmondsworth: Penguin).
Goodman N. (1978). *Ways of World-making* (Indianapolis: Hackett Publishing).
Gordon, M.E., Kleiman, L.S. and Hanie, C.A. (1978). Industrial-organizational psychology: open thy ears O House of Israel. *American Psychologist*, **33**, 893–905.
Gould, S.J. (1983). *Hen's Teeth and Horse's Toes* (New York: Norton).
Gould, S.J. and Lewontin, R.C. (1979). The spandrels of San Marco and his Panglossian paradigm: a critique of the adaptationist programme. *Proceedings of the Royal Society of London*, **B205**, 581–98.
Habermas, J. (1972). *Knowledge and Human Interests* (London: Heinemann).
Hare, R.M. (1981). *Moral Thinking: its Levels, Method and Point* (Oxford: Oxford University Press).
Harré, R. (1980). Man as rhetorician. In A.J. Chapman and D.M. Jones (eds) *Models of Man* (Leicester: British Psychological Society).
Harré, R. (1986). *Varieties of Realism* (Oxford: Blackwell).
Harris, R. (1987). The grievances in your head. In Colin Blakemore and Susan Greenfield (eds) *Mindwaves* (Oxford: Blackwell).

Hearnshaw, L.S. (1979). *Cyril Burt: Psychologist* (London: Hodder and Stoughton).
Herrnstein, R.J. (1970). On the law of effect. *Journal of the Experimental Analysis of Behavior*, **13**, 243–66.
Herrnstein, R.J. (1977a). The evolution of behaviorism. *American Psychologist*, **32**, 593–603.
Herrnstein, R.J. (1977b). Doing what comes naturally: A reply to Professor Skinner. *American Psychologist*, **32**, 1013–16.
Hesse, M. (1980). *Revolutions and Reconstructions in the Philosophy of Science* (Brighton: Harvester).
Hippler, A.E. (1984). Review of E. Gillner (ed). *Soviet and western anthropology. Journal of Psychoanalytic Anthropology*, **7**, 433–4.
Hofstadter, D.R. and Dennett, D.C. (eds) (1981). *The Mind's I* (Brighton: Harvester).
Holland, R. (1977). *Self and Social Context* (London: Macmillan).
Hudson, L. (1989). Recalling a scapegoat. *Times Literary Supplement*, 3–9 November, p. 1201.
Hull, C.L. (1943). *Principles of Behavior* (New York: Appleton-Century-Crofts).
Humphrey, N. (1987). The inner eye of consciousness. In Colin Blakemore and Susan Greenfield (eds) *Mindwaves* (Oxford: Blackwell).
Husserl, E. (1928). *Phenomenology* (Encyclopaedia Britannica).
Husserl, E. (1970). *The Crisis of the European Sciences and Transcendental Phenomenology* (Evanston: Northwestern University Press).
Israëls, H. (1988). *Schreber: Father and Son* (New York: International Universities Press).
Jahoda, G. (1982). *Psychology and Anthropology* (London: Academic Press).
Jahoda, M. (1980). One model or many? In A.J. Chapman and D.M. Jones (eds) *Models of Man* (Leicester: British Psychological Society).
Jakobson, R. and Halle, M. (1980). *Fundamentals of Language* (The Hague: Mouton).
Jensen, A.R. (1969). How much can we boost IQ and scholastic achievement. *Harvard Educational Review*, **39**, 1–123.
Jensen, A.R. (1980). *Bias in Mental Testing* (New York: Free Press).
Jones, E. (1961). *The Life and Work of Sigmund Freud* (London: Hogarth).
Joynson, R.B. (1989). *The Burt Affair* (London: Routledge).
Kazdin, A.E. and Wilson, G.D. (1978). *Evaluation of Behavior Therapy: Issues, Evidence, and Research Strategies* (Cambridge, Mass.: Ballenger).
Kelly, G.A. (1955). *The Psychology of Personal Constructs* (New York: W.W. Norton).
Kendler, T.S. (1979). Toward a theory of mediational development. In H.W. Reese and L.P. Lipsitt (eds) *Advances in Child Development and Behavior*, Vol. 13 (New York: Academic Press).
Kimble, G.A. (1984). Psychology's two cultures. *American Psychologist*, **39**, 833–9.
Kline, P. (1977). Cross-cultural studies and Freudian theory. In N. Warren (ed.) *Studies in Crosscultural Psychology* (London: Academic Press).
Knorr-Cetina, K.D. (1983). The ethnographic study of scientific work: towards a constructivist interpretation of science. In K.D. Knorr-Cetina and M. Mulkay (eds) *Science Observed* (London: Sage).
Knorr-Cetina, K.D. and Mulkay, M. (1983). *Science Observed: Perspectives on the Social Study of Science* (London: Sage).
Kohler, W. (1929). *Gestalt Psychology* (New York: Liverwright).

Kolakowski, L. (1978). *Main Currents of Marxism: its Rise, Growth and Dissolution* (Oxford: Clarendon Press).
Kozulin, A. (1984). *Psychology in Utopia: Toward a Social History of Soviet Psychology* (Cambridge, Mass.: MIT Press).
Kuhn, T.S. (1970). *The Structure of Scientific Revolutions* (Chicago: University of Chicago Press).
Kuhn, T.S. (1977). Second thoughts on paradigms. In F. Suppe (ed.) *The Structure of Scientific Theories* (Urbana: University of Illinois Press).
Kuhn, T.S. (1979). Metaphor in science. In A. Ortony (ed.) *Metaphor and Thought*. Cambridge: Cambridge University Press.
Kupfersmid, J. (1988). Improving what is published: a model in search of an editor. *American Psychologist*, 43, 635–42.
Lakatos, I. (1978). *The Methodology of Scientific Research Programmes* (Cambridge: Cambridge University Press).
Lakatos, I. and Musgrave, A. (1970). *Criticism and the Growth of Knowledge* (Cambridge: Cambridge University Press).
Lakoff, G.A. (1987). *Women, Fire and Other Dangerous Things* (Chicago: University of Chicago Press).
Lakoff, G. and Johnson, M. (1980). *Metaphors We Live By* (Chicago: University of Chicago Press).
Langer, W. (1972). *The Mind of Adolf Hitler: the Secret Wartime Report* (New York: Basic Books).
Latour, B. (1983). Give me a laboratory and I will raise the world. In K. Knorr-Cetina and M. Mulkay (eds) *Science Observed* (London: Sage).
Latour, B. (1988). *The Pasteurization of France* (Cambridge, Mass.: Harvard University Press).
Latour, B. and Woolgar, S. (1979). *Laboratory Life: the Social Construction of Scientific Facts* (London: Sage).
Laudan, L. (1977). *Progress and its Problems: Towards a Theory of Scientific Growth* (London: Routledge and Kegan Paul).
Lazarus, A.A. (1971). *Behavior Therapy and Beyond* (New York: McGraw-Hill).
Lemaine, G., MacLeod, R., Mulkay, M. and Weingart, P. (1976). *Perspectives on the Emergence of Scientific Disciplines* (Chicago: Aldine).
Lettvin, J.Y., Maturana, H.R., McCulloch, W.S. and Pitts, W.H. (1959). What the frog's eye tells the frog's brain. *Proceedings of the Institute of Radio Engineers*, 47, 1940–51.
Lewin, K. (1935). *Dynamic Theory of Personality* (New York: McGraw-Hill).
Lichtman, R. (1982). *The Production of Desire: the Integration of Psychoanalysis into Marxist theory* (New York: Free Press).
Lifton, R.J. (1986). *The Nazi Doctors: Medical Killing and the Psychology of Genocide* (New York: Basic Books).
Littlewood, R. and Lipsedge, M. (1986). The culture-bound syndromes of the dominant order: psychopathology and biomedicine. In J.L. Cox (ed.) *Transcultural psychiatry* (London: Croom Helm).
Lodge, David (1977). *The Modes of Modern Writing* (London: Edward Arnold).
Lotman, J.M. (1977). Problems in the typology of culture. In Lucid, D.P. (ed.) *Soviet Semiotics* (Baltimore: Johns Hopkins Press).
Louw, J. (1986). This is thy work: a contextual history of applied psychology and labour in South Africa. Doctoral thesis, University of Amsterdam.
Lubek, I. and Apfelbaum, E. (1987). Neo-behaviorism and the Garcia effect: a

social psychology of science approach to the history of a paradigm clash. In M.G. Ash and W.R. Woodward (eds) *Psychology in Twentieth-century Thought and Society* (Cambridge: Cambridge University Press).
Luijpen, W.A. (1966). *Phenomenology and Humanism: a Primer in Existential Phenomenology* (Pittsburgh: Duquesne University Press).
Luria, A.R. (1976). *Cognitive Development: its Cultural and Social Foundations* (Cambridge, Mass.: Harvard University Press).
Luria, A.R. (1979). *The Making of Mind: a Personal Account of Soviet Psychology*. Edited by M. Cole and S. Cole (Cambridge, Mass.: Harvard University Press).
Maddi, S.R. (1974). The victimization of Dora. *Psychology Today*, 8, 91–100.
Marchetti, C. (1985). Swings, cycles and the global economy. *New Scientist*, 106, (1454), 12–15.
Marchetti, C. (1987). The future of natural gas: a Darwinian analysis. *Technological Forecasting and Social Change*, 31, 135–71.
Martindale, C. (1984). The evolution of aesthetic taste. In K.J. Gergen and Mary M. Gergen (eds) *Historical Social Psychology* (London: Lawrence Erlbaum).
Marx, K. (1967). *Capital* (New York: International Publishers).
Marx, K. (1975). *Early Writings* (Harmondsworth: Penguin).
Masterman, M. (1970). The nature of a paradigm. In I. Lakatos and A. Musgrave (eds) *Criticism and the Growth of Knowledge* (Cambridge: Cambridge University Press).
Mauer, K.F. and Lawrence, A.C. (1988). Human factors in Stope productivity – a field experiment. In J. Mouton and H.C. Marais (eds) *Basic Concepts in the Methodology of the Social Sciences* (Pretoria: HSRC).
Maynard Smith, J. (1974). The theory of games and the evolution of animal conflicts. *Journal of Theoretical Biology*, 47, 209–21.
Maynard Smith, J. (1979). Game theory and the evolution of behaviour. *Proceedings of the Royal Society of London*, B205, 475–88.
McClellan, D. (1971). *The Thought of Karl Marx* (London: Macmillan).
McCullogh, J. (1985). *Black Soul White Artifact* (Cambridge: Cambridge University Press).
McDowell, J.J. (1981). On the validity and utility of Herrnstein's hyperbole in applied behavior analysis. In C.M. Bradshaw, E. Szabadi and C.F. Lowe (eds) *Qualifications of Steady-State Operant Behaviour* (Amsterdam: Elsevier/North-Holland).
McDowell, J.J. (1982). The importance of Herrnstein's mathematical statement of the law of effect for behavior therapy. *American Psychologist*, 37, 771–9.
McDowell, J.J. and Kessel, R.A. (1979). A multivariate rate equation for variable-interval performance. *Journal of the Experimental Analysis of Behavior* 31, 267–83.
Mead, G.H. (1934). *Mind, Self and Society: From the Standpoint of a Social Behaviorist*. Edited, with an introduction, by C.W. Morris (Chicago: University of Chicago Press).
Medawar, P. (1963). Is the scientific paper a fraud? *The Listener*, 12 September pp. 377–8.
Medawar, P. (1967). *The Art of the Soluble* (London: Methuen).
Meehl, P.E. (1954). *Clinical Versus Statistical Prediction* (Minneapolis University Press).
Merleau-Ponty, M. (1962). *The Phenomenology of Perception* (London: Routledge and Kegan Paul).
Minsky, M. and Papert, S. (1968). *Perceptions* (Cambridge, Mass.: MIT).

Munz, P. (1977). *The Shapes of Time: a New Look at the Philosophy of History* (Middletown: Wesleyan University Press).
Musil, R. (1979). *The Man Without Qualities* (London: Picador).
Neimeyer, R.A. (1985). *The Development of Personal Construct Psychology* (Lincoln: University of Nebraska Press).
Nesfield, J.C. (1899). *Manual of English Grammar and Composition* (London: Macmillan).
Newell, A. and Simon, H.A. (1961). Computer simulation of human thinking. *Science*, **134**, 2011–2017.
Ortony, A. (1979a). Beyond literal similarity. *Psychological Review*, **86**, 161–80.
Ortony, A. (ed.) (1979b). *Metaphor and Thought* (Cambridge: Cambridge University Press).
Osgood, C.E., Luria, Z., Jeans, R.F. and Smith, S.W. (1976). The three faces of Evelyn: a case report. *Journal of Abnormal Psychology*, **85**, 247–86.
Paivio, A. and Begg, I. (1981). *Psychology of Language* (Englewood Cliffs, New Jersey: Prentice-Hall).
Papert, S. (1980). The role of artificial intelligence in psychology. In M. Piattelli-Palmerini (ed.) *Language and Learning* (London: Routledge and Kegan Paul).
Piaget, J. (1967). *Biologie et connaissance* (Paris: Gallimard).
Piaget, J. (1970). *Genetic Epistemology* (New York: Columbia University Press).
Piaget, J. (1972). *Insights and Illusions of Philosophy* (London: Routledge and Kegan Paul).
Piaget, J. (1977). *The Origin of Intelligence in the Child* (Harmondsworth: Penguin).
Piaget, J. and Inhelder, B. (1969). *The Psychology of the Child* (London: Routledge and Kegan Paul).
Piatelli-Palmerini, M. (ed.) (1980). *Language and Learning: the Debate between Jean Piaget and Noam Chomsky* (London: Routledge and Kegan Paul).
Platt, G.M. (1980). Thoughts on a theory of collective action. In M. Albin (ed.) *New Directions in Psychohistory* (Lexington: Lexington Books).
Pollio, H.R., Barlow, J.M., Fine, H.J. and Pollio, M.R. (1977). *Psychology and the Poetics of Growth* (Hillsdale, New Jersey: Lawrence Golbaum).
Popper, K. (1963). *Conjectures and Refutations* (London: Routledge and Kegan Paul).
Popper, K. (1972). *Objective Knowledge: an Evolutionary Approach* (Oxford: Clarendon Press).
Popper, K. (1976). *Unended Quest* (London: Fontana).
Popper, K. (1987). Natural selection and the emergence of mind. In G. Radnitzky and W.W. Bartley (eds) *Evolutionary Epistemology, Rationality, and the Sociology of Knowledge* (La Salle, Illinois: Open Court).
Popper, K.R. and Eccles, J.C. (1977). *The Self and its Brain* (Berlin: Springer).
Potter, J. and Wetherell, M. (1987). *Discourse and Social Psychology* (London: Sage).
Premack, D. (1971). Language in chimpanzee? *Science*, **172**, 808–22.
Putnam, H. (1960). Minds and machines. In S. Hook (ed.) *Dimensions of Mind* (New York: New York University Press).
Rachlin, H. (1971). On the tautology of the matching law. *Journal of the Experimental Analysis of Behavior*, **15**, 249–51.
Rachlin, H., Green, L. and Tormey, B. (1988). Is there a decisive test between matching and maximizing? *Journal of the Experimental Analysis of Behavior*, **15**, 249–51.

Radnitzky, G. and Bartley, W.W (1987) (eds). *Evolutionary Epistemology, Rationality, and the Sociology of Knowledge* (La Salle, Illinois: Open Court).
Reichenbach, H. (1938). *Experience and Prediction* (Chicago: University of Chicago Press).
Ricoeur, P. (1977). The question of proof in Freud's psychoanalytic writings. In C. Reagan and D. Stewart (eds) *The Philosophy of Paul Ricoeur* (Boston: Beacon).
Root-Bernstein, R. (1983). *History of Science*, 21, 275.
Rosch, E. (1973). Natural categories. *Cognitive Psychology*, 4, 328–50.
Rosch, E. (1978). Principles of categorization. In Eleanor Rosch and B.B Lloyd (eds) *Cognition and Categorization* (Hillsdale, New Jersey: Lawrence Erlbaum).
Rumbaugh, D.M. (ed.) (1977). *Language Learning by a Chimpanzee: the LANA Project* (New York: Academic Press).
Russell, B. (1961). *History of Western Philosophy* (London: Unwin).
Sartre, J.P. (1957). *Being and Nothingness* (London: Methuen).
Sartre, J.P. (1960). *Critique de la Raison Dialectique* (Paris: Gallimard).
Sartre, J.P. (1962). *Sketch for a Theory of the Emotions* (London: Methuen).
Sartre, J.P. (1963). *Saint Genet: Actor and Martyr* (New York: New American Library).
Sarason, S.B. and Doris, J. (1969). *Psychological Problems in Mental Deficiency* (New York: Free Press).
Scarr, S. (1980). *IQ: Race, Social Class and Individual Differences* (Hillsdale, New Jersey: Lawrence Erlbaum).
Schafer, R. (1976). *A New Language for Psychoanalysis* (New Haven: Yale University Press).
Searle, J. (1987). Minds and brains without programs. In Colin Blakemore and Susan Greenfield (eds) *Mindwaves* (Oxford: Blackwell).
Sears, R.S. (1944). Experimental analysis of psychoanalytic phenomena. In J. Mc V Hunt (ed.) *Personality and the Behavior Disorders* (New York: Ronald).
Seedat, M., Cloete, N. and Schochet, I. (1988). Community psychology: panic or panacea. *Psychology in Society*, 11, 39–54.
Seidenberg, M.S. and Petitto, L.A. (1979). Signing behavior in apes: a critical review *Cognition*, 7, 177–215.
Seligman, M.E.P. and Hager, J.L. (1972). The sauce-bearnaise syndrome. *Psychology Today* (August) 59–87.
Sève, L. (1974). *Marxism et Theorie de la Personnalite* (Paris: Editions Sociales).
Sève, L. (1975). *Marxism and the Theory of Personality* (London: Lawrence and Wishart).
Sherwood, M. (1969) *The Logic of Explanation in Psychoanalysis* (New York: Academic Press).
Siegel, M.H. and Zeigler, H.P. (1976). *Psychological Research: the Inside Story* (New York: Harper and Row).
Sinclair de Zwart, H. (1967). *Acquisition du Langage et Developpement de la Pensee* (Paris: Dunod).
Skinner, B.F. (1957). *Verbal Behavior* (New York: Appleton-Century-Crofts).
Skinner, B.F. (1969). *Contingences of Reinforcement: a Theoretical Analysis* (New York: Appelton-Century-Crofts).
Skinner, B.F. (1972). *Beyond Freedom and Dignity* (London: Cape).
Skinner, B.F. (1977). Herrnstein and the evolution of behaviourism. *American Psychologist*, 32, 1006–12.
Slobin, D.I. (1979). *Psycholinguistics* (2nd edn). (Glenville, Illinois: Scott, Foresman).

Smolensky, P. (1988). On the proper treatment of connectionism. *Behavioral and Brain Sciences*, **11**, 1–74.

Spence, K.W. (1937). The differential response in animals to stimuli varying within a single dimension. *Psychological Review*, **44**, 430–44.

Spindler, G.D. (ed.) (1978). *The Making of Psychological Anthropology* (Berkeley: University of Los Angeles Press).

St James-Roberts, I. (1976). Are scientists trustworthy? *New Scientist*, 2 September, pp. 481–2.

Stein, H.F. (1986). Cultural relativism as the central organizing resistance in cultural anthropology. *Journal of Psychoanalytic Anthropology*, **9**, 157–75.

Stevens, S.S. (1957). On the psychophysical law. *Psychological Review*, **64**, 153–81.

Stich, S. (1983). *From Folk Psychology to Cognitive Science; the Case against Belief* (Cambridge, Mass.: MIT).

Taylor, J.G. (1958). Experimental Design: a cloak for intellectual sterility. *British Journal of Psychology*, **49**, 106–16.

Taylor, J.G. (1962). *The Behavioral Basis of Perception* (New Haven: Yale).

Taylor, J.G. (1968). The role of axioms in psychological theory. *Bulletin of the British Psychological Society*, **21**, 221–7.

Taylor, J.G. (1970). Phantom theories: a reply to Mr. Vine. *Bulletin of the British Psychological Society*, **23**, 281–5.

Terrace, H.S. (1979). *Nim* (New York: Knopf).

Thigpen, C.H. and Cleckley, H. (1954). A case of multiple personality. *Journal of Abnormal and Social Psychology*, **49**, 139–51.

Thinés, G. (1977). *Phenomenology and the Science of Behaviour* (London: Allen and Unwin).

Tschudi, F. (1977). Loaded and honest questions: a construct theory view of symptoms and therapy. In D. Bannister (ed.) *New Perspectives in Personal Construct Theory* (London: Academic Press).

Uexküll, J.V. (1921). Cited in Irenaus Eibl-Eibesfeldt (1970). *Ethology* (New York: Holt, Rinehart and Winston).

Valle, R.S. and King, M. (1978). *Existential – Phenomenological Alternatives for Psychology* (New York: Oxford University Press).

Van den Berg, J.H. (1961). *The Changing Nature of Man* (New York: W.W. Norton).

Van den Berg, J.H. (1971). What is psychotherapy? *Humanitas*, **7**.

Van den Berg, J.H. (1974). *Divided Existence and Complex Society* (Pittsburgh: Duquesne University Press).

Van Strien, P.J. and Dehue, T. (1985). A relational model of the historiography of psychology. *Proceedings of the Fourth European Meeting of Cheiron, Paris 1985* (Leyden: Psychologisch Instituut RUC).

Verhave, T. and van Hoorn, W. (1984). The temporalization of the self. In K.J. Gergen and M.M. Gergen (eds) *Historical social psychology* (Hillsdale, New Jersey: Lawrence Erlbaum).

Vygotsky, L.S. (1978). *Mind in Society: the Development of Higher Psychological Processes*. Edited by M. Cole, V. John-Steiner, S. Scribner and E. Sourberman (Cambridge, Mass.: Harvard University Press).

Warner, M. (1989). Against parents and plenty. *Times Literary Supplement* 21–7 April, p. 420.

Wächtershäuser, G. (1984). Light and life. Paper to AAAS Annual Meeting, New York.

Watzlawick, P., Beavin, J.H. and Jackson, D.D. (1968). *Pragmatics of Human Communication* (London: Faber and Faber).
Weinberg, S. (1976). The forces of nature. *Bulletin of the American Academy of Arts and Sciences*, **XXXIX**, 13–29.
Wertsch, J.V. (1985). *Vygotsky and the Social Formation of Mind* (Cambridge, Mass.: Harvard University Press).
Winner, I.P. and Umiker-Sebeok, J. (eds). (1979). *Semiotics of Culture* (The Hague: Mouton).
Wolpe, J., and Lazarus, A.A. (1966). *Behavior Therapy Techniques* (Oxford: Pergamon).
Woodfield, Andrew and Morton, A. (1988). The reality of the symbolic and subsymbolic systems. *Behavioral and Brain Sciences*, **11**, 58.
Wuketits, F.M. (1984) (ed.). *Concepts and Approaches in Evolutionary Epistemology* (Dordrecht: D. Reidel).

Author index

A

Adams, D., 144
Agassi, J., 11
Allport, G.W., 130, 174
Althusser, L., 39
Apfelbaum, E., 134–6
Aron, R., 39
Aronson, R., 197
Ash, M.G., 4
Ashby, W.R., 60, 65, 168, 189

B

Bacon, F., 3
Bakhtin, M.H., 195, 201
Bannister, D., 169
Barker, P., 116–19
Barlow, H., 203
Barthes, R., 85
Bartley, W.W., 190, 210
Bateson, G., 206
Bazerman, C., 10
Beardsley, T., 62
Begg, I., 75
Berlin, I., 40
Bettelheim, B., 132
Bhaskar, R., 6
Billig, M., 193, 198–200
Black, M., 75
Blakemore, C., 172
Bock, P.R., 156
Boden, M.S., 38
Bolles, R.C., 134
Boss, M., 30
Botha, R.P., 170
Bourguiqnon, E., 156
Bowlby, J., 152–3
Boyd, R., 23, 76, 181
Brentano, F., 33
Brown, R., 147
Bruner, J.S., 141
Brush, S.G., 118, 170

Bryant, P., 38
Bulhan, H.A., 133, 141–2

C

Campbell, D.T., 123, 137–8, 160
Chomsky, N., 144–7, 163, 170
Cleckley, H., 188
Cohen, G.A., 42
Cohen, L.G., 83
Cole, M., 126

D

Danziger, K., 5, 7, 8, 120, 129, 136, 171
Dasen, P.R., 148
Dawkins, R., 109, 210
Dehue, T., 130
Dennett, D., 34, 63, 172, 183, 186–8
Devereux, G., 141, 194, 199
Dewey, J., 3
Dirac, P., 118, 180
Donaldson, M., 38
Doris, J., 143
Douglas, R.J., 83
Du Preez, P., 170

E

Eccles, J.C., 83
Einstein, A., 72
Ellis, B., 178
Evans, R.I., 119, 120
Eysenck, H.J., 123, 127, 148, 168

F

Fanon, F., 132–3, 195
Farr, R.M., 156
Farrell, B.A., 148

224 AUTHOR INDEX

Feberabend, P.K., 115, 117, 164, 173
Fodor, J.A., 63, 64, 120, 146
Forrester, J., 151
Foucault, M., 12
Fox, R., 128
Fransella, F., 169
Freud, S., 85–8, 107–8

G

Galileo, G., 173
Garcia, I., 134–6
Gardner, B.T., 147
Gardner, H., 146
Gardner, R.A., 147
Garfield, E., 160
Gazzaniga, M.S., 189
Geertz, C., 127
Gergen, R.J., 15, 16
Geuter, U., 174
Gholson, B., 116–19
Goffman, E., 55–9
Gordon, M.E., 177
Gould, S.J., 110, 112, 122, 124
Greenfield, S., 172

H

Habermas, J., 26
Hager, J.L., 135
Halle, M., 84
Hare, R.M., 162
Harré, R., 121, 178, 183–4, 193
Harris, R., 184, 185
Hearnshaw, L.S., 179
Heron, A., 148
Herrnstein, F.J., 100, 105–6
Hesse, M., 16
Hippler, A.E., 127
Hofstadter, D.R., 172
Holland, R., 140
Hudson, L., 179
Hull, C.L., 168
Humphrey, N., 202
Husserl, E., 31, 170

I

Israëls, H., 152, 168

J

Jahoda, G., 138
Jahoda, M., 26, 193

Jakobson, R., 84
Jensen, A.R., 127
Johnson, M., 74
Joynson, R.B., 179

K

Kamin, L., 127
Kazdin, A.E., 158
Keaney, B.P., 83
Kelly, G.A., 130, 141, 169–70, 175, 198, 200, 202
Kendler, T.S., 117
Kessel, R.A., 101
Kimble, G.A., 174
King, M., 32
Kline, P., 148, 156
Knorr-Cetina, K.D., 6, 11
Kohler, W., 158
Kolakowski, L., 143
Kozulin, A., 132, 166, 179
Kuhn, T.S., 5, 16, 18, 29, 45, 46, 82, 116–19
Kupfersmid, J., 130

L

Lakatos, I., 24, 116–19, 149
Lakoff, G.A., 60, 62, 74, 86, 120
Langer, W., 174
Latour, B., 9, 10, 114, 128
Laudan, L., 45–7, 116–19, 163
Lawrence, A.C., 129
Lazarus, A.A., 157, 158
Lemaine, G., 141
Lettvin, J.Y., 190
Lewin, K., 171
Lewontin, R.C., 110, 112
Lichtman, R., 153–6
Lifton, R.J., 188, 195–6
Lipsedge, M., 176
Littlewood, R., 176
Lodge, D., 86
Lotman, J.M., 12, 13, 81
Louw, J., 129
Lubek, I., 134–6
Luijpen, W.A., 31
Luria, A.R., 43, 126, 143

M

Maddi, S.R., 157
Marchetti, C., 210
Martindale, C., 198

AUTHOR INDEX 225

Marx, K., 41, 89–93, 142
Masterman, M., 20
Mauer, K.F., 129
Maynard Smith, J., 110–111
McClellan, D., 42
McCullogh, J., 133, 143
McDowell, J.J., 101–3
Mead, G.H., 57
Medawar, P., 10, 114
Meehl, P.E., 130
Mendel, G., 149
Merleau-Ponty, M., 30
Minsky, M., 65
Morton, A., 66
Moscovici, S., 156
Mulkay, M., 6
Munz, P., 150
Musgrave, A., 149
Musil, R., 83

N

Neimeyer, R.A., 141, 169
Nesfield, J.C., 80
Newell, A., 171

O

Ortony, A., 76
Osgood, C.E., 188

P

Paivio, A., 75
Papert, S., 65
Petitto, L.A., 147
Piaget, J., 36–8, 69, 136–7, 210
Piatelli-Palmerini, M., 146
Platt, G.M., 42
Pollio, H.R., 71
Popper, K., 24, 60, 83, 97–8, 123, 148, 160, 190, 203, 209
Potter, J., 156, 205
Premack, J., 147
Putnam, H., 63

R

Rachlin, H., 103–5
Radnitzky, G., 211
Reichenbach, H., 182–3
Ricoeur, P., 150

Root-Bernstein, R., 149
Rosch, E., 120
Rumbaugh, D.M., 147
Russell, B., 40

S

Sarason, S.B., 143
Sartre, J.P., 30, 31, 32, 40, 58, 61
Scarr, S., 127
Schafer, R., 181–2
Searle, J., 68, 184
Sears, R.S., 157
Seedat, M., 132
Seidenberg, M.S., 147
Seligman, M.E.P., 135
Sève, L., 41, 99, 143
Sherwood, M., 150
Siegel, M.H., 119
Simon, H.A., 171
Sinclair de Swart, H., 47
Skinner, B.F., 61, 103, 105–6, 120, 144–5
Slobin, D.I., 118
Smolenskey, P., 65, 67, 172
Spence, K.W., 137–8, 158–9
Spindler, G.D., 156
St James-Roberts, I., 179
Stein, H.F., 127
Stich, S., 61
Swift, J., 10

T

Taylor, J.G., 60, 130–1, 166–8, 171, 204–5
Terrace, H.S., 147
Thigpen, C.H., 188
Thinés, G., 31, 203
Thompson, E.P., 42
Tolman, E.C., 137–8
Tschudi, F., 194

U

Uexküll, J.V., 31, 190
Umiker-Sebeok, J., 12
Valle, R.S., 32
Van den Berg, J.H., 32, 156
Van Hoorn, W., 174
Van Strien, P.J., 130–1
Verhave, T., 174
Vygotsky, L.S., 201

W

Wächtershäuser, G., 190
Warner, M., 176
Watzlawick, P., 206
Weinberg, S., 163
Wertsch, J.V., 125
Wetherell, M., 156, 205
Wilson, G.D., 148, 158
Winner, I.P., 12

Wolpe, J., 157
Woodfield, A., 66
Woodward, W.R., 4
Woolgar, S., 10, 114
Wuketits, F.M., 211
Wundt, W., 5, 8

Z

Zeigler, H.P., 119

Subject index

A

Abstracta, 183, 185–90
Alienation, 90–93
Altruism, 109
Axioms, 96–113, 167, 204–208
Axioms – how they change, 105–6

B

Behaviourism, 43–5, 120, 144, 158

C

Carnegie Commission, 129
Causal explanation, 175–7
Challenge and response, 158–9
Climate of thought, 12–18, 127–8
Codes, 12–16
Community psychology, 132
Competition between theories, 140–62
Conceptual objects, 182
Concreta, 183, 185–90
Connection machines, 59–68, 172
Consciousness, 167, 202–208
Consciousness – and communication, 203, 204
Consciousness – reflective, 203
Contexts of theory, 4, 6
Cullture-bound syndromes, 176

D

Disciplinary matrix, 5, 6, 19, 24–7
Discourse, 9–12, 187–8, 204–8
Dishonesty in science, 179–80

E

Ecology of theory, 210–11
Exemplars, 27

Eurocentric psychology, 141–2
Evolution by natural selection, 108–113
Evolution of theory, 123–39
Evolutionary epistemology, 123, 160–2, 189–90, 209–211
Existential phenomenology, 29–32, 156–7

F

Fetishism, 90
Formal theory, 166–70

G

Genetic epistemology, 35–8
Gestalt challenge to behaviourism, 158
Grammar, 146–7, 184–5

H

Hybrid discourse, 201, 206
Hysteria (Dora's case), 153–7

I

Ideal cognitive object, 121
Identity, 186–9
Illata, 183, 185–90
Intellectual climate, 12–18, 127–8
Interpretation, 175–7
Isolation, 140–1

J

Justification, 165

K

Knowledge matrix, 4, 6–18

SUBJECT INDEX

L

Laws in science, 24–5, 96–7
Law of relative effect, 100–5
Leadership, 137–8
Legitimacy, 131–4

M

Marxism, 89–93, 175–6
Marxist social psychology, 38–43
Mathematization, 170–1
Metaphor, 25–6, 51–77, 84–8
Metaphors and intellectual space, 71–4
Metaphors – how they work, 74–7
Metaphysical research programme, 97–9
Methodology, 148–53
Metonymy, 80, 84–7, 88–94
Misrepresentation, 141–4
Model solutions, 27
Moral discourse, 189
Myth, 81–3

O

Observation, 149, 173
Overextension, 166, 177

P

Paradigm, 19, 20–4
Paradoxical communication, 206
Paranoia (Schreber), 151–2
Personal construct psychology, 169–70
Political movements and theory, 125–6
Polyphonic being, 193
Power structures, 134–7
Prediction, 177
Problem-solving, 114–162
Professional opportunities, 129–131
Programmability of theory, 171–2
Pseudo-causal language, 182, 184–5
Psychoanalysis, 32–5, 87–8, 107–8, 148–53
Psychoanalysis and behaviourism, 157–8
Psychoanalysis and Marxism, 153–6

R

Raising the bid, 144
Range of convenience, 177
Rational choice between theories, 47–8, 164–6

Realism, 'the real', 181–90, 210
Reflexivity, vii–viii, 194–208
Reification, 182
Relativism, 6–7, 23, 27, 127
Research traditions, 29–48
Rhetoric, 193–202
Rhetoric and cognition, 198
Rhetoric and consciousness, 204
Rhetoric and social change, 202
Rituals for testing beliefs, 138, 162
Rules, 72–3

S

Satisfactory answers, 164–6
Selection factors in the evolution of theories, 125–62
Self, 186–9, 193, 194–8
Seville declaration on violence, 128
Showing how to do it, 153–8
Social matrix of knowledge, 6
Social structure and knowledge, 6–9
Sociorationalism, 15–16
Stable strategies, 110
Stimulus generalization, 158–9
Symbol machines, 59–65, 171–2
Symbolic generalizations, 24–5

T

Tautology, 98, 99, 104–5
Theories,
 and codes, 13–15
 and discourse, 9–12
 and intellectual climate, 12–18, 127–8
 and observation, 149, 173
 and research traditions, 45–8
 and social context, 6, 134–7
 changing, 115–23
 formal, 166–76
 typology of, 183–4
Theory-driven research, 174–5
Truism, 95–6
Truth, 177–8
Typology of theories, 183–4

U

Utility, 174–5

V

Values, 26, 163–180
Voice, 195, 201